J.W.ORR N.Y.

THE HOMESTEAD—FRONTISPIECE.

# RURAL HOMES;

OR

## SKETCHES OF HOUSES

SUITED TO

## AMERICAN COUNTRY LIFE,

WITH

ORIGINAL PLANS, DESIGNS, &c.

BY

GERVASE WHEELER.

NEW YORK:
CHARLES SCRIBNER, 145 NASSAU STREET.
1851.

C. W. BENEDICT,
STEREOTYPER AND PRINTER,
201 William Street.

# PREFACE.

---

To the Reader—

In the pages I respectfully offer for perusal, I would have you look for no very new or critical remarks, or learned and technical disquisitions. Of course it may be presumed that, in studying the profession of an architect, I have, to the extent of my ability, mastered the elementary rudiments, technicalities, and theories of the science; and, although I might show learning in discoursing of the nice distinctions between this and that school of ancient art, and quote Latin and Greek in support of my own peculiar tenets, I should very little interest you, and do nothing towards supplying your want of a plan for your house.

I therefore modestly present a few notes of things that in the course of a varied architectural practice have come before me, and which have left certain conclusions impressed upon my mind. In this, I claim no title to originality; others, long ere now, have written useful and learned books about houses, and how to build them; this, however, I do claim—an intention of directing the thoughts of all interested in country-life, to the embodiment of a fixed principle in rural architecture.

Heretofore, too generally, country houses have either been on a stereotyped plan, or have shown an unmeaning whimsicality: the true way is, to make the building exactly what its parts, uses, material, and extent require—ornamental or plain as you will—but every portion suggestive of a meaning and a use.

Perhaps this is more easy to direct than to do; the designs presently following will best show how far in my case the attempt has been successful. I can only urge that they have at least the merit of study; and every plan—the practical value of either having been tested by erection, or of having been reduced from drawings as elaborately drawn out as if for actual use by some cautious and very particular builder.

The contents of the book itself will be found to be but short, simple, and comprehensive directions to all desirous of building—embracing every variety of home usually needed. It commences with the first foot tread upon the spot chosen for the house; details the considerations that should weigh in selecting the site—gives models of buildings, differing in character, extent, and cost, and suited to particular localities, and to circumstances, fully enlarged upon—shows how to harmonize the building with the surrounding scenery, and to reconcile economical expediture with truest refinement of taste—teaches how healthfully to warm and ventilate—assists in selecting furniture, and the innumerable articles of utility and ornament used in constructing and finishing—with remarks upon the adjuncts to a house—its entrance lodge, and its numerous out-buildings. It concludes with final practical directions to building amateurs, giving a few useful hints as to drawing up written descriptions, specifications, and contracts.

In conclusion, I would say that, in the hope of infusing something of its spirit therein, I have mentally headed every page with a sentence suggested as a matin and even song to every architect and amateur—Mr. Ruskin's great maxim, "Until *common sense* finds its way into architecture, *there can be but little hope for it.*"

G. W.

NORWICHTOWN, CT.

# CONTENTS.

## CHAPTER I.



## CHAPTER II.



## CHAPTER III.



## CHAPTER IV.

## CHAPTER V.



## CHAPTER VI.



## CHAPTER VII.



## CHAPTER VIII.



## CHAPTER IX.



## CHAPTER X.



## CHAPTER XI.

## CHAPTER XII.



## CHAPTER XIII.



## CHAPTER XIV.



## CHAPTER XV.



## CHAPTER XVI.

# RURAL HOMES.

---

## CHAPTER I.

### THE EXCELLENCIES OF A HOUSE—CHOICE OF A SITE.

All who build, desire to build well; if cheaply,—still, to the best of their knowledge and ability,—they desire to build well.

Unfortunately, however, there are very few who understand in what the excellencies of a house consist; nor in the effort to construct a house, do their ideas at the highest soar above a point somewhat beyond what their last building neighbor has achieved. By the help of monthly periodical, or other reading, they have arrived at the conclusion that better professional aid can be obtained than the skill of the village carpenter, and so they instruct some architect to prepare plans; not, however, until wearied in the endeavor to concoct such for themselves. In directing him, their minds are generally so obstinately settled upon some rudely-digested but pet plan, that the professional adviser is obliged to defer to the opinions of his employer, and patch up something by way of a compromise between what his judgment would approve, and what his client insists upon; or else risk the withdrawal of his commission—and this, as architects must live, he is not desirous to do.

At length, some plan for the internal arrangement of the house and the character of the exterior settled upon, the drawings and working directions for the mechanics provided, and the building is fairly commenced. It is then, and as the structure gradually developes itself, the gentleman begins to wish he had given the subject closer attention before; for even he can see what improvements might have been made, and how much better it might all have been. At this stage of proceedings he probably blames his architect, forgetting that his own obstinacy denied his adviser a voice, when it could have spoken to advantage. Finally the building is completed, to the but cold satisfaction of its owner, who is only glad to get so much trouble off his hands, and to the relief of the architect, whose professional pride (if he have any) and personal feelings (if he can afford the luxury) have been perpetually jarred upon and mortified, from the first pencil-stroke upon paper, to the last nail driven home in the finished building.

Now, all this might be changed, if the public would themselves seek information on the principles that should guide them in the selection of a plan upon which to build. A man builds generally for a lifetime, not to gratify the whim of a moment. "*Build* in haste, repent at leisure," is a maxim of which many ere this have found the truth; nor is the character of a house so much a matter of mere taste as many assert; the planning of a building requires calculation, science, experience, as I dare say all have found who have endeavored to reduce their fanciful ideas into tangible form upon paper. It is not necessary every one should receive the education of an architect, but it is necessary every one should know something of the elementary principles of the architect's noble art, not, it may be, of its technicalities, or the differences, or history of its various styles and epochs, but something of the excellencies he would incorporate in his contemplated dwelling.

So much by way of introduction. Now, dear readers, I will plunge at once into the subject that I have to grapple, and begin by drawing a distinction between *houses* and *homes.*

Houses may tell very well in advertisements, and speculating builders know to make them look sweetly pretty upon paper; but, dear friends, take care that you thoroughly satisfy yourselves that you can make them homes, before you commit yourselves to a choice you may afterwards repent.

The excellencies of a home may be briefly stated thus:

CONVENIENT ARRANGEMENT.

FACILITY OF CONSTRUCTION AND OF REPAIR.

PERFECT PROTECTION FROM HEAT AND COLD.

ADEQUATE MEANS OF WARMING AND VENTILATING.

CONGRUITY WITH THE SCENERY AROUND.

In these may be summed up all that has to be studied in the contriving and the building of a house. To discuss with advantage the several points that present themselves under each head, I will suppose a friend about to commence the initiatory steps towards erecting himself a home, and so will first say a few words about selection of the site.

Think more than once, before selecting too large a tract of ground. Space is desirable, undoubtedly; but a ramble in country lanes, and in woods skirting your place, is as pleasant as if in your own grounds, and enjoyed at a far cheaper rate.

If you really, soberly understand farming, and wish to devote your time and attention to agricultural pursuits, well and good; purchase, then, just so much land as you feel you can control; or if you have wealth enough to permit you to play at farming, and to raise potatoes at four dollars a barrel, when you can send to the city and buy them at three, and to cultivate other charming crops at a like scale of expense, get as many broad acres as you have a mind to; but for the particular spot where you mean to place your house, choose as follows:

Rather prefer a quiet, smiling, little nook, with a rolling surface of natural grassy slopes, tenderly shaded with many trees, than a rocky, bare, quasi-picturesque territory.

Notice particularly how you are sheltered, by hills around, from the quarter whence cometh the wintry wind, and so prefer rather the gentle slope of a long hill to its summit. Many will tell you, it is true, of the "fine views" you may enjoy from thence; but distant prospect is monotonous—I repeat monotonous, though, in so saying, I hazard the infliction of the title barbarian. Saving some certainly beautiful effects of aerial *chiaro-scuro*, which lighten and quench the gray of the mountain, the view varies but little, however extensive may be the panorama.

It is the foreground—the familiar objects near the eye that are varying ever—change of leaf, growth of twig upon twig—budding and fading of flower—constant shifting of the margin of the near winding brook, that make a *coup d'œil* that is never monotonous, for the relation and the aspect of each atom are perpetually varying.

Apart from these artistic reasons, there are others of very

simple and matter-of-fact character, that would lead to the preference I advise.

On the summit of the hill, water is difficult to be obtained without great expense; on the side it may be found in abundance. On the summit, stone, and sand, and timber have all to be slowly and painfully hauled from below; on the side, perhaps, all of the materials may be almost at hand, and, at any rate, are more easily reached.

There are some beautiful places (I have one now in my memory), where, with ravine, and waterfall, and forest trees, and evergreen groves, below and on either side, the most eligible spot for the house seems to be on a large extent of level tableland, that without being on the summit of a hill is yet elevated above the surrounding surfaces. In such a case, carefully avoid so placing the building as that it appears to stand alone, unsupported by stately trees or rising hills in the midst. Nothing can look more bare and un-home-like than an edifice so situated; if there are positively no trees near, and you have, after careful pondering over every foot of ground about your place, been forced to the determination to build your house on such an open space, all that can be done is, to surround your dwelling as much as may be with architectural shade, and to give it base upon the ground by spreading its verandahs, porch, and ombra widely on either side, trusting to the growth of the young trees you have liberally scattered around, and to the success of your efforts at removal and transplanting of larger trees from elsewhere, to provide a natural shade that will relieve the bareness of the building and give its outlines connection with the landscape.

Again, there are often situations in which you have to climb some craggy peak and perch your building upon its very summit, where it is difficult to determine the character of the parasitical house that would be appropriate, but as this is not a case of frequent occurrence, and as future chapters will treat of this class of house in detail, I will dismiss its consideration, and return to sites more usually adopted.

Say, then, you have selected a few acres of land, prettily wooded, and on or near a good country road, and you have stuck a peg into the earth as the spot where your house is to be; you have been moved by the arguments I have used, and have wisely determined to make the summit of the hill only a barrier to guard you from wind and cold, taking your place for building at an humbler elevation—to which determination you have been perhaps assisted in coming by some one's applying, to those who perch themselves on a mountain's peak,

> "Their pleasure greatest seems, I ween,
> In viewing landscape—to be seen."

The stake that marks the spot where your house is destined to stand, has been driven, of course, after due deliberation; you have probably had some idea of about the kind of house you intend erecting, and have pictured to yourself how the window of your library will peep upon yon pretty sunny dell, and the curl of the stream you have the good fortune to possess running through your place; a stately tree is not far off, and you think how, on a bright day, you will step out from your window upon the grassy slope, and stretch yourself beneath its limbs, and build castles in the air, no less substantial than those we are fabricating now. You cast your eye to an opening in the belt of trees that skirt the side of your grounds nearest the road, and you see at once how your carriage drive will wind through there, and bring you to the level flat, that you have at once decided shall be before your door. You see that there is a plentiful growth of trees towards the north and north-east, so plentiful as to allow of your cutting its margin back a little; for, you remember to have been told, trees on the north side of the house must not be too near, or they will harbor damp; they must be only near enough to screen the wind.

The same trees, too, will hide your kitchen offices and humbler buildings from view in approaching the entrance front of your house; and still walking on and admiring the many pretty vistas that open upon you as you change the point of sight, you mentally resolve that in such a room you will have a projecting window looking three ways, that shall command views as varied as they are pleasant.

You delight in finding that the level flat on which the house shall stand, is large enough to permit glorious verandas on the west, and on the south a spacious ombra or shade room (for the coining of which long wanted word, I claim a patency), and which (see Frontispiece) open to every breeze that blows, and roofed over at the top, will make you a charming place for a *siesta* in the afternoon, when the summer sun is looking a little too curiously upon the exposed sides of your dwelling.

Of course you have noticed that the spot is abundantly supplied with good water. Perhaps you have found some plentiful spring in the hill-side above you, the superior level of which will permit the luxury of water carried to every part of your house, bed-rooms, bathing-rooms, etc., and that, too, clear, fresh, spring water, and not stagnant roof-wash in a cistern; or some engineering friend has shown you how, from your never-failing brook below, a hydraulic ram will, at an expense of a hundred and twenty dollars, convey its liquid treasures up to your door, and into all your rooms; and you think of the pleasant splashing of a little fountain in your plant cabinet or ombra, until you can almost hear the tinkle of the drops as they patter in the vase brimming over with its sparkling contents.

You are not going to "lay out your grounds," as it is called—at least, not yet; you think nature has done very well so far, and that all you will venture upon at present is to assist her; and so you devise how a parterre there, and a clump of shrubs here, and a little cleaning of the ground generally, and a week's labor in clearing out the too luxuriant growth of under-brush in your woods, will do all you care to do at present. So all you undertake just yet, by way of preparation, is to mark out the line for your carriage drive, and to have the stones you collect off your grounds thrown thereon, and to have the earth turned up and well dressed, that you destine for your flower-garden and lawn—meaning, after the latter is made, to let a few sheep be your gardeners, knowing that the expense of an invisible wire fence will be far less than the maintenance of a man to mow and keep in order, and that your sheep will pay for themselves.

The fruit and vegetable garden, with a small, sheltered patch for herbs, you place near the kitchen and servants' offices, and are not very anxious they should be in sight; for, horticulturize it as you will, a row of bare bean-poles is not a very sightly object from a window.

You have now turned over all these things in your mind, and are ready to hear something more about the house; so at this point I will close this chapter, for I can scarcely go further in my capacity of architect, or I shall have the landscape gardener step in and say I am trenching on his ground.

# CHAPTER II.

## GENERAL ARRANGEMENT OF A HOUSE UPON THE GROUND—DISTRIBUTION OF ITS APARTMENTS.

THE planning of a house comprises, not only the arrangement of its rooms and offices, but the occupation also of the ground upon which it is to stand. Hence, a plan may be very well arranged in itself, so far as the convenience of rooms, passages, stairways, and domestic accommodations is concerned, and yet be ill adapted for erection upon a particular spot.

Thus, many books that give illustrated descriptions of villas and cottages sadly fail, when a reader endeavors to practically carry out any one of the designs they contain. He finds, however suitable it may appear at first sight, yet, when his ground comes to be fairly mapped before him, and he pencils his plan thereon; or, when better still, he goes upon the ground itself and pins out the outlines of his house, he generally has to abandon and change so much of the design in the book, as to involve the trouble of beginning almost *de novo*, as, in fact, it would prove ultimately more satisfactory if he did.

The designs that illustrate this book are not offered for actual embodiment and execution. They are merely given as models of what, under certain circumstances explained in detail, would afford good studies for those about building. So far only as the exigencies of the case in point are met by the examples herein contained would I counsel their adoption—no farther. There probably will be many hints and fragments of detail that can profitably be employed by those who may be about to construct a home; but I do not desire any of the plans to be considered as patent medicines suited to every disorder.

It is scarcely possible to do justice in designing a house, without study upon the spot where it is to stand. A carefully prepared map even, is not sufficient, so many considerations affecting the composition of a plan, which it is impossible a map should fully present.

Not merely the style and general character of a house are influenced by the contour and aspect of features in the landscape around, but its outlines on the ground, its arrangement in masses, equally are subject to the same laws that would direct the form of its exterior. So that it is almost impossible to find a design which, perfectly suited to one spot, shall, in every respect, be entirely appropriate in another.

The first thing to be done upon the ground towards planning a house, is to secure it a good aspect.

In England, it is very common to face the building, not due north and south, east and west, but to place it diagonally, so that the sun shall, in a greater or less degree, have access to each side of the house. This plan has advantages, which recommend its adoption in some cases here.

Although the southern side of the house has, in warm weather, the sun upon its front for a longer portion of the day than any other, it is nevertheless the most desirable for occupancy. A breeze almost always, even in hottest sunshine, rustles from the south, and the even, steady light, although bright and accompanied with heat, is cheerful. Properly contrived blinds will screen the sun, and due regard to the position of doors, windows, and ventilating valves, will secure a constant change of air within the rooms.

As a general rule, the entrance hall should not open towards the north, but towards the east, south, or west; if, however, any local peculiarity obliges the necessity of the northern side being chosen, take care that the hall door is screened by a porch, closed towards the north, and open through on the two sides, as then though the door be thrown back, the entrance of the cold air will be prevented. A carriage porch might easily be so arranged, the northern side filled in, and the eastern and western open with a broad arch—affording space enough for a carriage to be driven through, and allowing the travellers to alight under cover, and screened in winter from the nipping wind.

The kitchen and domestic offices may jut out towards the north, and stretching towards the belt of trees and shrubs the previous chapter described as screening the northern exposure, would leave the more desirable points of the compass for the main building.

If your destined home-life is going to be that of one at leisure, or a seeker of rest and refined and refining ease, you will probably desire your choice room to be a sort of snuggery, half-library, half-saloon, but wholly comfortable.

And so you take a sunny southern aspect for its one side; and if your room be very large, you divide its unity somewhat by a bay-window at one end, probably the eastern. In this, when the noonday blaze is pouring on your exposed side, you may sit ensconced, and read quietly with untroubled eye in the shade of its recess. Or you only occupy one outer wall—the southern—as a side to your room, shading that by a widely extended veranda, or an ombra, as represented in the frontispiece; thus having always perfect seclusion, with a cool and shady retreat, at the hottest portion of the day.

Your next thought will be of your dining-room, touching the aspect and position of which I have a few words to say.

If you are going to be an early-feeding, unsitting-after-late dinner family, let the room look east, and for this reason. In the middle of the day, when you sit down to table, a room *darkened* to exclude the sun, is both inconvenient and uncomfortable for purposes that, like carving, demand a steady light. By noon the sun will be off the eastern side, so you may dine in comfort, without interposing a blind as a barrier between your table and his scrutinizing glance.

If, however, you make the late afternoon or early evening meal the principal event of the day, a room with an end looking west through a bay in which the golden, glowing light may stream cheerfully in, richly touching up the crystal and the china upon your table, and adding another depth of mellow beauty to your apricot and peach, will, I think, be more pleasant; and so the question, touching, as I conceive it to do, upon these two points, I will leave, if you please, open for your consideration.

You, of course, will provide a little gem of a room—if octagonal, or oval, or quaintly cornered, so much the better—for the lady of the house; and whether boudoir, book-room, or work-room, as its fair presiding deity may determine, let it have the sunniest aspect, the most charming prospect you can give it; for there will the taste that can best enjoy the enjoyable—in outer view—

and inner elegance, mostly congregate. Place it south or southwest, opening into a plant cabinet or an ombra, not, I think, directly leading on to the main piazza, or its sweet seclusion would be marred; but yet in reach of all the agreeable adjuncts to the house which you have been able to attain.

The room answering to the *saloon*, drawing-room, or best parlor, is difficult to treat in a country-house. That a large, cheerful, gay, and airy room is desirable, I am not disposed, of course, to deny; but a room opened only occasionally, filled with finery, which is covered up from vulgar gaze three-fourths of the year, seems to me too party-ish and pretentious for the country. Still, a room for the evening accommodation of a large family, and for the occasional reception of company, is at least a convenience; and so, cautioning against the vulgar error of sacrificing all the comfort of the other rooms in the house to the attainment of a showy parlor, we will consider the provision of such a room a necessity, and trust to the good sense of its occupants to appropriate it properly.

Make a large, well-lighted apartment, facing south or west, with windows opening upon a spacious piazza; it may be *en suite* with the dining-room and boudoir, but not, to my taste, with the library. Any feature that will break the regularity of its outline, as a projecting bow or bay window, will take from the too dressy character of the room, and will be desirable, not only on that account, but from the increased cheerfulness of internal aspect it will impart.

In all good houses should be a gentleman's dressing-room; near the hall and the dining-room; but yet so cunningly contrived, as, whilst easy of access, to be nevertheless retired, and its entrance secured from observation.

The principal staircase should be roomy and easy of ascent, I would advise that it be *off*, though connecting immediately with. and not *in* the main entrance hall, as the latter could give an area of unobstructed space, very desirable if the house, as in holiday times, be filled with many dance and frolic-loving people. The first landing on the stairway leading to the chamber-story, should be so arranged as to come on the same level as the floor of rooms and passages over the offices, as it will then be handy to the back, or servants' staircase, and to the bathing-rooms, etc.

The sleeping apartments, I will only speak of here just so much as they are influenced by the distribution of the rooms in the floor below. They should be spacious, well-lighted and ventilated, and should all have separate means of access to the hall or corridors.

Dressing-rooms, linen-closets, housemaids'-closets, bathing-rooms, etc., etc., should be thought about in arranging the chamber floor, and the servants' stairway and passages ought, if possible, to be entirely distinct from those used by the family.

Some few directions as to the proportions of rooms seem necessary to accurately plan the outlines of the building upon the ground, which, dear reader, is all we will attempt at present, and then, when the excellencies of a house as laid down in the last chapter have been understood, examples of houses, and ground and chamber plans filled out in detail, can be discussed with greater profit.

The height and proportion of rooms must, in a measure, depend upon the size of the building; there are, however, certain restrictions that may be stated.

A dining-room, to secure the comfort of the diners, should not be ever less than sixteen feet, though, provided the fire-place be at the end, and not the side of the room, if needs must be, a less width will do; but fifteen is the minimum even then for servants to get comfortably between the table and the wall.

The drawing-room should not be square, but rather long than otherwise. The fireplace should be at the side of this room, unless its situation in reference to other rooms opening in connection with it, would render that position objectionable.

As a rule, endeavor not to have windows at opposite sides or ends of rooms, (unless only one end be kept open at a time,) or they will produce cross lights and some unpleasant phenomena of shadows and reflections, very trying to a fair face or a cherished picture.

The absolute proportions and heights of rooms have caused a good deal of argumentation and writing amongst those learned in such things; but, as a general rule, I may state to you that the height of a room, to produce a good effect, should never be less than three-fourths of its width; or, as a still better and more consequent guide, it should be one-third of the sum of the width and the length added together.

Thus, in an apartment sixteen feet by twenty, by the first rule, the height would be twelve feet; and the sum of the width and length being thirty-six feet, one-third of that would again give the height as twelve feet; and by either rule the result would be the proper altitude for such a sized apartment.

These rules, however, will not apply to long galleries, corridors, etc., of which the proportions are generally as varied as they are arbitrary; but as a basis for determining the proper height of rooms, as usually proportioned, their guidance may very safely be trusted.

The kitchen and domestic offices should be so arranged on the ground as to afford ready access to the vegetable garden, the farm yard, and the lane or road. Their adjuncts, as wood-shed, out-house, and the like, should be enclosed within a high wall or fence, that may shut them from view, unless the screen of trees and shrubs will do so effectually.

It is very desirable that there should be abundant space for all culinary and domestic operations; this may be gained, not so much by large rooms or yard, as by convenient arrangement of the different portions of the offices. A large kitchen is not nearly so really useful as one of moderate size, with proper conveniences of pastry-room, store-closet, cook's room, sink-room, and scullery attached. A kitchen, even for a very large household, need not be more than fifteen or sixteen feet by twenty, provided it has all these adjuncts conveniently near. The fire-place should be at the end rather than the side of the room; it is then more easy to avoid the heat, and greater room is given to move about, and more wall space for shelves.

The domestic offices should so join on the main body of the house, as that a pantry may communicate with the dining-room, and a passage may be preserved from the kitchen or servants' hall into the principal vestibule of the dwelling.

These hints will suffice to show what must be thought about in mapping out the house upon the ground; we have now the skeleton. In the next chapter, the materials in which to embody the design that is thus far framed, will be described.

## CHAPTER III.

### SELECTION OF MATERIALS—HOW SUITED TO PARTICULAR STYLES.

Now for the house itself. The best way to set about building a country house, I suppose I ought, with Abernethy, to say, is to "take advice"—put yourself under the guidance of a professional man. We will suppose that already done, and so I, standing in the light of architectural adviser, will proceed to the best of my ability to give the requisite information—as fully as if my retaining fee had been secured in the shape of a promised "five per cent." upon the cost of the proposed erection.

The true way to commence, is to first consider the subject in its common-sense, working-day light. You are going to put up what you mean as your home; you want screening from the sun, and sheltering from the cold; you desire to be at all times snug and comfortable, and free from all harassment, in any way traceable to your dwelling's external character or internal accommodation.

You have a wholesome dread of the horrors of a leaky roof, and of possible weekly repairs; you shudder at the idea of a damp bed-room, or a mouldy cupboard; and you have misgivings touching the amount of your Saint Anthony-like forbearance under the broiling tortures of a stifling July night, beneath a metal roof, and in an unventilated bed-room; and so all these thoughts make you reflect very deeply before choosing your material and your style. You notice I class these two together because I hope to show that the one influences the other rather more than it is the fashion, just now, to allow.

In choosing your material you are, of course, influenced by the selection your neighborhood affords. Wood and stone are those generally used; brick not being introduced so often into country buildings as I think it might be with great advantage.

For a house on a very large scale, wood seems unsuitable, because, in a greater or less degree, it is suggestive of temporary intention in the erection.

Stone is of many characters, and needs varied treatment. Its use is often a source of very great expense, where a character is attempted the particular specimen of material will not allow.

Brick does not seem as yet to have had a fair chance of trial: and though, where stone and timber are in abundance, I would not, of course, prefer its adoption; still there are many places in this country where it is both cheap and readily obtained, and in such places I conceive a far better use might be made of it than has, so far as my personal observation goes, been attempted.

England, France, and Germany abound with charming cottages, entrance lodges, and manorial residences constructed of this material; and those who only associate with the mention of its name a rectangular oblong three inches and a half by eight, would have a much more respectful opinion of its capabilities were they to see Holland House, l'Hotel Choiseul, or the innumerable pretty things dotted about the sunny lawns of Western Germany.

If your building is of moderate dimensions, and with timber conveniently near, you prefer to use wood, do thus: Let timber, and timber only, be evident in every part of your building. Don't veneer it all over with a thin ceiling of inch boards, nicely planed and fitted, and then sanded, and painted, and lined off, in imitation of stone; because if you do, no one will really be deceived by it but yourself. Especially, don't heap Pelion on Ossa, and glue up fluted monsters of carpentry in front, and fancy because they have the outline and proportions of Doric columns, and have painted white lines at even distances thereon, running round them at about the height courses of stone would be cut, you have shown your classical taste, and possess a Grecian edifice. You have no such thing; you have only a great deal of unnecessary and expensive wood-work constantly to paint and keep in repair, and which the sooner you sweep away the better.

If you like a smooth, unbroken surface, and prefer ceiling your house to clap-boarding or upright planking and battens, well and good. Ceil it and sand it also, if you will, (and sand is an admirable addition to your whitelead and pigments,) trusting to your verandas, projection of roofs, window caps, sills, and other features, to cast shadows and reflexes enough to break the monotony of a level surface of tint, which you will find by these natural causes more varied than if lined off into blocks with white paint and a rule stick.

A rustic treatment of this material is often effective. The veranda may be supported with cedar or cypress posts, upon which the bark has been left, farther preserving its adhesion by small tacks driven in here and there, and the whole varnished with a pitchy varnish to preserve from the weather. The house itself must be less architectural and finished in its details to conform to this style; and by covering externally with upright planking and battens, by projecting the roof at least four feet, and by avoiding everything that looks like pretension, a very pretty and economical dwelling may be constructed.

A building so contrived should be rather low than high; should be spread upon the ground; should have high-pitched roofs, with the gables free from the decoration admissible in more ornate styles. The rafters and roof-timbers that project may be simply finished by cutting their ends into the form of an S, as in the annexed illustration, and by substituting a deep roll moulding,

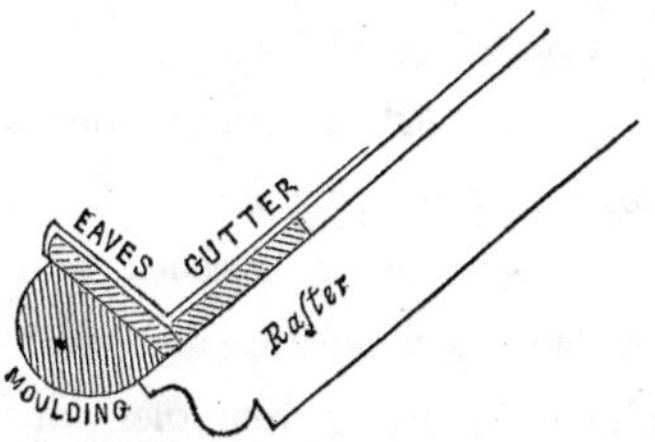


from six to twelve inches deep, running alike under the eaves and up the gables, in lieu of a cornice. The windows should be low and broad, rather than of their usual proportions; and many of my friends will thank me for telling them that to such a house outside blinds will be not only not unsightly, but a source of beauty, if properly managed; which I would do in this wise: Cut the outer or lower side of the slats to a curve, or some variation from a horizontal line, and make the frames broader than usual, and paint them a shade or two darker or lighter than that of the house.

Such a building, roofed with shingles, and painted a quiet

gray, with its veranda and ombra wreathed with graceful creepers, I can picture now before me as a very pretty home.

One constructed in accordance with these principles will be found exhibited in detail in a subsequent chapter.

Another style, for which wood is a suitable material, is that called "Gothic."

Unfortunately this beautiful and eminently rural style has been vulgarized and greatly abused; and I know that many persons of pure taste are hence frightened when the idea of "Gothic" is presented to them as the style suggested for their home.

Excuse me now, if I speak a little scientifically. Gothic is an architectural classification of principles of erection now determined simply to mean *pointed*, in contradistinction to those principles which recognized rectangular lines as their fundamental basis; thus classic architecture, as it is called, with its upright columns and pilasters, and its entablature and cornice resting on them at right angles, or springing from them in semi-circular curves, is very easily distinguished from that style which has its lines all tending upwards to a point, and of which its curves, in every instance, meet in a point. The different periods at which certain styles of pointed architecture prevailed, give the name to its various classes now in use. Rural Gothic is wrought out from these different styles, and though the peculiarities of each period of pointed architecture are very marked, they have become universally so blended in modern domestic architecture, a description of the points of difference in each period is scarcely needed.

But the great principle upon which all were based, and in which all agreed, was reality: every form of even the simplest moulding; every line and portion of the building was contrived exactly to answer the purpose for which it was intended; and in this we will gladly follow the mighty artist-minds of old whilst we scorn the petty trickery of servilely copying a bit here and there of their immortal works, and leaving unnoticed the inborn principle which made each bit of detail beautiful.

A Gothic house, then, is a building, the character of whose architecture is distinguished by the upward direction of its leading lines, and by such curves as may be introduced meeting, or having a tendency to meet, in a point. It may be highly ornamental, or left perfectly simple; but true taste will be outraged if ornament, beautiful as it may be in itself, is introduced where it does not serve some purpose of construction.

The gables, and the windows, and the doors, and the veranda, and ombra, may all be decorated as richly as you like; but it must be their composing parts that receive the decoration; there must be no ornamental work stuck on here and there without meaning and use: too much ornamental wood-work about a house, any way, is a nuisance, and a source of continued expense.

In arranging the outlines of your plan upon the ground, the selection of wood as the material will permit of a more varied and irregular shape than stone or brick, the corners, which, in mason-work, add so considerably to the expense, not being a source of greater outlay. But irregular outline on the ground is apt to involve intricacy of roof; be therefore thoroughly satisfied the latter is going to give you no trouble before you commence.

Dormer windows on the roof are greatly in favor with those who design Gothic houses. Unless they are clear above the eaves, so as to allow the eaves' gutters to run below them in unbroken line, they will, in heavy rains, or after a thaw, be sources of great trouble.

A very pretty effect may be attained by cutting off the corners of the shingles before nailing them on, or by rounding them off, or giving them any other form that will work in such a manner as to present the appearance of an ornamental pattern on the roof. The covering of the veranda is generally of metal, but where the slope will allow similar shingles to be used, the effect is not only more pleasing, but the chambers whose windows overlook, are less exposed to the radiated heat from the large surface of metal below.

Those who have noticed recently erected Gothic country houses, will probably remember that the windows seemed a source of some difficulty; they were either ordinary sash windows, that did not seem to harmonize with the house, or they were such as gave great trouble to the inmates. I would advise, where the character of open tracery is attempted to be given, that it be made solidly and as a fixture outside; being, in fact, as it may well be supposed to be, the ornamental support of the lintel above; and that the part filled with glass be behind and independent, having, however, divisions similar in character to the outer frame. This method of executing an ornamental window will, I think, be found productive of more external and internal effect, and certainly remedies the difficulties I have, in the course of my experience, found to exist.

The modern Italian bracketted style is one which has been frequently adopted for wooden buildings.

It demands more regularity of external outline upon the ground, and hence is better adapted for a villa, in finished garden grounds, than for a rural home in a picturesque and natural situation.

Its element consisting in the constant recurrence of horizontal lines, a flat roof seems almost indispensable; a high pitch, or pointed gables, are therefore out of place.

It permits great variation in the heights of different parts of the building; but the breaks must be made vertically from a horizontal line—not by slope pointing above slope, as in the spire and tower of a Gothic structure.

The species of buildings whence this style, as used now, originated, abounded in *campanili*, or bell-towers, the form and character, though not the uses of which are retained—the upper story of said towers being finished as an observatory, affording a cool and pleasant retreat, from the open windows of which an extended prospect may be commanded. In a house of mine on the Hudson, this portion of the tower is intended as a billiard-room. For small and unpretending country dwellings, this style is desirable equally with those on a large scale, and in many situations would be found to look more home-like than, perhaps, almost any other.

The great objection is the necessity for a flatter pitch of roof than a shingle covering will allow; and there are many reasons that a metal roof should not be resorted to, where shingles can be used. A sufficient pitch of roof to permit covering with shingles would give an entirely different character to a house erected in this style; but a modification may be resorted to, which will render such a pitch perfectly admissible. In such a case, the slope of other roofs, such as veranda, porch, etc., should agree with it; and it may farther be harmonised by making the brackets much longer or deeper than if the roofs were flatter.

Circular-headed windows are found very generally in the various examples of buildings from which this style has been derived. They are often introduced in modern buildings here; but where outside blinds are to be used, they do not look very well, as each half of the blind, when open, presents an unsightly appearance.

One advantage this style possesses is the adaptation it affords to internal furnishing and decoration. Gothic furniture is too apt to look outré; but any species of modern cabinet work, excepting Gothic, looks well in a room of this character.

Wood when selected for the construction of a dwelling of this character, has one disadvantage connected with it, in the too great temptation to introduce ornamental work, which in this facile material is apt to lead into the putting up of a great deal of unnecessary carpentry, the maintenance of which will be attended with expense.

In speaking of these three different classes of country houses—the Rural, the Gothic, and the Italian—I have comprised all those that are generally seen. Other varieties there are, I know; but they all have so much in common with some one or other of these three, that my readers will not wish me to describe them.

Stone, with its pleasant associations of moss and fretted surface, seems the material for a quiet, rustic home; there is something in its aspect, of appeal from the long, long past, and of promise of endurance in the future, that must make it especially sought after by those who preach a crusade against the ephemeral pretensions of the present day.

Where it is found in abundance upon the spot, and its character is such as a respectable mason would recommend for building purposes, I would say, use it for your house, by all means.

If you are from the city, do not, however, fancy, because stone is your material, that you must have a Fifth Avenue front. If your stone is susceptible of dressing and tooling, as it is called, and your purse and the character you mean to give to the architecture will allow cut stone to at least portions of the erection, there can be no objection to artistically displaying the material to the best advantage; but even then, unless you are seeking to build a palace, do not think of having your building faced with cut stone. Rough stone, as it comes from the quarry, and laid in its natural bed, for the walls, and cut stone for your door and window dressings, and your plinth and porch, if you will; and the one will give contrast and value to the other.

If, however, the texture of the stone should not prove sufficiently fine for working, and you desire to build the walls simply in a durable and substantial manner, use the stone as follows:

Let the quarrymen split it off just as the veins of the stone make it most easily worked. Select such pieces as, from their length and *even* quality, seem adapted for sills and lintels, and use the remainder just in the shape it naturally comes upon your ground from the quarry. In building your walls, lay the stone in its exact bed as it lay in the quarry, and here and there let long pieces be introduced, the length of the thickness of your walls; these, lying across, would serve as *bonders* to the walls, and will materially strengthen the work. A wall built in this manner, in irregular courses, looks remarkably well for country buildings, and it is the method in which the time-honoured rural churches of England have been built, than which more simply beautiful or more durable erections cannot be found.

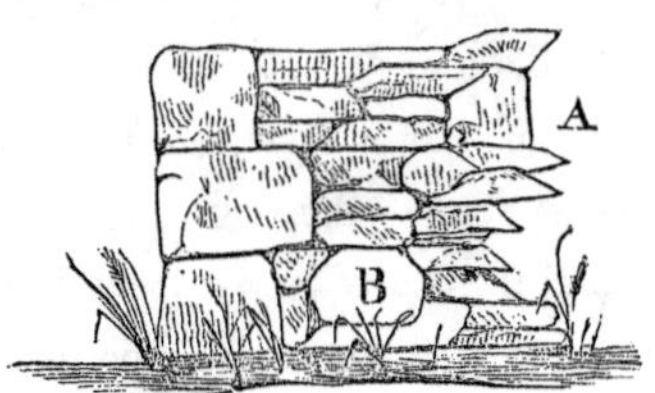


This sketch shows the wall laid in the manner described; solid "quoins" as they are called are built into the corners, one alternately overlapping the other. The other stones are placed in layers with the direction of their lamina as imbedded in the quarry, and at certain distances apart "bonders"—indicated by letters A and B—pass solidly through, and give union and adhesive connection to the masonry.

Many builders will tell you to place your stones edgeways or upright, instead of in the solid manner I have described; and it is true the masonry will look as if constructed of larger blocks, and will have a more regular appearance, but it is by no means so durable—the walls, in fact, being no more than shells of outer and inner veneering of smoothly-fitted slabs of stone placed on end, and filled in with loose bits of rubbish and mortar. A wall can even be built more rapidly if laid as I direct; because no time is taken in selecting the stone, and of course the stone is quarried and built into the walls at less expense.

Persons complain of stone houses in the country being damp. This inconvenience is caused by the walls not being properly built, rather than by the nature of the material itself. Such dampness as may be found in a stone building, comes, not from surface exposure to the weather, but from wet arising in the walls by capillary attraction from the ground. A wall built as I speak of, would prevent this; because the pores of the grain would be horizontal, and the possibility of dampness finding its way by any means through the interstices upwards, may be guarded against by building a course of slate into the walls above the ground, and immediately under the joists of the first floor. This, where slate can easily be procured, is an infallible method; and where it is not within reach, a course of large stones, of the width of the thickness of the walls, and about four inches thick, laid in hydraulic cement, will do equally well.

A wall may be plastered inside, without any furring out, as usually done, if built as above, and without any fear of wet finding its way in.

A country house, to be built of stone, in the rural manner described in my last, would require to be of very simple form; there should be few breaks in the outline, and the effect called by artists "breadth" must be that sought.

The veranda, windows, doors, and roof, may be treated in a manner similar to that recommended for the rural home sketched in the commencement of the chapter. The windows should be set deeply in the walls, and the roofs have a greater projection, and their timbers that show be somewhat heavier in their scantlings. Let the stone be rough, just as the masons lay it, knocking off, here and there, with a hammer, any fragment that seems to jut out too prominently, and I would much prefer that the walls be not rough-cast.

In building on a Gothic plan, the style would have to be less ornate in its details than if the material were wood, and the minutiæ of the building should be more massive in their character.

Bay-windows, or other projecting portions of the plan, only partially extended up the walls, may be more easily and always more economically constructed of wood than of stone. Indeed, unless the piers between the openings be very large, the latter material can scarcely be used unless cut, and then entailing considerable expense. But so constructed, (of wood) a different treatment must be sought; stone must not be imitated, but the character of the design of such a feature be evidently appropriate to the material;—harmony with the rough stone walls being obtained by the wood-work being sanded to protect from the weather, and painted to suit the tone of coloring of the stone. By the means thus taken to *preserve* (a mode perfectly allowable and no wise approaching the vulgarity of imitation), the tint of the rough wall and the quality of its texture will be assimilated with.

Outside shutter-blinds never seem to match with rough stone walls; and as the thickness of the latter is such as in all cases to permit of their being arranged inside, I would advise their being so contrived, and a pent roof over the window will add as much to the picturesque external appearance, as it will to the internal comfort of the building.

An illustration is here given of such a window covering. The roof, a simple lean-to, is supported by brackets built into the walls of the house, and made of wood. This covering should be so placed as that the head of the window would be about one foot above the drop of the roof.

The modern Italian, as described in this chapter, is as suitable for erection in stone as in wood, but the masonry should generally be more regular and finished than would be requisite for either of those described before. Hence the expense will be greater, but

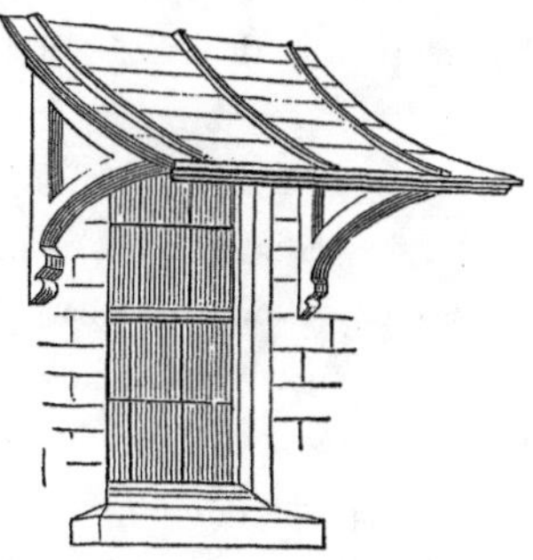

provided the simplicity of the wood-work and other portions of the house were agreeable, a rough stone building would look very well, even if its outlines and its general form were in strictest accordance with the severest requisitions of the style.

Open arches are prominent features in an Italian rural building; the veranda, the porch, ombra, and window-openings, especially those of the upper story of the tower, may take this beautiful form, and the massive nature of the material of the house will blend delightfully with the ideas of strength the arch conveys.

Terraces are constantly associated features with this style, and if the ground upon which your home is to be, naturally presents a terraced appearance, a very little aid from art will soon convert it into the beautiful form that is so suitable to an Italian villa.

Moulded brick might be frequently used upon a country-house; and brick, as a suitable material for building, must receive a few moments' attention before I bring this chapter to a close.

It is not so suitable for Gothic as for other styles, though the Tudor, as it is called, which is but a later period of Gothic architecture, seems well adapted to its use, and England and the western portion of the Continent of Europe abound in examples.

Brick walls should be built *hollow*. They will be cheaper, drier, and afford room for sliding-shutters, windows, and blinds, and, above all, give the opportunity for thorough and easily-controlled ventilation. Insist upon your builder wetting the bricks before laying them on the walls, if even you have to pay the labor of an extra man on purpose to do so. Your walls will be stronger and drier if you do.

Do not, as a general rule, permit any smoke-flues in outer walls. They are the cause of an extravagant waste of heat, and of unsightly seams and stains down your external walls, particularly if painted. If you have a cistern in your roof, build a kitchen or some constantly-used flue through it. You will then not fear frost; and if, once every six months, you will place therein a bushel of powdered charcoal, you need not have stagnant, fetid water, breeding corruption in your home.

If your brick house is to be painted, cover it with two coats of paint in the fall. The bricks will be thoroughly dry then, and the quantity of paint will be amply sufficient to repel all wet during the winter, and will be ready-toned down to receive the finishing coat or coats in the spring.

Whilst in this connection, a few words upon the painting of a brick building, and I have done.

The color chosen should be one that will suit the objects around. If there be many lichen-covered rocks near, or grey mountains in the distance, against which the building is seen, the tint should be a cool grey, which may be made with any blue that will stand, mixed with one tenth part Venetian red, and lowered with white as requisite; and I have frequently used sand upon brick buildings with great advantage, by mixing it with the last two coats, or even the last, and applying it with a wire-brush, which, though requiring a strong arm, is much more satisfactory in its effect than if the sand were dusted on, which leaves a number of shining particles to catch the light, and by their dazzling appearance, destroy the quiet, even tone of color a house should possess, and which the former method will secure.

If the house be surrounded by trees, many of which are evergreens of dark foliage, a lighter and more distinguishing color may be used. Cream color, made by mixing one part raw umber, two parts raw sienna, one fourth part burnt umber, to one hundred parts white lead and oil. The last coat, mixed with silver sand, is a very beautiful tint for a building in such a situation.

The taste of the owner will no doubt lead to the selection of a proper color, particularly as I have said enough to guide him; and I will conclude, by quoting the advice given by a noted English landscape painter under similar circumstances: "Pluck up a tuft of grass near you, observe the tone of coloring the earth adhering to its roots possesses, and paint your house the tint you see there."

The gist of this remark lies in the fact that the tone of coloring of natural objects immediately around you is the best possible pattern-card from which to select the pigment you desire your painters to use.

# CHAPTER IV.

## HEALTH IN A HOME;—AS DEPENDENT UPON VENTILATION, AND ON MEANS OF OBTAINING ARTIFICIAL HEAT.

A COMFORTABLE home must be both a warm and a sweet one.

Its warmth is dependent in winter upon its provisions for artificial heating; its sweetness, at all seasons, upon its ventilation; its thorough comfort, upon both.

Dickens's "Household Demon," an air-tight stove, will afford the one, so far as certain degrees of the thermometer are any indication, and an open door and window, when its hot breath has become a little too searching, will, according to generally received country practice, supply the other.

The cold air thus admitted is soon weakened by its battling with the stifling heat, and another reinforcement from without becomes necessary; and so, in severe weather, the temperature is constantly jumping from extremely hot to extremely cold. After a while, the decomposed air gathers upon the ground, where its weight has taken it, and heaps itself up, layer upon layer, until it reaches the mouth and nostrils of those sitting in the room, who, in every eighteen respirations, inhale in the course of a minute, a gallon of stuff so foul, as, could it be made sensible to sight in the form of a refreshing draught, would fill them with loathing and dismay.

With an open fire, the evil is somewhat lessened, but not removed; with a furnace, it is changed. What is to be done? Would you cut off all means of artificially warming? Certainly not; but, in warming—*purify!*

The simple principle upon which this purification must be effected is this: Provide a means for withdrawing the debris of every gallon of warm air you admit, and you may do so in the following manner:—

Say you are sitting in a room eighteen feet wide by twenty-six feet long, and that the fire-place, or register, is in the centre of one of the longer sides; the windows are at one end, and the doors at the other, or in the side opposite the fire-place.

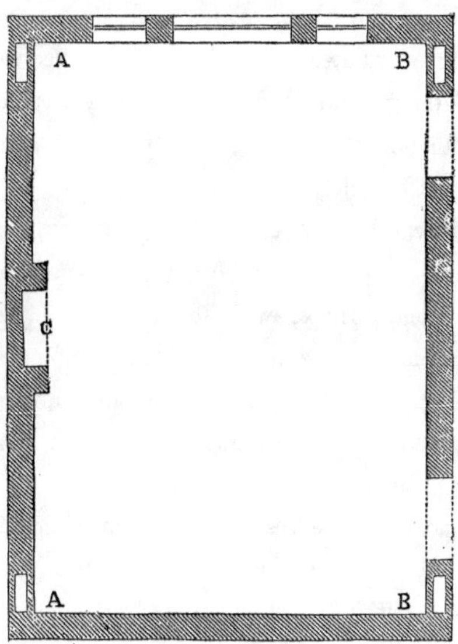


By the help of the annexed plan, I can make the method I would propose apparent.

In this, the letter C represents the position of the fire-place or hot air supplying register; the doors into the room are, we will say, upon the opposite side, and the windows at either end.

As the freshly warmed air comes into the room it will gradually ascend, and in its ascent will incorporate with itself the lighter portions of decomposed air that have escaped from the lungs, leaving the heavier but equally impure gases to settle near the floor. For the escape of this upward flow of foul air, openings are made in or near the ceiling, at the points indicated by the letters A, A;—these openings communicate with air-ducts or flues, which I will presently describe.

If, however, the aperture for the escape of foul air be solely at the ceiling, much of the warm, good air will fly off, as well as some of the upper vitiated atmosphere, and hence lower the temperature of the room, and demand an increased supply of heat. The ventilation, therefore, of the apartment given as an example, is not yet complete.

Many persons who have furnaces or other heating apparatus in their buildings, complain of not being able to obtain a sufficient heat, not being, perhaps, aware, that the fault very probably lies in a want of means for escape of the dense impure strata of air that are stagnating just above the floor, and through which the fresh warm air cannot penetrate in sufficient purity and volume to raise the temperature of the room.

This was found to be the case at the Patent Office in Washington. An excellent warming apparatus had been used, but in a certain room, about forty feet square, tightly closed, and with (I think) but one window at the end, it was found impossible to attain a heat exceeding forty degrees Fahrenheit, with the furnace turned on to its full blast; when some one suggested to cut a hole in the floor, which was no sooner done than the confined ponderous gases plunged down the aperture, and in a few minutes the thermometer showed the excessive heat of ninety degrees.

These remarks I introduce to show the necessity of providing some downward conducting flues, as well as those leading upwards. At the letters B, B, are openings in the wash-board immediately above the floor of the room conducting into air passages that discharge themselves below.

The action of the air in the room thus provided with apertures for escape and supply of air will be as follows: As it rolls in volumes of warmth into the room, it will expand and ascend, moderately, however, because the top openings must not be too large for undue escape of heat. As it becomes used, the deoxygenated portions having a heavier specific gravity than the pure air, will fall towards the floor, and be drawn off by the air-ducts and dissipated below. The lighter, heated air also expelled from the lungs, will escape into the apertures above, as will also all superfluous heat, the apertures in the ceiling being provided with regulating valves, so that, guided by a thermometer within the room, its occupants may graduate the supply *from* the register and escape *through* the flue.

These apertures for the upward escape of air must be furnished with one of Arnott's Patent Ventilating Valves, a simple and most effective little article recently introduced from England, and now furnished by the Berrians, 601 Broadway, with great improvements in external form and appearance, and in the method of acting.

This ventilator is provided with a balanced valve, which

closes instantly at the slightest puff of air from above; hence effectually preventing downward draught, or the escape of smoke into the room if placed in connection with an ordinary smoke-flue.

A regulating lever is also attached by which the opening of the valve and consequent size of the aperture of escape may be adjusted at will.

A cut is here given showing this little machine. The outer portion which comes flush upon the wall might be made of any form or ornamented at pleasure.

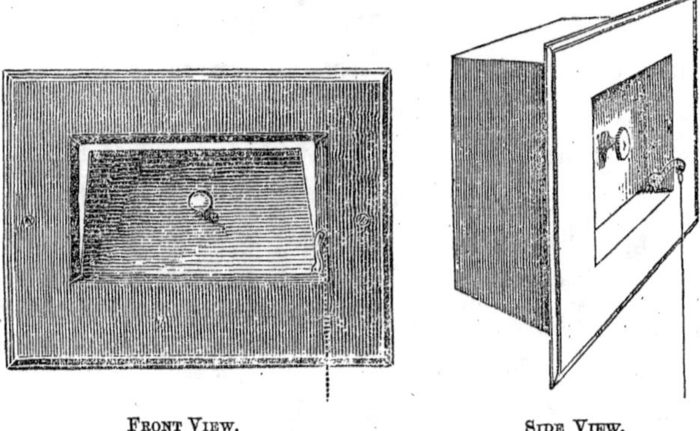

FRONT VIEW. SIDE VIEW.

The box is let into the wall, so that the outside face may come even with its surface. The price for one as here represented is three dollars, other and more ornamental forms are in proportion.

The flue for downward escape of impure air may conduct into any part of the cellar, or even into the open air, and an ordinary register, or simply a perforated metal front, would be all that is needed within the room.

In making these flues, abrupt turns or shoulders, or any other direction than a perpendicular one, must be carefully avoided, unless the current be very strong.

If the house is warmed by a furnace, a very perfect means of ventilation may be adopted by providing an escape-flue and air-chamber of large dimensions, through which the smoke-flue from the furnace may be led, the spare heat from which would, by its radiation, cause expansion and consequent rapid motion of the air contained in the flue and air-chamber around it, and hence provide a current sufficiently strong to draw off all impure air from the various rooms which, by means of air-ducts, communicated with it.

But these air-ducts must equally be means of escape for impure air, both from the upper and lower portions of the room, or the ventilation will be very imperfect.

The form and nature of the flues themselves require attention. If built of stone or brick, their inside surfaces should be pargetted or plastered, or the roughened sides will too greatly impede the passage of the air by friction. A circular, elliptical, or square with bevelled corners are more desirable forms than the narrow parallelogram usually employed, but on account, not so much of expense, as the unwillingness of masons to depart from established usage, although cylindrical flues are very commonly used in England, and are found to be more cheaply built. They are, I believe, almost unknown here.

But the mere provision of these flues is not all that is necessary, nor would the method of ventilation here described be sufficient except during such seasons as will allow the use of a furnace or fire.

The air will not ascend of itself into these flues, nor will it descend and be discharged without some motive power being given to it.

This motive power, when a furnace or fire is in operation, can be obtained by the radiation of the artificially heated air, and all that will be necessary is to terminate the flues that lead above the building with a "cowl" or "wind-guard," to protect from draughts of air. In his admirable and invaluable report upon "Ventilating Buildings," Dr. Bell, of the McLean Asylum for the Insane, near Boston, says: "Any flues depending wholly upon the action of cowls or turn-caps in any of their numerous forms, are totally unequal to the demands of a constant, reliable ventilation." Those ventilators which are so constantly advertised to the public as *at all times* causing circulation of air within the building cannot therefore be depended upon—they will only assist—but unless used in conjunction with other means (presently to be described) their action will only be when there is a current of air flowing across the roof, and bearing upon the sides of the ventilating cap employed. Of these numerous machines, that made by Janes, Beebe & Co. of New York, is undoubtedly the best, and will take advantage of the slightest breath of air that stirs.

The reliable means, therefore, to be employed is this: One of the escape flues from the room must lead into a shaft which may ventilate the whole house very easily and economically, and in the following manner: At all times of the year culinary operations demand a heating apparatus, giving a constant, though, perhaps, varying degree of warmth. The discharging smoke-flue from this, conducted into a large shaft, would *at all seasons* produce motion in the column of air therein contained, and this, aided too by a ventilating cap o' extra size placed at the top of the shaft, would draw off from all the rooms that could be brought in connection with it the vitiated air, from both *above* and *below.*

To exemplify this, let me refer again to the little plan given. Let one of the upper apertures communicate with the shaft, to be used during summer—let one of the downward shafts also so communicate—and the other, left as before, but *kept always open,* would supply cold fresh air to the lower portion of the room, a thing so necessary, that it seems strange builders should only permit cracks, or the occasional opening of doors, to admit what the first principle of pneumatics requires, it being impossible that vitiated air can escape, when no fresh air can take its place.

Open windows are not always desirable, nor to ventilate successfully and reliably are they at all to be wished for; but as this involves an explanation of a system of ventilation more thorough and elaborate than ordinary dwelling houses would require or permit, I will content myself with saying, that it is best to consider windows as only auxiliary aids to ventilation, securing perfect circulation of air in the apartment without.

The shaft spoken of in connexion with the kitchen fire may be thus supplied with hot air:

A large metal chest or chamber, supplied with fresh air from behind, should be built into the chimney of the kitchen, or other room where fires are daily used. This chamber must be placed back of the fire-place, stove, or other cooking apparatus, or over the boiler, if hot-water bathing apparatus is provided. It must be capable of containing not less than ten cubic feet of air, and from its top a pipe, not less than six inches in diameter, would lead into the discharging flue intended for ventilation, and then diminished so as to leave around it, in the shaft, a space of at least two inches in the clear, each way. Thus diminished, it should extend upwards in the flue for at least ten or fifteen feet.

The radiation thus caused will produce a sufficiently strong current to draw off from the rooms connected with it all impurities of atmosphere, as before explained.

In many parts of this country, and especially in the Southern States, a summer kitchen is used, which is detached from the house. In such a case, it is more difficult to obtain the necessary motive power for successful ventilation, but as the smoke-flue from the kitchen might be led sufficiently near to the house to permit the erection of a lofty shaft for the especial purpose of drawing off its foul air, the same principle can be employed. The air-ducts cannot be led to the kitchen if detached, on account of the almost impossibility of drawing air without an immense force in a horizontal direction, but the hot escaping air from the fire-place can more easily be led, and if the shaft be lofty (which some such feature as a tower or corner turret would allow it to be) and its top be terminated with one of Janes' most powerful ejectors, there will be little difficulty in obtaining the motive force requisite.

A very simple means of ventilating a room only occasionally used, is by placing a lighted lamp in an ordinary flue, providing the aperture with one of Arnott's valves to prevent downward draught. The heated air from the combustion of the lamp will produce an upward current, and thus ventilate the room without in any way producing increase of temperature by the burning of the lamp.

I have contrived a little apparatus for this purpose—of which the following is a description.

The whole apparatus is comprised in a metal screen, intended to supply the place of an ordinary fire-board at such times when the grate is not used. The lower portion is open, for the escape of the foul air from the floor of the room, and above is a door, inside of which on a small shelf is the lamp. This lamp can be made to burn camphene, lard oil, or any cheap combustible, as the formation of the trumpet-shaped tube or chimney which encloses it, is such as to prevent carbonization. When shut, the lamp is covered above the flame with a metal trumpet-shaped funnel, opening as wide as the flue will permit at its mouth, and reduced to four inches diameter above, extending up the flue at least *one foot above* the height of the room. The radiated heat from this would suffice to give motion to the column of air within the flue, and a cap at its top would secure, with this little machine, a perfect and always reliable ventilation. Near the ceiling, into the same flue is an aperture furnished with Arnott's valve for escape of warm air from the upper portion of the room. The tube within the flue need not be removed at any season, as it would not interfere with the draught of any grate or stove that in winter might be used, but would rather increase it; the lower portion of the funnel, which could be made in a length of three feet, might easily be detached and connected when required. This apparatus can be supplied by Janes, Beebe & Co. of New York, or ordered through the Messrs. Berrian, and its cost need not exceed twenty-five dollars.

It is very necessary to the comfort of a home that the kitchen should be thoroughly ventilated; and though my readers will see, from what I have said, that this room may be more readily purified than any other, they will agree with me in condemning the want of attention that has so often permitted a nuisance, from escaped effluvia of cooking, that might so easily have been avoided.

A ventilating flue should be provided, not only in the kitchen itself, but in the vestibule, hall, or pantry, connecting it with the main body of the house, and the store-room, vegetable-room, larder, and, of course, bathing-rooms, etc., should each have an air-duct for supply and escape.

Chambers immediately under the roofs of country houses are frequently rendered scarcely habitable, in consequence of the heat.

This excessive heat may be greatly lessened by making a double roof; that is, by furring out a space all over the roof, from the under side of the rafters to the line of the ceiling. This space, say of about a foot deep, would, if made perfectly tight, afford a receptacle for a stratum of dead air, than which a more perfect non-conductor cannot be found. External heat could not penetrate through this double roof, and in cold weather, internal warmth would not be lessened by contact with the cold inner surface of the roof.

Houses artificially heated, are usually supplied either with hot-air furnaces, of which there are several kinds, by steam, or by hot water.

Heating by means of hot-water apparatus is deservedly attracting great attention now, and when constructed on scientific principles and the *radiating surface is sufficient* (the want of this being the common fault), is an agreeable, healthy, and economical method, and one I would, from experience, recommend in preference to any other.

There are many machines for effecting this end before the public, but I have rarely found that the pretensions of the greater number have been justified by their actual operation.

An Italian villa erected in Connecticut from my designs, was provided with a ventilating and heating apparatus in which hot water was used, which, after a trial of eighteen months, has given such entire satisfaction, that I am induced to make mention of it here, particularly as its manufacturers, Janes, Beebe & Co., of New York, have so distinguished a reputation, I can refer to their work without incurring any suspicion of intention to "puff."

The building has a frontage of nearly ninety feet, is built of brick and stone, and upon a somewhat exposed situation; every room is ventilated and most pleasantly warmed, by a heat which, though capable of increase to almost any degree, is yet so soft as neither to warp the wood-work of the building nor the furniture, and is produced by an expenditure of fuel so trifling, as would surprise those who are accustomed to the hot-air furnaces in ordinary use. The working of this apparatus is the subject of praise from all who have witnessed it, and it has now been in action sufficiently long to thoroughly test its merits.

In another chapter, before closing this little treatise on Rural Homes, I shall detail at length the peculiarities of this apparatus, and recur to the subject of ventilation and of heating. At present, I wish merely to say just so much on the general principles of the former, as will enable my readers to understand the allusions made here and there in subsequent portions of the book ;—thinking, too, that ventilation is so important a means of attainment of comfort, it ought to be thought of from the first, so that the "home" to be contrived may be "both a warm and a sweet one."

# CHAPTER V.

## HOW TO BUILD TO SUIT THE LANDSCAPE—EXAMPLES OF RURAL HOMES.

The right to look upon beautiful scenery, is a privilege all possess in common: those whose means have enabled them to claim ownership in some lovely garden-spot of this beautiful country, have no right to mar the fair harmony of nature by the intrusion of a discord of their own. The purchasers of land therefore, in the country, cannot, in building themselves a home, follow the bent of their own inclinations so entirely as many would have us suppose. A man has no right to disfigure some noble scene by an unharmonious dwelling: how often this has been done, those who have rambled on the banks of the Hudson (this but as an example near home) can testify. Congruity between home and landscape is secured by no necessarily increased expenditure. On the contrary, those buildings of most economical and simple character generally possess the charm of fitness which costly structures attempt in vain.

Undoubtedly, the excellence and charm of a home consist in the perfect keeping of the artificial construction with the natural objects and the scenery around. The uniform Palladian Villa, that would be out of place in the mountain gorge, or beside the rocky glen and leaping torrent, will be perfectly in congruity with broad lawns, grouped trees, smooth, widely-stretching glades, and the placid lake. This perfect congruity between home and scenery would be easy of attainment, if the operations of deciding the character and arrangement of the building were less mechanical. The owner of the ground is generally content, if the builder to whom he shows his plans tells him he can deliver to him, by a certain day, and for so much money, a house like the one delineated. How have these plans been probably obtained? If the gentleman or lady about to build possess at all a literary, or even only a picture-book-loving taste, some "Architectural Design-Book for the Million" has been turned over, and, after many tea-table discussions upon the merits of the "Swiss Cottage" style, the "Anglo-Norman," the "Etruscan," or the "Castellated Gothic," some pretty picture-house has been selected. Armed with that, an architect from the city has been called upon, the picture shown to him, the ground-plan of the house determined, and, finally, a "set of drawings" engaged to be furnished by a certain day, and at a stipulated price.

Probably even this small call upon professional aid would not have been made, had not the builder advised to get some "archy-tect" to "draft the plans," knowing that even the most wretchedly slender skeleton of a plan, if framed by a draughtsman, will be easier to work from than the artistic performances of the amateur employer. The architect has neither a voice nor an interest in the matter—the drawings are ordered and paid for, as a bale of goods. He has not seen the spot selected for the building;

knows nothing of the tastes or habits of life of its future occupants, and is naturally only desirous to get the job done as quickly as possible, knowing, by past experience, that, should he venture any departure from the instructions given him—however essential they may, to his cultivated judgment, seem—the drawings will probably be returned to him for correction, and his labor lost. How tame, common-place, and unsuitable the building must be when erected, my readers will be able to judge. What, then, should be done?

The building should, even to its minutest detail, be studied and determined on the spot; and an architect who has the interests of his noble science at heart, will *always* insist upon the necessity for this very first step. Both the architect and the contemplator of the building must be guided by such simple rules as I will here attempt to state. Endeavor first to be impressed with the suggesting influences of the spot. If the range of vision be limited, the scenery quiet, and possessing a self-contained charm of beauty or grandeur complete in itself, the character of the house may be left more to the bent of the owner's taste, than were the building a prominent feature in an extended range of landscape—a connecting link in the chain of beauties around. If the first be the case, the house—governed, however, by certain rules—may be more fancifully developed, more profuse in details, and more whimsical, than in a situation like the latter. There every outline must accord with the prevailing character of the natural forms around, and the details and architectural features must be bolder, more marked and expressive, in order to be defined by the eye that views them after a scale formed upon the bold fragments of nature's architecture. These considerations are the text from which all rules for the choice of styles may be deduced. General outlines and effects, rather than minutiæ of details, are to be studied, to secure congruity between art and nature; the niceties of particular styles are only to be so attended to that they may not conflict with the first great truth of harmony of the general masses. Almost any style may, in the hands of a master, be made suitable for a given location; and there are few modern styles that may not architecturally be moulded to the requirements demanded.

So, then, I come once more to a definition made before, that the style must grow out of the circumstances bearing upon the building, upon the nature of the materials, the peculiarities of climate, of domestic habits, and, above all things, upon the prevailing influences of the scenery around. In high mountain scenery, where the outlines of the forms around all point upwards, and shoot into pyramids of beauty towards the skies, the building, in its lines, must not contradict this tendency: the prevalence of horizontal lines and parallelisms must be cautiously avoided, and the style chosen must be such as, without violation of its attributes, will permit this character. Thus, we see, in olden times, the builders on the plains erected flat-roofed, widely-extended dwellings, with row upon row of parallel lines; but in mountain lands, up soared the gable, and high-pointed pinnacle and spire, until the architect seemed emulous of soaring aloft with the mountain peaks and stately hills.

Let me now sketch a scene such as my readers will be able to picture before them without any effort. Here is a road leading from a country town. At a distance of two or three miles from the busy market-place, a quiet lane leads from the more frequented public road, and a quarter of a mile down this lane we will enter a gate, and walk upon the grass within. The lane we have left continues its winding and tree-shaded course to a bridge which, half a mile off, stretches across the stream that originally induced the settlers to choose the town below, where its waters flow in greater volume, as their site. The ground is tolerably level, and has trees scattered here and there; but, as is generally the case, not very much has been done towards its cultivation. We have progressed to the centre of a field of about ten acres bounded on one side by the lane, which we will say is east; on the north by a row of trees, that divides the land from that of the neighbors; on the west by a small stream, that is seeking the river below; and on the south by the land skirting the river's banks, and by the rising country and hills beyond. There is nothing particular about the place: its surface is undulated, and the scenery and distant view are only just so beautiful as the environs of every town will show. What is the suggesting influence of the place? Simply, quiet occupancy; the more exalting influences must be induced by the home itself. In my first introduction to you, dear readers, I sketched the preliminaries I would recommend in forming a home, so that I will say nothing about pegging out the house, etc., but will try and describe the building that will best suit the ground that we have imagined.

We are going to build on a moderate scale—say five thousand dollars have been left, after purchasing the ten acres of land—and we wish to make that sum serve to complete our home in every particular, excepting inside furniture of the house. Great care and economy must of course be used; for the more void of particular interest the site appears, the greater necessity there is to avoid an appearance of baldness. The entrance upon the

A COUNTRY HOUSE—elevation  p. 60

ground is from the lane, at the nearest point to the northern boundary line. All I would do at present, would be to measure off four hundred feet south of said line, and to plough up a strip thus wide from east to west, leaving a cart road close to the northern boundary, which may serve as approach to the stable and yard which will terminate the strip spoken of on the north-west. The house will be somewhat exposed. It will be seen from the public road on the north; though, excepting from the upper windows, the road itself will not be commanded from the house. It will also be seen from the lane, and from the opposite side of the river. The position for the house is determined to be at about one hundred and fifty feet from the lane, there being no local reasons to demand placing a greater distance between, which would only require a more expensive means of approach. The sum at disposal will permit a building of comfortable dimensions; its form on the ground may be thus arranged: The main portion—which would contain a library, seventeen feet by fifteen; a drawing-room, sixteen by twenty-five; a hall, nine feet wide and seventeen long;—would make a block thirty-six feet south by twenty-seven feet east and west. This block would be carried higher than the wing, containing a dining-room, fifteen by twenty; a small boudoir, or morning-room, ten by fourteen; a staircase, store-rooms, pantries, etc., and a commodious kitchen, which would all be contained in a block thirty-six by thirty-four. These dimensions, which include thickness for walls, chimneys, etc., enclose an area of about two thousand feet, and the division of the space is adjusted so as to afford the most economical form for erection.

The plan here given represents the arrangement of the rooms

upon the ground or principal floor, No. 1 being the entrance hall with its coat closet C.

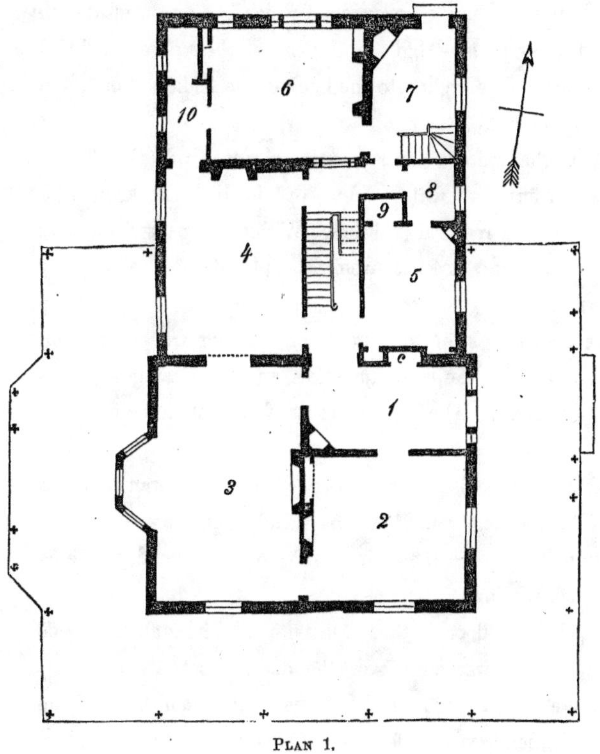


PLAN 1.

2. Is the library, with a fire-proof safe inserted in the wall, right hand of the fire-place.

3. The drawing-room, with a projecting window or bay on its western side.

4. The dining-room, with sliding-doors between it and the drawing-room.

5. The boudoir or morning-room with a large store-closet

No. 9, and a work and book-closet in the other end of the room.

6. Is the kitchen—on one side of which is a screen filled with ground glass to give light to the end of the staircase-hall and to the small entry leading to the kitchen, the scullery No. 7, and the store-room No. 8.

10. Is the waiter's pantry, communicating with the dining-room, and furnished with a sliding opening into the kitchen for the serving and removal of dishes. Within this pantry is a large china and plate closet conveniently placed and adequately lighted.

The staircase is in the inner hall, leading from the main entrance towards the domestic offices, and is privately and conveniently placed. The back or servants' stairway leads from the scullery.

Round three sides of the house stretches a veranda twelve feet wide, breaking round the bay-window on the western side and stopping against the dining-room, so as to extend to one of its French windows.

The chamber floor is thus distributed: The staircase lands first upon the lower level over the dining-room, kitchens, etc., which are not as high as the rooms in the main body of the house; it then ascends a few steps and opens into an octagonal vestibule lighted by an opening filled with stained glass in the attic floor, immediately over which is a skylight in the roof.

No. 1. Is a large chamber, sixteen by twenty-five, over the drawing-room, so large as to allow of division if necessary, the partition extending to one of the mullions of the window on the western side, and enclosing a convenient dressing room. In this room is a very large closet at its northern end.

No. 2. Is a chamber, same size as library below, provided with two closets, one of large size, and connected with it as a dressing-room or child's-room, No. 3.

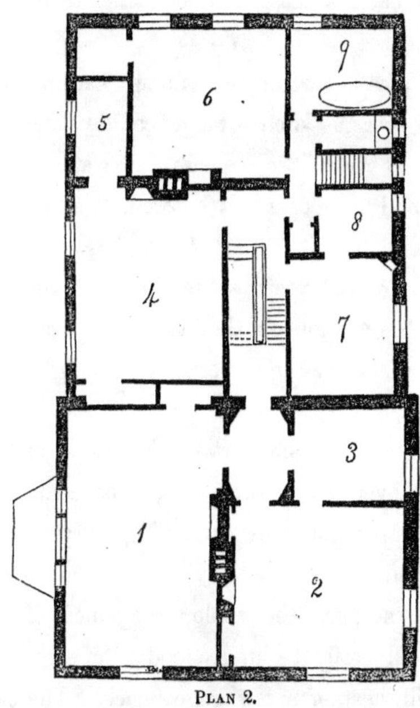


PLAN 2.

No. 4. Is a large chamber over dining-room, with a dressing-room or child's sleeping-room, No. 5. This room is provided with a very large closet in its southern end, and under the closet next to it, which opens into room; No. 1, is a space formed by the different levels of the floors of the two rooms, which might very advantageously be occupied by deep drawers for linen, etc.

No. 6. Is a servants' sleeping-room over kitchen, with a deep closet therein.

No. 7. Is what might advantageously be used as the nursery,

containing a fire-place, and an inner room, No. 8, which might serve as a sleeping-room for the nurse, or as a dressing-room if No. 7 be used as a chamber. Near to No. 8, in the vestibule leading from the back staircase, is a large linen-closet for the use of the housemaid.

No. 9. Is a pleasant room containing bathing apparatus, which, being so near the kitchen range, could easily be supplied with hot water at very little expense. A water-closet is conveniently close, and yet separately entered, as being more commodious for use.

The entry by the back staircase might be lighted from the roof, though, as the window on the staircase opens immediately upon the centre of the passage, the amount of light would probably be found sufficient.

In the roof over the main part of the house, an additional sleeping-room, or even two or three might be contrived for servants, and in the open garret over the wing a drying-room could readily be obtained.

By looking at the plans, the whole arrangement of the interior of this house will easily be understood; the exterior is represented in the illustration a few pages back. The elevation is that of the eastern front, and the design is delineated geometrically instead of in perspective, in order to give a more useful representation of the character of its architecture.

On looking at the illustration it will be seen that one portion of the house is much higher than the other. This is caused by the superior elevation of the rooms in the main portion of the house, their height being as follows: Rooms 1, 2, 3, are each twelve feet six inches high from floor to ceiling, and the other portion of the house but eleven feet. In the floor above 1, 2, 3, are eleven feet high, and the rest ten feet high. In the main portion of the house also, the walls are carried above the ceiling-line over chambers three feet high all round, so as to form a half attic, making a good deal of available room in the roof, and a cooler and more easily ventilated building.

The veranda is twelve feet and a half high where it comes against the wall, and drops to eleven feet three inches, making a slope of fifteen inches in its entire width on the under side. The rake of its roof outside would be greater, the rafters being deeper against the walls than at their feet, a mode of framing which is lighter and may be made more pleasing in effect.

The roof of the main building is hipped each way towards the stack of chimneys in the centre. It projects over the walls four feet, and is supported by brackets. The roof over the wing is also hipped on its northern side, and projects two feet on the east and west, and three feet on its northern end.

Thus far I have given the general distribution of the parts of the house, and the external features of its design—I will presently describe them in detail, after I have endeavored to give the reasons that induce the selection of a particular character or style.

The nature of the scenery is simply rural. The features are not marked or bold; the lines are mostly parallel, though the surface occasionally undulates; the house, therefore, to harmonize with it, must be simple, rather regular than picturesque; must seem stable and permanently fixed upon the ground; every accessory must be fitting; and although, if the means permitted, ornamental construction would be perfectly admissible, the general contour of the building, of the details or the masses of decoration, must be such as not to disturb the eye, or break the simple charm of quiet, unobtrusive beauty. The vicinity of the building to a town, the small means allowed for expenditure, and, we will say, the readiness with which the material can be obtained, determine the selection of brick as the substance of which the house shall be principally built; and as the use of this material obliges the necessity of a simple, regular plan, and uniform outline, we will conclude to adopt a building in the modern Italian style as our type for erection.

I will first detail the entrance, or eastern front. The hall doors should be simple, heavy doors, divided down the middle, and each half, say two feet three inches wide. On each side are side windows, and a transom window across the top. This arrangement I prefer to making the doors themselves sash-doors filled in with glass. The latter look a little more stylish, but are more easily broken by a sudden slam-to from gusts of wind. These windows, especially those at the top, should be made to open, in order to secure a circulation of air without the necessity of constantly open doors.

The eastern window, under the veranda, from the library, should be a French window, closing in the middle, and either hung upon hinges or made to slide into the walls on either side. If hinged in the ordinary manner, take care to direct your carpenter to provide Woodbridge's Patent Weather-Strip, which will not only make them tight at bottom, and exclude all dust, wind, and most driving storms, but will make them more easily opened and closed, from the simplicity and durability of the apparatus that both fasténs and protects them. Over this window, another would be required in the chamber of the floor above, and another over the hall. These windows may be as simple as you please.

Above them again, I would make a small semicircular break in the line of the roof, running over a circular window which would give light to the attic; this window is placed in the centre of the main building.

Here, with the kitchen buildings, stretching out north, and of course of a lower elevation, are all the features we have on the eastern side of the house; now let us see what can be done with them, to obtain the desired effect.

In the first place, we will settle the character of the veranda, which we can now do, having grounds to go upon. The building being necessarily regular and of even surface, from the nature of the material, a rough, rustic veranda would be out of keeping, as would also be a classic colonnade, or a light trellis work. The posts supporting its roof may be thus made. Put together studs, two inches by three, in the form of a cross, around a centre stud, four inches square; the outer studs to be furnished with cut brackets at top and bottom, extending say four inches at the bottom and six at the top, so as to form caps and bases, and the edges to be chamfered off until within three or four inches of the top and bottom. The cornice of the roof to be very simple, consisting of a fascia, and above that a heavy roll moulding, and, if means will afford, to be enriched with brackets. The roof to be covered with metal or shingles, and the under side to show the rafters, and to be ceiled above them, and not straight across. These posts would be so arranged as not to come in the way of windows in the rooms, and might be placed in pairs, close together, and each pair about nine feet from the next. Where the veranda runs around the bay-window in the drawing-room, on the western side, the space above would afford a good opportunity for a balcony entered from the chamber floor, which might again be protected by a light roof, supported on brackets, over the window leading upon it. Simply directing that the floor of the veranda would look best if laid in narrow strips of southern yellow pine, oiled, and that some of the beautiful seats procurable at the Berrians' be scattered here and there, I shall not have occasion to refer to this portion of the building again.

The roof needs very simple treatment in order to secure a desirable effect. The chimneys in the main house are gathered exactly into its centre, around a ventilating discharging flue, which may be terminated with an ejector, as described in the preceding chapter on ventilation. The projecting cornice of the roof will be supported by blocks following its rake and surrounding the foot of each rafter. These blocks, in fact, would be formed by casing out the feet of the rafters to about eight by six, and by cutting them at the ends into the form of the letter S, (as described in chapter iii.) The cornice to be nothing more than a heavy roll moulding containing the gutter, and of the simplest character.

A good effect may be given to all of the windows in building the walls, by making a projecting face of two inches thick and one foot wide, all round the opening, resting on the stone sill below the window; this face, however, would be only in the way if outside shutter blinds were used; but as the manner in which I have in a former chapter directed brick walls to be built, namely, hollow, would allow of blinds to slide right and left, I suggest this mode of finish, and advise that the blinds should be made inside, and to slide.

We have now before us all the outside features of the house —the building is simply treated—breadth of effect has been gained by the avoidance of all obtrusive features, and the character of the home is perfectly congruous with that of the landscape. The quiet tone of coloring that pervades the natural objects around will best be harmonized with by painting the brickwork of the house with a warm, gray sanded paint, as spoken of before, and by giving to the wood-work a more lively tint, marking the difference of the materials without producing too violent a contrast.

The wing containing the offices and rear buildings, must of course be of the same character as the main house; the roof and cornice similar in treatment, though subordinate in design. The stabling, barns, etc., should also present the same character of finish, though only where such finish is essential, and not merely ornamental. The barn, etc., may be built of wood—the planking at the sides perpendicular, and the joints covered with battens, the roof projecting, but without any cornice, the rafters being cut at the ends into the form of an S.

Now, I have given the house and all its details, and in sketching them have thought of the nature of the scenery that surrounds, let us, dear reader, walk down the lane, and see how such a house deserves the character of a home; how it will meet the requirements I have, from the first insisted, constitute the claim to that title. We open a substantial gate, heavily framed, and its timbers chamfered, and walk towards the house. Its view is at first concealed by a belt of shrubs and trees, around which the road makes a slight detour. As we walk on, its front opens out upon our sight, cheerful, light, and yet massive, like the stately trees and sturdy hills around. We step upon the veranda; and as we take a seat beneath its shade, a peep through a window discloses a cheerful room, fair, not fine within. Seated in our chairs, we look down the green grassy meadow, sloping towards the boundary dividing us from our neighbor's lands on the south; and we notice how, by means of a sunk fence, and by the skilful planting of a few trees here and there, similar in character to those beyond, we have connected his grounds with ours, and how, without robbing him of a single acre, we have increased our sense of occupancy, in looking around. A few sheep are quietly grazing, and birds are hopping about near the house, and twittering as they light upon a crumb or an earth-worm; the stream is heard fitfully in the distance as the soft wind comes and goes, and all we see and hear increases our sense of simple beauty and quiet enjoyment.

Stepping out upon the lawn, we turn and look upon the house. The broad veranda seems like a base to the building, and gives massiveness and apparent firmness to its foothold upon the ground, equally as it imparts lightness and variety to its outline. The overshadowing roof, with its varied light and shade, seems a fitting finish to the building; and the leading parallel lines of the veranda are reproduced in its unbroken horizontal line of cornice, and in the uniform elevation of the windows. There is a peculiar stamp of fitness upon the whole; and the building and the grounds, the natural objects and the result of art, are in perfect congruity, and their union produces a sense of that most charming of all excellencies—home-beauty.

In this ideal scene I have thus erected a house, which may be found to contain elements useful to those who desire to construct a house of about the size and character of this for themselves.

The simplicity, economy, and convenience that I have attempted to embody therein, would probably make it favorably received by many, and if the scenery or the circumstances any where be identical with those I have described, the fac-simile copy of this design might perhaps with advantage be made. The cost of construction would certainly not exceed four thousand dollars, leaving one thousand for the out-buildings, gates, and fences, thus appropriating, as I at first supposed, five thousand dollars to the erection of a country home.

---

I will now take another scene, and sketch therein another class of home.

Near a small country village, a road leads from its main street, screened on either side by trees from the sun, and slightly undulating in surface, giving here and there a pleasant glimpse of landscape, varied in beauty and extent. Here and there along this road are homes of the village gentry, and those families of more wealth and leisure, whom love of the country, and the convenient contiguity of the village to the town wherein the gentlemen are professionally employed, have caused to select this neighborhood as their place of abode.

The class of house, of even the wealthy, has hardly attained the dignity of the Suburban Villa, nor has it the wide stretch and informal arrangements of the genuine country house. The legitimate cottage seems the proper model for such a house—not the modern, pert, and inconvenient structure filled with odd corners and all sorts of vulgar prettinesses; but the "little house"—the true synonyme of the word cottage.

In the State of Connecticut, about a mile and a half from the

OLMSTEAD HOUSE—View from the S, E. p 72

village town of East Hartford, leads a road nobly shaded with spreading trees, and on either side are such residences as I have spoken of. Amid a beautiful orchard, and backed by shade trees, stands a cottage home, erected two years ago from my designs, for a gentleman, who finds himself so entirely satisfied with its arrangements, and is so proud of its picturesque appearance, I will close this chapter by giving a description. The building is framed of wood—has a high pitched roof, and is substantially and thoroughly built. A large cellar of brick runs under the whole house, extending even under the verandas, thus making the building at all seasons thoroughly dry, and in the summer pleasantly cool. The occupant of the house, Mr. Henry Olmsted, required a building half farm-house, half residence—with rooms spacious, and entries convenient both to the domestic offices and to the residence part of the house; a sort of two buildings under one roof—a style of house in very frequent demand in the country.

The illustration shows a perspective sketch from the south-east, taken by a daguerreotype from the building itself.

It will be seen that the peculiar feature about the house is the extreme projection of the roof. In fact, the veranda is shaded by the main roof itself, the latter being supported by framing of a very simple and effective character on the end, and by posts, formed of studs put cross-way together, and cut and moulded top and bottom, at the sides. The sharp gable over the side is framed so that the construction shows externally—this being no sham, but the actual framing of the roof within, the chamber ceilings of that part of the house being lathed upon the curved beams that support the roof. The sides of the house are planked, and their joints covered with battens, the roof being shingled. The heads of the doors and windows are protected from the weather by moulded labels, upon which the battens rest, and though the detail about the building is very effective, no ornamental work is any where introduced which does not serve some constructive purpose of design.

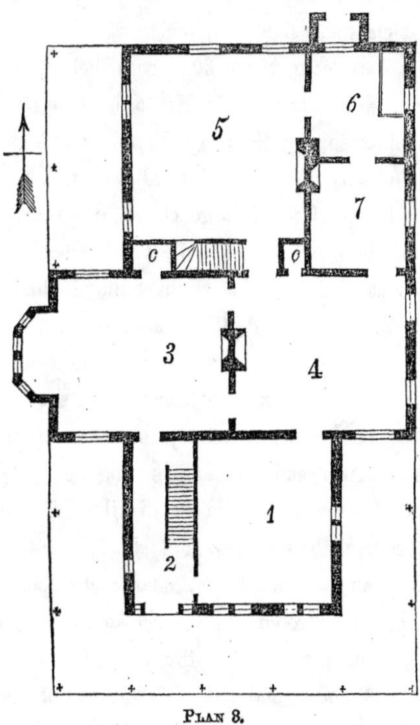


PLAN 8.

The plan is thus arranged: A veranda floor is on the front and two of the sides, shaded by the overhanging roof above. The house is entered by a door at the south-west angle; this leads into the entrance hall, No. 2, in which is the principal staircase of the house.

On the right is a sitting room, No. 1, which is fifteen feet by seventeen feet six inches. From the hall is a parlor, No. 3, sixteen by nineteen, in which is a large bay-window, and of which the French windows open upon the verandas on either side. Behind this, communicating with the sitting-room, is a dining-room, No. 4, which is also sixteen by nineteen, and opening from which is a large store-room, No. 7, fitted with shelves, and store, and china, and glass-closets, etc. No. 5 is a large kitchen, twenty-one by nineteen, and No. 6 is the scullery and sink-room. A back staircase leads up to the floor above, as shown on the plan, and on each side of it are large closets, one into the parlor, and the other into the dining-room. The kitchen has a door-window on its western side, so that entrance may be had without going through the house, and a similar door, protected by a porch on the northern end of the scullery, which leads towards the farm-yard. The rooms on this floor are all spacious, their arrangement has been found extremely convenient by the occupants, and the plan will readily make it intelligible.

The chamber floor is similar in its distribution to the floor below. No. 1 is over the sitting-room. No. 2, over the parlor. No. 3, over the dining-room. No. 4, a large chamber over the kitchen. No. 5, a long room over the scullery, etc., lighted on the east by a dormer-window on the roof. There are large closets in Nos. 2, 3, and 4, and a large additional one might be made from No. 1, over the entrance hall, unless, like Mr. Olmsted, the builder preferred the open, unobstructed, and cheerful light, obtained by leaving the end unoccupied. In a portion of No. 5, a bath-room might very easily be partitioned off, as the space is ample to allow it, and the nearness to the kitchen below would permit the bathing apparatus to be supplied with water at a trifling expense.

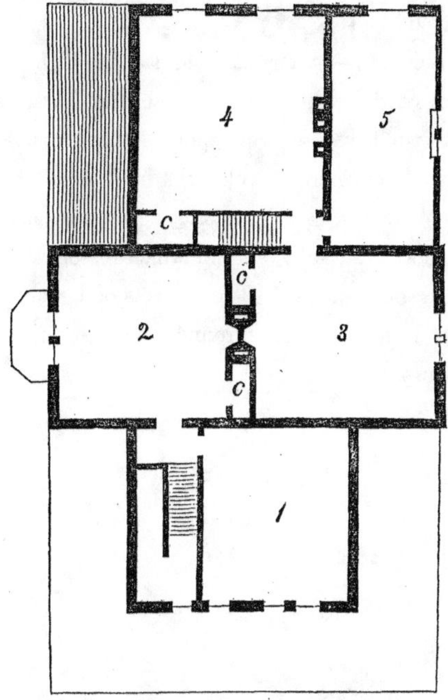


PLAN 4.

The cost of this house may be stated at from twenty-five hundred to three thousand dollars, the margin being left for the amount of labor expended on the outside and inside finishings. As erected in Connecticut, its cost was nearly three thousand dollars, but the workmanship and materials throughout, were all of the highest quality, and the extensive cellaring before alluded to, might not by other builders be deemed necessary, and would, of course, if curtailed, reduce the expense.

Its picturesque appearance attracts great attention, and as

creepers become trained upon the open tracery and posts of the frame in front, the cheerful aspect of its southern end will be greatly improved.

Its style is Gothic—so far at least as the high roofs, the pointed arches of the tracery in front, and the character of the labels over the windows—determine any distinctive style. The whole is painted a deep cream color, the bold projections of the roofs, posts, and tracery, casting interlacing lines of shadow that vary the tint most beautifully, and for which reason a light tone of coloring has been chosen. These effects of light and shade would be lost if a darker background had been given as the color of the house.

# CHAPTER VI.

## ACCOMMODATION SUITED TO A SHORT SUMMER RESIDENCE IN THE COUNTRY—THE SUMMER LODGE.

THERE are doubtless other scenes than those outlined in the last chapter, which might advantageously be sketched, and the means to obtain congruity therewith detailed; but in the examples given, a character of scenery very commonly encountered, and a class of house constantly in demand having been considered, I propose in this and subsequent chapters to select rather buildings not so usually met with, hoping that the designs given may prove proportionately more valuable.

There are homes which are only homes of a season—homes no less dear than those lived in at all times, but intended only for occupancy during such portions of the year as the leisure or the taste of their owners will permit. Many spend the winter in the city, the summer in the country; and a home suited to summer life is the one I will attempt to sketch here. The house should be roomy—that is, the limit of hospitable accommodation having been set according to the means of the owner—the rooms, the passages, the chambers, and the domestic offices,

SUMMER LODGE—p 78.

should all be of liberal dimensions. There is no necessity to be cramped in the country; and a house with a few but large rooms in it is much better deserving the title of a Summer Lodge than one with many but small chambers. It should be spread upon the ground—rather low than high, with spacious verandas, and with shading and projecting roofs. The hall should be roomy, and so opened in the house as to be used as a sitting apartment, its position always at some portion of the day making it cool and sheltered from the sun. The staircase should either be distinct in itself, and carried up independently of the house, or should be a means of thorough ventilation to the building if placed in a more central position. The chambers should be especially contrived with a view to perfect ventilation and lowest attainable summer temperature, and this object may be assisted by a means which perhaps many of my New England readers will at first doubt—that is, by having as few windows as possible. The more glass there is in a room, the hotter it will be in sunshine. Have just so much light as is needed; the position of the window or windows, and the use of other means, will secure ventilation and coolness more effectually than windows on all sides, as I *have* seen. So much by way of preface for the inside—now for the outside.

Let me here sketch a scene that I have often studied, and which is resembled, no doubt, by many a familiar spot in the reach of most of my readers.

Little more than fifty miles from New York, away from railroads or North River, and yet within an hour's drive of either, is an inland lake. There is nothing particularly grand, or wild, or beautiful about the spot, and yet it has a charm that endears it to all who have lingered upon its margin. The sheet of water is three or four miles long, and its surface is broken by many rocky and tree-crowned islands, that give variety and increased extent to the views from shore to shore. The margin is rocky, and pretty well wooded; here and there is an acre or two of natural lawn, stretching into the woods, and on the other sides the road, in points nearly touching the water, and again hid from view by an avenue of trees, winds along. But few houses are in its vicinity—a small and quiet country hotel, a store, a wheelwright's shop, and a grist mill, the wheel of which is turned by the overflow of the lake, are all that mark civilization and man around. Its level is very high—so high as to be a matter of curiosity, increased, too, by the fact that on one side of the lake a narrow ledge of rocks separates it from a smaller pond, which is one hundred and twenty feet below. I am thus particular, because, doubtless, many of my readers will recognise the description of the lake, and will be able to tell how far the house I am going to sketch would be suitable upon its banks.

There is plenty of wood around—much that would make timber for building, and, at all events, sufficient to justify the use of timber as the material. The character of the scenery is natural; wild, without being grandly magnificent; smooth spots here and there, suggestive of quiet, effortless cultivation; and the massy rocks and old trees seem to plead that no pretentious modern dwelling be allowed to thrust its tricksied face for reflection upon the silver lake they frame. On one side of the lake, the rocks and trees have drawn themselves away, and have left an open lawn of an acre or more, sloping gently to the lake, and extending along its bank for three or four hundred feet; then come rocks again on either side, and then another opening or two, but not so clear as the larger one, which will be the site for the house. As far back from the water as the space will permit, the house lifts up its eastern front. The entrance is on the eastern front, and the kitchens and offices stretch towards the north, where also is the road by which access to the house can be gained. The southern end looks across a varied prospect of rock, and tree, and glen, parallel to the winding margin of the lake, and the west looks upon the woods, and through them upon glimpses of noble prospect of hill and other distant lakes, miles and miles beyond; upon this side the trees have been cleared away just sufficiently to make a little parterre and a vegetable garden, a small dry lawn, and a shaded walk, and the morning of a hot July or August day may, on this side of the house, be passed without fear of sun or heat.

The ground plan here given will fully explain the internal arrangements of this floor.

The entrance is in the centre of the eastern front. A recess covered over by a light roof, supported upon brackets, will allow a carriage to drive up to the door and its occupants to alight under shelter. The hall, No. 1, which is so large as to admit of being used as an occupied apartment, extends throughout the whole space between the two wings of the main building, and is ten feet by twenty-six. At its one end are sliding doors opening into a spacious drawing-room, thirty-three feet by sixteen, No. 2, a truncated bay-window at its southern side, making the apartment of pleasing proportions. In front of the hall is a dining-room, No. 3, twenty-six by sixteen feet, and communicating therewith is a large waiters'-pantry under the staircase, and beyond it the domestic offices. No. 4 is a library, sixteen feet by fourteen, with a projecting window in its eastern side. This room would scarcely be required any longer, as the spacious

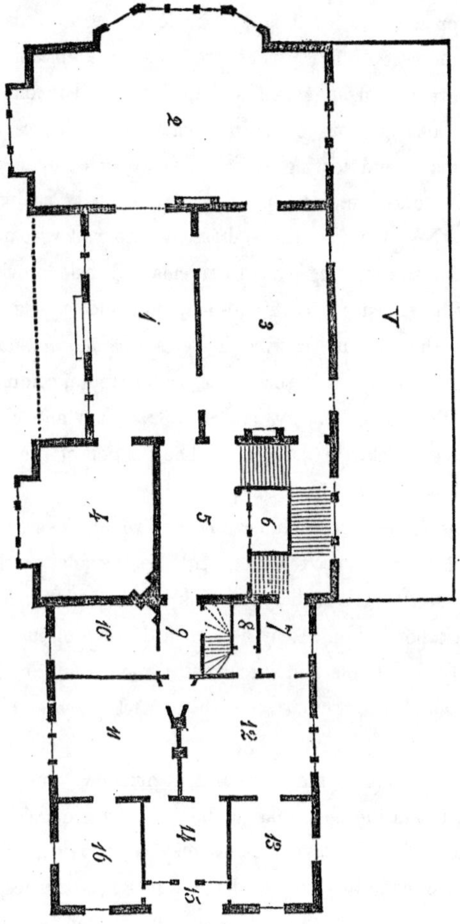


PLAN 5.—SUMMER LODGE.

hall would afford room (if more be needed) for recessed book-cases and niches filled with old china or honored busts.

The staircase is in the inner hall, No. 5, and is of ample size and grand appearance. No. 9, is a vestibule leading towards the kitchen and domestic offices, which are of most ample dimensions and convenient arrangement, and are distributed as follows:

No. 10 is a large store-room, to be filled with shelves and presses as needed, and leaving sufficient space for occupancy as a morning or work-room, a fire-place being provided "against a rainy day." No. 6, under the staircase, is the waiters'-pantry, and in drawing the working-plans to an enlarged scale, provision could easily be shown for coat, and hat, and shoe-closets, etc., all of which the present drawing is necessarily too minute to exhibit in detail. No. 7, is the cooks' serving-room, communicating with the waiters'-pantry, and No. 8, a plate and china-closet for those articles in daily use. The position of the back staircase will be apparent from the plan.

No. 12, is the kitchen, communicating with which the servants' hall, No. 11—a very necessary, though not usually provided apartment. No. 13, is a scullery and sink-room, opening upon an enclosed back porch, No. 15, by a door in the end of its inner side. No. 14, is a larder and kitchen store-room, and No. 16 a laundry, which also communicates with the back porch and with the servants' hall.

These domestic offices are of unusually generous dimensions and variety, but in the hope that the necessity for a more liberal accommodation for culinary purposes may be apparent to my readers, I have made this summer lodge a model in this respect. I would in this connection say, that the plan here given for the distribution of the domestic buildings is one that has received from me long study, and has been commended by very many competent judges. In Mr. Downing's country houses, a standard authority on such subjects, especial attention has been called to a somewhat similar plan, and the slight changes I have in this example made from the design published in that excellent book, have been determined upon from the desire to concentrate the arrangement of the adjuncts to a country kitchen.

The ventilation of the servants' portion of the house, where other than the usually provided circulation of air by doors and windows, might readily be secured by the construction of an air-exhausting shaft at the back of the kitchen fire-place. The radiated heat from the latter would cause an upward motion in the column of air within the shaft, and communication having been established therewith by means of openings provided with the *Messrs. Berrian's Ventilating Valve*, all impure and heated air, together with effluvia from culinary operations, would be carried off.

The arrangement of the chamber floor may be seen by reference to the chamber plans.

The principal staircase lands at its first flight upon a level with the floor over the domestic offices, opening upon which level is the back staircase. Then, as the superior height of the rooms in the main house requires a rise again above the rooms in the wing, a flight of stairs leads up to the floor of the hall and the chambers over the main portion of the house.

The staircase is very roomy, airy, and well lighted, and would have a grand and imposing appearance. Through an open arch-way leads a corridor over the entrance hall below. Out of this are partitioned off small rooms, No. 3 and No. 7, forming dressing-closets to the chambers with which they connect. In the centre of this corridor a large space is left which would permit a pleasant recess for sitting, and as its window would command a view of the lake below, this would be, particularly in the afternoons and evenings, an agreeable spot for chit-chat for the ladies of the house.

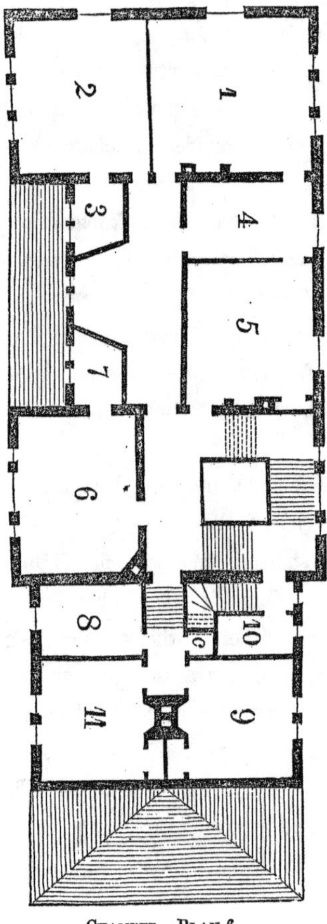


CHAMBER.—PLAN 6.

The sleeping apartments are all spacious—so spacious, that as dressing-rooms are plentifully provided, I have not curtailed their dimensions with partitions for closets, preferring in this case that wardrobes or other furniture conveniences be made their substitute. No. 1 is a large chamber, sixteen by nineteen, and communicating therewith is a room, No. 4, which might as occasion served, be used either as its dressing-room, a separate chamber, or as a dressing-room to chamber No. 5. No. 2 is a sleeping-room, sixteen by fourteen, communicating with which is a light, airy dressing-closet, six by eight, No. 3. No. 5 is provided with a closet, gained out of the thickness of the inner wall and the projection for the chimney-breast, and is sixteen by fifteen. No. 6, over the library, is sixteen by fourteen, and is provided with a dressing-closet, No. 7.

The position of the doors, windows, fire-places, etc., has been especially thought of, in reference to the convenient placing of a bed and the requisite articles of furniture usually contained in comfortable sleeping rooms.

Over the domestic offices, in the wing, are the following rooms:—

No. 8, entered after descending a wide flight of stairs in a corridor lighted from above, is for a bathing apparatus and a water closet. In this corridor is a large closet for the use of the house-maids, designated by the letter C on the plan. No. 10, off the back staircase, is a large, well lighted linen closet; and Nos. 9 and 11 are servants' sleeping rooms, each one provided with a spacious closet.

It will be seen that the chamber accommodation is upon the most liberal scale; but if the mode of life of its occupants demanded it, an increased number of rooms might be gained in the attic, the height and pitch of the roof permitting, in its centre, without any additional increase of height of the posts, several rooms, both with economy and advantage. The external appearance of such a house should be simple, rustic, and broad. The character of the exterior must be suited to the material. The covering should be plank, put perpendicularly, and secured with battens. The roof covered with shingles, projecting four feet at the eaves and gables, and supported by simple brackets, as shown in the perspective sketch at the commencement of the chapter.

Without intending to carry out the style into any ornate excess, I would suggest a modification of that called Gothic, as appropriate to the scenery and material. The gables might be relieved by showing some open framing, and some ornamental construction, the details of which, however, should be simple and bold. The eaves may be supported by simple brackets, following the rake of the roof, and resting on corbel blocks, and a string course, against which the upright battens may terminate. The windows should be simply square-headed, with mullions in each, dividing the aperture into openings or bays; and in the library I would make a projecting bay-window on the eastern end, giving a cheerful sitting-place for a book, and occasional peep across the lake, and affording on enrichment to the general appearance of the eastern front. The verandas and the porch would be simply made of wood—the posts of the trunks of trees, with the bark thereon, (nailed and varnished as described in a previous chapter,) and the seats upon the verandas of similar character.

So much of effect may be obtained by the careful and artistic placing about the house and verandas of articles of rustic furniture, I have given some specimens of simple manufacture suited to the purpose. The chair here shown is of a simple but durable construction, and admirably suited to the veranda or to the

Rustic Chair.

grounds of a summer lodge. It is made strongly and compactly, and the bark is left on, so that it may be in keeping with the appearance and texture of surrounding objects. The price ranges from two and a quarter to three dollars. Cheap and good.

Rustic Table.

A rustic table is made to accompany the chairs given above, and is as pleasingly simple. It is very firmly made, and its price is five dollars.

For shady nooks here and there in the grounds, and for the centre or between the windows of the veranda, the subjoined

RUSTIC SOFA.

design of a rustic sofa would be found very appropriate. The price would be eight or ten dollars, according to the size. All of these articles, together with an infinite variety of other odds and ends suited to the embellishment and comfort of country life, can be found at the Messrs. Berrian's, Broadway; and the firm is daily adding to its stock, and keeps the run of every thing new.

The furniture and internal fittings of such a house should be very simple, but convenient; and in my chapter upon "Summer Furniture" will be found many examples of articles adapted to such a building. The whole building should be painted and sanded, and the entrance doors should be made of yellow pine, or other hard wood, oiled and varnished. The chimneys might be of brick, with a simple cap and base of stone, or of the former material. The verandas would look best constructed in the rustic method before described, and the detail of the whole of the external woodwork should be very bold and simple.

Thus the house and scenery would accord; and the building so treated would form no unfit model for a "Summer Lodge." The estimated cost of this building is eight thousand dollars. This has been arrived at by actual figuring upon enlarged drawings, by a competent builder, as if for actual execution.

# CHAPTER VII.

## THE HOMESTEAD.

There is a style of house needed in parts of this country, somewhat analogous in intention, though not in absolute purpose, to the *manor-house* of England. Although the absence of a law of primogeniture here necessarily tends to prevent the retention in one family of a "household-place," yet there are many large landed estates, of which at least some one central portion may safely be hoped to be preserved intact, and in which a homestead as a culminating point for the sympathies and gathered remembrances of the family, would be very desirable.

This want, without wishing even by implication to advocate any principle repugnant to Constitutional feeling, or Republican character, I will in this chapter seek to supply.

Perhaps it would be in such a class of house that a national architecture would most probably in time develope itself. Public buildings, edifices for trade and commerce, small residences erected by individual fancy and but for a temporary occupancy, are too much controlled by impulse, the fashion or the style of the moment, and other easily understood causes, ever to generate a specific style suited to the genius and the wants of a great people.

Therefore it is, I think, fairly to be supposed that the country-home of the landed or retired gentry, having to meet an universal want, will, as an universal taste is gradually attained, become the nucleus of a style of a People's Architecture.

It is not likely that the first efforts will be free from effects of the trammels of precedent and the stereotyped maxims of the architectural schools, but after a while the valuable principles only will be remembered that gave beauty to this and that by-gone style, and the details, peculiarities, and arbitrary rules be set aside unless subservient to the governing truth. But truth in art is progressive; it developes itself into perfect fullness only step by step; the germ may be with us now, but the glorious beauty of the complete flower can only be surmised. The mistake that is most to be guarded against is, unnecessary whimsicality on the one hand, and the difficulty of steering clear of old associations on the other.

For the rural home of a land-possessing family, a house must be contrived with reference to the following necessities:

In the first place, its character must be one that will attach the sympathies of its occupants. This too, not merely by its absolute and æsthetic beauty, but by inherent qualities of fitness and unison with the purposes of life, and with the tastes and principles of the owner.

The severity of the purely classical styles is certainly not congenial to modern American taste, nor are their examples practically adapted to the climate and nature of the country. The innumerable varieties of the styles that have been originated by the necessities and the changes of modern times from the classical model, have many of them excellencies that must commend their adoption here and there in this country. Yet there is nothing specific, nothing suggestive about any one of them, and therefore, for the universal adoption under local restrictions of a people's architecture, some other element of design must be suggested.

The Gothic, from a congeniality of origin with the race that controls this vast continent, has in its elements a principle that makes its adoption seemingly more fitting than the styles of Greece and Rome. And yet, in the strict sense of the term, a Gothic house is not the homestead that we are seeking; it approaches it more nearly it is true, but from causes I will attempt to explain, does not satisfactorily embody the characteristics that are required.

Gothic architecture as applied to domestic purposes requires, if properly carried out, a peculiarity and completeness of detail and finish that render the noble examples with which Europe is thronged unfitting for reproduction here, or indeed there. By this I do not mean that lavish decoration is indispensable; on the contrary, there are thousands of ancient buildings as simply, honestly plain as puritan could wish: but, pervading every minute detail, the governing principle of Gothic art must be plainly felt and seen. The principle alluded to was *then* a truth, but now from the development of fresh necessities the truth remains the same, but its working has become different. The great governing truth was then as it is now—*fitness.* But the genius of the age then was ecclesiastical, the suggesting influence of Gothic art reverential worship; and so deeply were its examples imbued with this, that whether in cathedral, chapter house, manse, or cottier's lodge, the all influencing spirit was at work. This gave in the upward, soaring tendency of all its leading lines the constant recurrence of features beautifully significant then, and fitted eminently to the most scientific principles of construction. But now the *forms* are merely copied, and a house is *made* Gothic "because it looks pretty," and does not any longer *become* Gothic, because the influence and feeling of the times would in no wise else find embodiment. Thus the source of beauty in Gothic art was the constant subservience to the truth of fitness; that fitness determined not only by the exact adaptation to constructive purposes, but by the pervading church feeling of the times.

This has now become changed. The once powerful concentration of thought to one specific end, that produced results so grandly and so wonderfully beautiful, is no longer amongst us. We do not deplore its departure, or weakly sigh for the "good old times;" we have other good, as a substitute, and the advance of time, and change and improvement in social and intellectual condition, demand now a change in the circumstances to which the ever-existing truth of fitness must be applied.

We of this Saxon race have, however, advanced with Gothic art rather than have left it. We have still congeniality with its principles, and we feel somehow always a home-whispering voice at the heart, when we gaze upon some crumbling beauty of its production in our nation's birth-place across the ocean, different and more dear than the emotions that fill our souls in Greece and Italy. I think this is so universally, and the growing fondness for modern "Gothic cottages" seems to show that the inborn feeling is seeking outer vent. But the best as yet attempted in this line has been scarcely more than meagre imitations of some Gothic building complete in itself, or of bits of detail copied here and there, and woven into a patchwork, generally more whimsical than skilful. I hardly know of one honest effort to take to pieces the machinery of Gothic art, and find out its working power, and then apply it here; and yet this is what should be done before essaying the introduction of a style so marked in its features.

Let me now attempt the task; and if not successful, the endeavor will perhaps interest my readers sufficiently to repay them for the time I would have them bestow upon this chapter.

Required to define a house suited to American life, manners, and climate; in which the element of design shall be exact fitness of every portion to the purpose for which it is intended. Decoration to be embellishment, and to grow out of the circumstances of treatment of construction as they may arise, rejecting all that does not serve some definite purpose, or carry out some specific idea. This is what I propose to do.

Material, climate, and method of carrying on the workings of domestic life are the first considerations to be thought about. We will suppose the scenery and *educated taste* to be sufficiently similar everywhere.

The natural materials of nearly universal provision in the States are timber and stone. The climate, though varied in different portions of the country, demands, however, nearly the same protection against its contingencies. The dreary snows of the north require the same form of roof, for instance, as the deluging rains and furious winds of the south, and it is a truism that "what will keep out the cold will exclude the heat." Stone and wood can be made equally subservient to the same principles of construction, although widely differing in character.

Thus, then, there seems no peculiar constructive difficulty in this country to the use of any consistent style of architecture; so far, therefore, there is no obstacle to encounter.

The first constructive want demands a steep, high pointed roof. That is easily given, but it will affect the rest of the building. How? It will require the general lines not to contradict the upward pointing tendency of this prominent feature of the edifice. So, then, we have a first element of design to work upon—upward direction of its main lines. But this, if universally carried out, would involve a form not suited to every situation, or congenial with every style of scenery. Therefore the design must in character present such a harmonious combination of the vertical line to accord with this soaring tendency, and the horizontal line, to accord with the ordinary features of every day landscape. But this can only be done, without danger of violation of one of the first laws of symmetry, by making the vertical character the main feature of the house, and the other subordinate, arriving, in fact, at the pyramidal form or an outline based upon its principle.

In the illustration serving as the frontispiece is a view of the building I have designed as an example of the class of houses I am attempting to describe. The general outlines of the mass, although broken up into bold features which embody the vertical principle, present a symmetrical, and really, almost a cubicular appearance. And yet the summit, or "sky line," as painters would call it, is varied in the extreme; the breaks, however, being formed by bold projections in plan, rather than by diversity of height. The pointed gables that crown the different portions of the structure are no less necessary as portions of the construction than of the composition. The tower, containing in its uppermost story a room for command of extensive prospect, is the most strongly marked feature of the building, at least as regards the first impression upon the eye, in viewing the general mapping of the parts of the edifice; but it is not only very useful in itself, as will presently be seen by reference to the plan, but its treatment and intention are such as to lift the building up, and give symmetry and meaning to its outlines. The high pitch of the roof tells its own story; wind and weather might assail it in vain, and as, on looking closely into a proof of the engraving now before me, I find that possibly the small projection I have intentionally made at the eaves might mislead into the supposition that I intended a parapet running around them, I would here remark that such is not the case. A gutter is provided, which extends so as to overlap the upper surface of the walls merely a few inches. Dripping eaves would be inconvenient, and the streams of water soon deface the walls, and a widely projecting roof would, in this particular case, add nothing to the provision for protection of the mason work, and would only cause the accumulation of a larger body of water from its additional surface; and by its projection, removing the gutter farther from the walls, would make a greater difficulty in conveying it into the cesspool or cistern into which it is to be conducted.

Next to the tower, the most prominent feature that would be likely to challenge remark is the large porch-like projection on the south. This is the ombra—the meaning of which word I have before explained; and it will at once be seen, on looking to the plan a few pages ahead, to be a very desirable and most comfortable addition to the house. A geometrical elevation of the eastern or entrance side of the house is given, drawn to a scale of one twentieth of an inch to the foot, a scale which, I will remark, is used to all the plans in this book, where no other directions are given.

In this, the general character of the architecture of the building is easily discernible. It will be seen to be simply what the forms of each part themselves suggest. The details, and such ornamented construction as is permitted, are merely embodiments of the leading principles of design already laid down. The entrance-way is through an arched opening into a vestibule; arched because the construction required it; and the material, which is assumed to be stone, permitted greater strength to be gained, and with superior economy and character by such a form than by a square-headed opening with its lintel and posts.

The rough edges of the stone are cut off at an angle,—chamfered, as such a process is technically called, and the radiating joints of the masonry round the pointed arch are protected from injury of water lodging therein, by a hood moulding a few inches above them, cut off abruptly on the under side, so as to at once throw off the water, and sloped to an easy curve on the upper side, so as to lead the wet along, and discharge it perpendicularly at the "*drip*," or termination of the moulding. Buttresses are shown to the angles of this projecting block of building. These are necessary, because so much of the stone-work has been cut away, to allow the opening to the door on one side, and the window on the other, that the superincumbent weight would be too much for the piers thus left, unless they were aided and strengthened by buttresses, or other such support. The bay window that projects on this side is a feature too commonly met with to demand remark. I would only call attention to the connection given therewith and the building, and the preservation

THE HOMESTEAD—elevation. p, 98.

of the unity of principle decided on from the first, by the arrangement of the windows above it, by which the pyramidal form is carried out, and the parallelism and horizontal tendency of the lines of the upper part of the window, blended into a return to the vertical expression. The same remark also will apply to the combination of the windows in the other gable, facing south. The central portion recessed, where is the ombra, has, you will observe, a uniform and intentional parallelism and strict adherence to horizontal lines. This, if the building were cut off here, would cause an unsightly want of symmetry in the whole mass; but the tower on one side, the connection of the ombra therewith, and the marked character of the pointed gable that flanks it on its other side, make it a subordinate to the whole mass, a necessary background to these prominent features, and a point of contrast that permits the boldness of the rest to be more apparent.

Thus much at present in regard to the exterior. Let me now direct attention to the arrangement within.

The plan of the principal floor is thus disposed:

No. 1 is the entrance vestibule, with inner doors shutting it out from the hall, No. 2. The vestibule is twelve feet square; the hall eleven feet wide by twenty-five in length. This hall is lighted by a large window looking north, and communicates through an opening also shut off by double doors, with the staircase hall and vestibule No. 7. The main hall would, from the nature of its light, be an appropriate place for the hanging of pictures, and would be also—as it should be—at all times a cool and agreeable apartment.

Immediately on entering the hall is a door leading into the library, a large and cheerful room, twenty-six feet by sixteen, on one side of which is a bay window, and at the end a stone fire-proof closet recessed and arched overhead, (No. 4,) in which books, plate, or valuable papers could safely be stored. The drawing room, No. 5, is entered from the main hall, and also

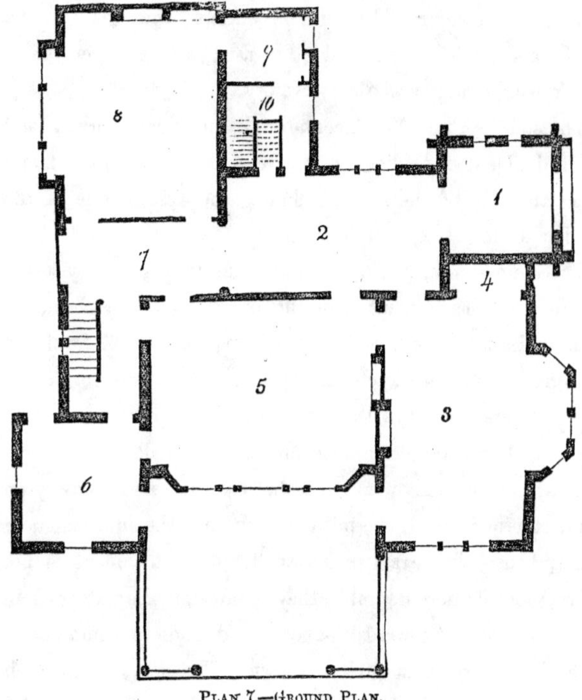


PLAN 7.—GROUND PLAN.

from the vestibule. It is twenty-six feet by about twenty in the clear, and its one side is, by means of large windows, made so as to be entirely opened to the ombra. Connected with the drawing-room is a small boudoir or ladies' room, being the first story of the tower, and is thirteen feet square. The boudoir, drawing room, and library, all open on to the ombra, a large and agreeable shade room, the natural artistic development of the progress from the ancient "stoup." This is a delightful place for sitting in, and as an easily obtained addition to a suite of rooms, cannot be too strongly advocated as a feature in American domestic architecture. It could be enclosed with glass in the winter, and artificially warmed; thus used as an enlargement of the drawing-room, or as a conservatory.

The staircase hall, No. 7, contains the principal stairway, and also a double door leading on to a veranda which might extend along the side of the house, including the western side of the boudoir or not, as seemed desirable.

The dining-room, No. 8, is a large room, twenty-four by seventeen in the clear, exclusive of the projecting western window. Communicating with this is a waiters'-pantry, No. 9, furnished with glass and china closets, and opening into a vestibule, No. 10, in which are stairways leading to the kitchen below, and to the floor above, and also a door into the main hall.

I have in this design assumed that the land so falls away on the northern side as to permit the kitchens to be in a basement below, hence the arrangement of the domestic offices is not shown; but if more desirable, they could easily be extended in a wing jutting out towards the north, and made to communicate with the pantry as at present shown. The spot upon which this design was studied had the ground so falling away, and induced the arrangement I have given.

The chamber plan gives ample accommodation for a large family, and with a due regard to rooms for guests. It is thus arranged:

The staircase leads to a landing on which is a door into chamber No. 1, over the boudoir, which, not being so high as the drawing-room, etc., is entered upon a different level above, to that of the floor over the main portion of the house. Above this is another room of similar size, and then a space in which is a stairway leading to the observatory or upper story of the tower.

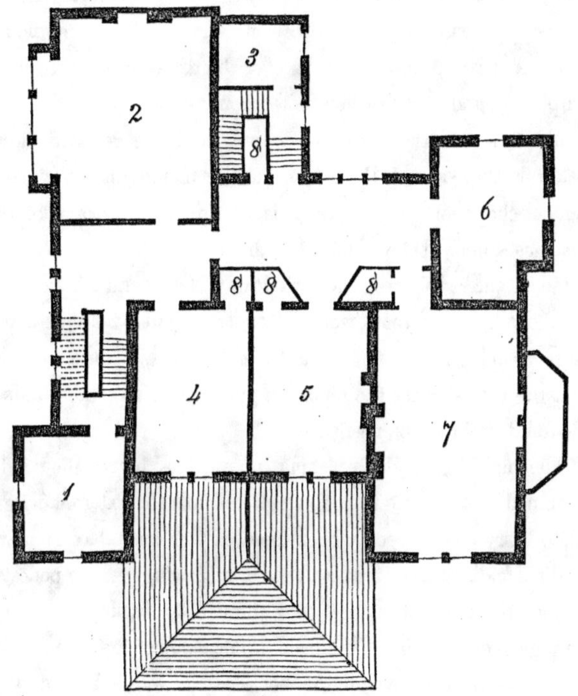


PLAN 8.—CHAMBER.

Continuing up the main entrance, the vestibule shown upon the plan is reached; this is nine feet by nineteen. A door in this leads to a large sleeping-room, No. 2, the same size as the dining-room below, and to which is a dressing-room, not shown upon the plan, but occupying the place designated by No. 3.

This room (No. 3), containing a bathing apparatus, etc., is on a level with a landing on the servants' staircase, and is entered by descending a few steps from the spacious hall or corridor over the hall below. As this room need not be more than eight feet high, a dressing-room might be contrived over it from the chamber last spoken of, a step or two being made between the floors. No. 4 and No. 5, are chambers over the drawing-room, each of ample size and well provided with roomy closets.

No. 6, is over the entrance vestibule, and the recessed closet below is thrown into the room, thereby making it a very convenient shape for a bed. No. 7, is a room the full extent of the spacious library below, and over the bay-window, a balcony is obtained entered from French windows. Nos. 8 and 9 are closets.

Above this the roofs would permit cool, well-ventilated, and large sleeping-rooms for servants, and it will at once be seen that the provision for the repose of guests is as hospitably ample as would probably be needed.

The finishing and furnishing of such a house should be governed by the same intention that controls the external design. The library with its roomy book-cases, easy-chairs, tables, and two or three folding-stands for portfolios of engravings, with a pedestal and a bronze or a bust here and there, only requires a natural arrangement to be in perfect taste. The doors of the room, of the lower presses or closets, of the book-cases, may be hinged with some such massy hinges as the annexed cut represents.

These are of American manufacture, and can be procured silver plated, brass, or bronzed. I saw them a few days ago, and was so pleased with their appearance, that, thinking a representation would be valuable, I have introduced one into this chapter.

They can be procured of *Baldwin & Many*, 49 John Street,

New York, where is kept constantly an unusually large and varied assortment of everything appertaining to the metal work and finishing of a house. At the same establishment, among the

HINGE.

many articles of ingenuity, beauty, and utility I examined, I selected a number of things that I thought would be a means of making these directions for the perfecting of a home more practically useful, and in different portions of this work I shall, from time to time, introduce such as seem worthy of notice.

An immense variety of beautiful articles manufactured in porcelain could very advantageously be selected from in im-

DOOR-KNOB.

bellishing and finishing a homestead, amongst them, door-knobs, of which a specimen is here given, display some truly artistic taste in their designs, and are no less elegantly than firmly and durably made.

A great improvement has been introduced by Baldwin & Many in the manufacture of the shanks of these articles—the old objection of the knob being liable to become detached from the shoulder, being in those made by this firm entirely removed.

The windows opening out of the drawing-room, boudoir, and library into the ombra should be made to close in the centre, either swinging back upon hinges, or sliding into the walls. There is frequently a difficulty in properly securing the two halves of such windows without a complication of bolts and locks that renders their use objectionable. A simple and beautiful little machine invented in Paris, where these windows are greatly used, has recently been introduced into this country, and as I have found it effectively to answer its purpose, I give here a representation. It is called the "Espagnlette Bolt,"

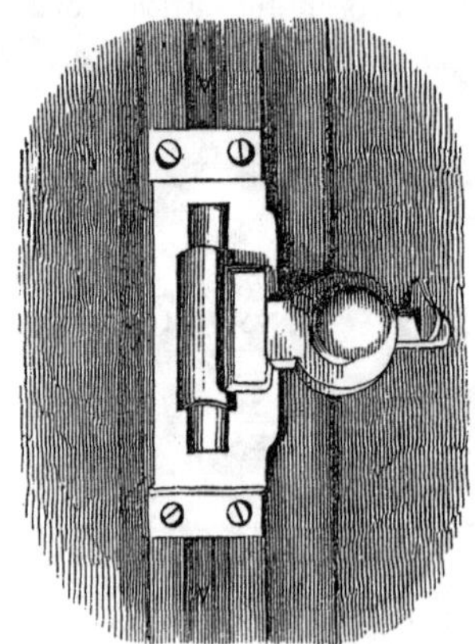

ESPAGNLETTE BOLT.

and is procurable at the warehouse of the same firm I have

just alluded to. Its working is very simple, the leverage bringing the two parts of the window together, and constantly drawing them as closely as their construction will permit. This and *Woodbridge's Patent Weather-Strip* are very valuable for French windows.

The drawing room and boudoir will permit such enrichment as taste and means will suggest, taking care, however, that the room be not too much cumbered with light or useless articles of *fine furniture*, and that the effect of breadth which the simple grouping together of a few choice pieces here and there would easily induce, be not frittered away. The wood for the doors, the staircases, the library and dining room furniture, should all be national—Southern pine, black walnut, American oak, and chestnut, oiled and polished, (not varnished,) will afford a sufficient variety, and the design of all these accessories should accord with that of the house.

The glazing of the windows might be made a means of imparting considerable character to the house. The old glass used in Gothic times could then only be manufactured in small pieces. Hence the minute "quarries," (as they are called,) and the leaden reticulated casements found in churches and domestic buildings of olden times. The servile copying, however, of such forms into modern buildings, when the improvement in the manufacture of glass renders suchs mall lights unnecessary, is a miserable mannerism, and I have seen many a really sensible house spoiled by the ridiculous embodiment in its design of an obsolete mode of construction. Furthermore, the leaden strips which held the glass in old windows was small and unobtrusive, and projected so little from the glass, that the outline of its intersection was scarcely seen, the decoration generally running all over, the window being usually so cunningly wrought that the black cross lines formed by the lead bindings seemed portions of the embellishment rather than constructive parts of the window. Here wooden sashes supply the place of the lead; and when diagonal or other geometrical forms are introduced into modern Gothic windows, the necessity for making the work sufficiently strong obliges the use of wood-work so thick and heavy, that the light is obscured, and the appearance of the whole casement is clumsy. The beauty of our clear modern glass, the unobstructed view its large and clear panes afford, plead for an honest and sensible use. Therefore let the panes be large, and as the square or parallelogram is not always a harmonious outline in such a house as I am describing, let some variation in its form be attempted. This may be done by leaving some large and unobstructed glass opening for view and light, and surrounding it with a simple border of framework, made of right lines disposed at various angles, and the spaces between, if wished, filled with stained and mosaic glass, of such dainty device and sparkling hues as will best harmonize with the decoration and tone of coloring within.

But I cannot pause, or there will not be space left for other matters no less important or interesting than the homestead. Remarking only, in conclusion, that the masonry of the house should be rough, if of stone, and that a porch under which a carriage could drive might, without violation of the principles of the design, be erected before the entrance door [I omitted this in the views, for the sake of making the marked feature of the ombra still more prominent], that broad lawns should be left before its fronts, with shade trees placed in accordance with preconceived design, not spotted here and there as if their planter had sailed over in a balloon and shaken them out of a pepper-caster; and that such a building finished substantially and consistently would cost twelve thousand dollars, or might be so treated as to be built for less,—I commend this study of a homestead, and these ideas of the elements of design, suggestive of a national Rural Architecture, to the attention of all lovers of the beautiful, the real, and the true.

SUBURBAN VILLA p 107

# CHAPTER VIII.

## THE SUBURBAN VILLA.

THE immediate vicinity to a town seems to require or permit a more ornate and less utilitarian style of building than would suit the broad and open country. The evidences of advanced civilization, wealth, and spendor around justify, in the home for retirement from the cares and turmoil of the city, a modest putting forth of the position, consequence, and taste of its occupants. The neighborhood of many of the manufacturing and commercial towns of England abound in beautiful examples of the Villa Rustica. The environs of London, particularly St. John's Wood, and the neighborhood of the Edgeware Road, are studded with handsome places and pretty cottages well arranged for the purposes of the life for which they were built. The Continent of Europe is full of them, though of a different type to the Anglicised villa suggested by the home efforts of Palladio and Vitruvius, who drew their inspiration from the pure taste of the courtly Roman gentlemen, the once fathers and patrons of art in Italy.

Less progress has, perhaps, been made in the suburban villa, in this country, than in almost any other branch of architectural study, not for want of opportunities for experiment—every town and city in the Union more or less abounding in them—but from the prevalence of two great mistakes, which I think most of my readers will admit to exist. A gentleman desirous of building a family home in the outskirts of the city, is apt to fall into one of these two errors, either that of endeavoring to drag the city out to his door-step, (evinced by the high three windows on each floor, back and front, a house the type of which exists in any newly attempted settlements in the distant wilds of far away up-town): or he falls into the other error, and erects him a house, too large on the ground for his lot, too whimsical for contrast with the necessarily many regular forms around, and too evidently, if good in itself, requiring a large, cheerful lawn and a background of forest-trees to set it forth to anything approaching to advantage.

The villa should always be retired, if even on a most constantly frequented street and road. Still, though the depth of the lot will not, in all cases, permit of the building being placed back, and the planting of a screening belt of evergreens and shrubs to shut it out from view, by placing the rooms most constantly used by the family, and the flower garden in the rear or side, (as the aspect will suggest,) the conveniences of privacy and retirement may be attained. I would not wish to shut a house into a well of tall trees and impervious fences, but neither would I counsel the bare and unprotected arrangement so generally in vogue, which permits each passer-by to command the movements of every one within.

Were I asked what should be the feature most prominent in an American villa, I would say "the veranda," for to no portion of the house are perfect comfort and effective appearance attributable so much as to its provision for shade. In fact, this may be considered the element of the character of the design, and the "veranda style" in this age of new nomenclature would be no unfit description of a class of house otherwise difficult to be placed in the list of recognised orders and styles. If my readers will permit me to decide this as the first important consideration in determining the character for the house, I will endeavor to suggest the treatment it should receive in different localities and under different circumstances.

Where the immediate neighborhood of a large city possesses considerable and varied natural beauty, with ground irregular, and with mossy rocks, and sparkling water here and there, to mark the links between the busy city within, and the wide range of nature without; the building should, in a measure, carry out the same feeling. It may be that the house stands on a natural terrace of mossy bank and rock; the surface of the road may undulate, dipping now suddenly down to the bridge over the river that brings wealth to the city, and now stretching far behind, up and down and right and left, until its course is lost in the distance. The probability is that the shape of the lot is regular—a rectangle parallel to the street, and so great irregularity of outline upon the ground would be both inconvenient and unnecessary; for the easiest way to reconcile broken surface of country around with form of building is by breaks in height, or, as it is called, in the "summit outline." A tower and lookout may shoot up somewhere from the block of the main building, and break lines else monotonous; and this or any other irregular feature may the more easily be ventured upon if the veranda base is ample, and by its bold appearance unite and keep down all that might otherwise have seemed too distinct or prominent. In such a situation, almost any style will be susceptible of adaptation in its details; perhaps the high-pointed Gothic might, unless very carefully treated, appear too positive, and challenge too much observation from the absence of that partial means of concealment which should not permit it to be seen all at once; or if so, only from a distance, and where there is a background or a balancing object beyond or near to it; and this, from the necessity of close proximity to a public road, and from the desire for careful and minute finish in details, is not easy here. The Italian is, perhaps, universally adapted to the purposes of villa building, and as the house now to be described originated in Italy, and has even given a name to the building itself as well as its style, it may be considered, in the absence of reasons, to demand a preference for any other, as the legitimate style for the suburban villa. This style I have before sketched, and as it is susceptible of infinite variety in its treatment, and is, moreover, one equally adapted to the simplest home and grandest mansion, its adoption for the purpose named, will, I think, appear suitable.

This style must not be confounded with the Roman or the classic, and no visions of lofty columns or of pediment must flit before the eyes of my readers on encountering the term Italian. It is a fact, that in the suburbs of Rome, Florence, Genoa, etc., the column was seldom or never seen in any relation to a domestic purpose. With the exception of a few graceful columns supporting the inner arcade of the atrium or court, a simple pilaster or antæ, here and there, and a truncated column affording a pedestal for a sun-dial, I am not aware of the existence of any ancient dwelling of the villa class, possessing column, pediment, or portico. It remained for us in modern times to combine the temple and the three-story front, and to disfigure a building, and bring opprobrium upon the classic style, by erecting the masses of unmeaning carpentry our every suburb shows. The ancient villa had a broad overhanging roof, spacious covered cloisters or walks, (answering to our veranda now,) and generally a means of covered carriage-approach to the hall of the dwelling. It had also a peculiarity seldom retained here (excepting in Mexico,) in an inner court of large size, covered over at the top on the same level as the roof, and decorated with fountains, mosaic pavement, parterre and statuary, and with an arcade of simple columns, or light open metal tracery, round the four sides, upon which the doors and windows from the apartments within looked, there frequently being no windows in the outside of the building that could afford any prospect without, the whole of the view being comprised of the objects in the court within. Many old houses in England, and several hotels here, (the Astor, for instance,) are built upon this plan, excepting the provision of outer windows, as well as those upon the court, and the arrangement has evidently been made from that of the ancient villa.

Within, the rooms should be spacious, and their heights somewhat greater than would be considered necessary in the country; the hall should have an outer vestibule, if there be no porch, and also an inner vestibule, communicating with the principal rooms, and capable of being shut off at times from the hall. I would here say, that a hall running through the house, if not so made as to afford a means of cutting off a portion as a screened vestibule from one suite of rooms to the other, is not only a great waste of space, but is really an inconvenience, and I can think now of many good houses spoiled by this one thing—the hall seldom being of noble enough dimensions to be considered as an apartment in itself, and only becoming a long, narrow passage-way, inconvenient to cross, and too small comfortably to sit in. The kitchen buildings, if stretching out in a wing, may be easily rendered an appropriate and even ornamental portion of the erection; or if below, as in such houses they sometimes are, a very sharp eye must be kept that the builder has not forgotten the provision of the most ample flues and ventilating air-ducts, for the prevention of the admission of the air and odors from below into the floors above. A conservatory is an ornamental, and, I am pleased to believe, is becoming a necessary adjunct to a villa. It may sometimes be placed on the second floor, (over the carriage porch, for instance,) with great advantage, though the capabilities of the house for reception of company are increased, by making it so that it can be used in connection with the rooms on the principal floor.

The house being required more frequently for the entertainment of a large number of persons, like the town-house, has to be contrived to meet such a want, and at the same time neither cramp the home comforts for the family, nor oblige them to build a larger house than their number or way of living may need. This excellence of adaptation to both purposes can be attained more by skilful arrangement of the rooms and passages than necessarily by great space. The ombra, or certain portions of the veranda, may be contrived in such a manner as to be occasionally, or at certain seasons of the year enclosed, and thus form, at little expense, and no increase of real size of the house, additional rooms for the reception of guests; and as the demand on such occasions for extra sleeping rooms has not to be met also like it would be in the country-house, such a facility of down-stair expansion would be a great excellence in the suburban villa.

I have incidentally mentioned the carriage porch; my readers will themselves see how desirable such an appendage at all seasons would be. This should extend sufficiently far to allow a carriage to drive and put down its load at the entrance door of the hall, under cover; and its roof might be made either a delightfully spacious balcony from the chamber floor, or, as suggested just now, would afford an opportunity for a conservatory at little additional expense.

In all the designs selected for the illustration of this little work, I have made the veranda, ombra, or other provisions for architectural shade a prominent feature; in the suburban villa such a portion of the building requires a somewhat more regular and architectural treatment than would be desirable in the country house; and as such a treatment can only satisfactorily be obtained by a scientifically detailed drawing of the building and its parts, I have preferred, in the villa that illustrates this one of my rural homes, to give one that has been erected, and which, from its internal arrangements, and picturesque, yet finished aspect, has given satisfaction to its owner and his neighbors. I will suppose the spot upon which it stands, describing the building itself, however, exactly as it is.

A mile or two from the city, just where the stone flagging of the pavemented town is merging into the neatly kept gravel walk of the suburbs, stands the house whose title heads this chapter. A thick belt of shrubs and evergreens, protected from injury by vagrant hands by an outer fence or paling, shuts out the lawn and garden between the house and the public road, a timber-framed gate and a handsome stone pillar on either side.

marking the entrance to the drive within. We will enter, dear reader. The road, ten feet wide, and as smooth as gravel will permit, curves towards a nearly circular space which sweeps before the arcade in front, which supplies the place of a projecting portico or carriage porch.

Within the porch, a flight of steps leads to the vestibule, and through double doors into a square hall, with, if you please, a marble floor, or, perhaps, one of encaustic tiles, and the corners are ornamented with niches and vases, or statuary. On the left, an open archway leads into another vestibule, containing the principal staircase and the entrance to the library, which is in a campanile, or tower, that will be presently spoken of. On the right, a similar archway leads into a vestibule leading to the offices and kitchen, in which is a door conducting into a gentleman's dressing-room, bath-room, etc., contained in a projection which answers to that of the tower, and between which is the entrance-porch previously spoken of. In the hall immediately opposite the entrance door, are double doors leading into a boudoir, or saloon, and which may be thrown into the hall when needed. On the left of this is a large drawing-room; on the right, the dining-room; and beyond it, the pantry, china-closet, kitchen, and other domestic offices. On the floor above are spacious sleeping and dressing-rooms, bath-rooms, etc.; and the tower is carried up a clear story above the roof, affording a cool retreat, where the breeze blows unmolested, and whence a cheerful and extended prospect of the town and the country beyond is commanded.

The aspect of the house is as follows: the entrance-front is east; the tower on the east and southern corner; the drawing-room south, with an end west; the boudoir and drawing-room west; and the kitchens, etc., protected on the north by an enclosed yard containing wood-sheds, etc., and extending to an avenue which runs along and bounds the northern side of the grounds. A large veranda is on the western side, and a smaller one (as being more exposed to view from the street, and consequently less desirable) on the south.

The grounds run back, in all, from the road about four hundred and fifty feet; the house is placed back one hundred feet, and as near as possible to the northern boundary, so as to permit as large a lawn and garden on the southern side as the space will afford. The stable and offices are at the extreme western end of the grounds, screened from view, by means of a thick plantation and a fence, and conveniently entered from the road or avenue on the north.

The external appearance of the building is designed to suit the situation. Being so near a city, and the objects contrasted with it being regular, and more or less ornate, a roughly-rural erection would be out of place, though not more so than would be a regular city-house. The ground undulating, and its level being considerably elevated, some harmony is desirable between these circumstances and the distribution of the parts of the building. Accordingly, the tower spoken of is placed at the south-eastern corner, where, as it is the object that first meets the eye on approaching from the city, it has a bold and picturesque appearance; and as the view of the scenery around is extremely fine, there seems every reason that means for an extended look-out should be so provided. The projecting portion of the front balancing this tower, and which contains the gentleman's dressing-room, etc., (which, you will see, I almost always insist upon in a *home*,) extends merely to one story, and terminates in a somewhat ornamental manner, with pedestals crowned with vases, and an open balustrade between; whilst between it and the tower, the projection of the porch affords an opportunity for making a large balcony, entered from the chamber floor, and in which many beautiful plants might be reared, as it would be very easy to enclose the top and sides with glass, removable at such seasons when the increased heat of so much glass in front of the windows might not prove desirable.

The style to be chosen for the house seems to me to be most readily met by the use of the genuine modern bracketed Italian, with projecting roof, somewhat flatter in its pitch than in a house farther in the country, and with the brackets, the cornice, the chimney-caps, etc., of a more finished and architectural character than I have heretofore described. The material selected to be brick, with stone dressings to the windows and chimneys, and to be painted and sanded a deep, warm cream-color, with those parts of the building which are constructed of wood, painted the same tone of color, but of deeper tint.

The southern end is pleasingly embellished by the addition of a large projecting bay window in the drawing-room, extended up to the chamber floor, and finished with pedestals, vases, and balustrade, in a similar manner to the projection on the eastern front. The veranda would be of wood; or I have occasionally seen some patterns in iron that are very satisfactory, although the extreme stiffness of design too often observable in articles of this material, generally makes them anything but desirable. Janes, Beebe and Co., of New York, have recently imported some patterns from Europe, of such great beauty, and which they are re-making in so exquisite a manner, I would recommend all interested in artistic smithery to call and see their extensive collection. The *Art Journal* has done much to raise the character of the designs of metal work in general; and such of my readers as have anything upon which they wish to exercise their taste, connected with the useful or ornamental in metal, will find the examples there given, and since reproduced by Janes, deserving a close study. The firm have, likewise, some ornamental tables, seats, flower-stands, fountains, vases, etc., of equal merit of design and workmanship.

The grounds of a villa near a city afford opportunity for the introduction of very many durable objects of art, which, if chosen with reference to their use and purpose, greatly enhance the pleasures of a stroll therein; though my readers will, I hope, not think this remark a justification for the admission of the vulgar "garden images" that the cockneys love to stick about their places, or of the quaint, though I think no less vulgar, conceits and practical-joke machines that degrade Chatsworth, in the shape of imitation men fishing, and tin trees that drench the gazer standing beneath them.

The ground plan here given will make the arrangement of the rooms on the principal floor easily evident.

No. 1, is the entrance arcade, recessed back a little from the projection of the tower, so that the line of its lower step may not protrude beyond the tower's base. This arcade is of a heavy, massive character, the columns with panelled recesses, and the soffits of the round-headed arches above sunk in a similar manner. Its ceiling is divided by beams into compartments also deeply recessed, and its floor and its widely spreading steps are of the Connecticut brown stone. No. 2, is the hall, about fourteen feet square, and provided with coat and hat closets on either side of the arched recess, in which are the double-doors to the boudoir, No. 6.

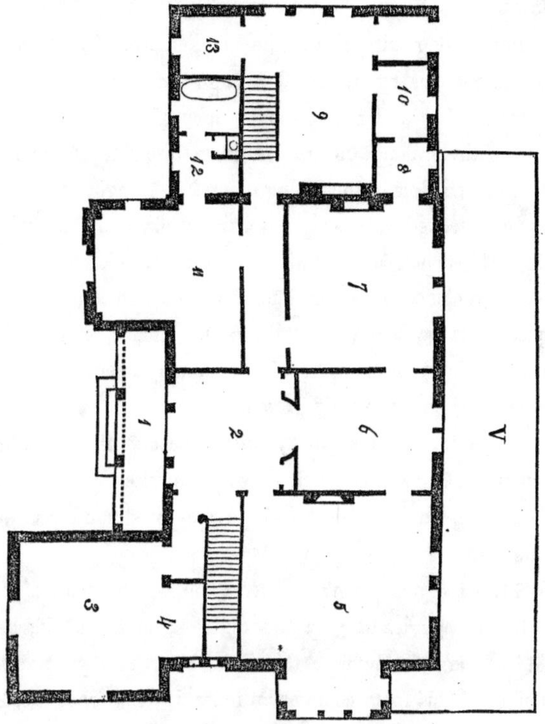


GROUND PLAN.—SUBURBAN VILLA.

No. 3, the library, sixteen feet square in the clear, its real accommodation being increased by a large recess, No. 4, under the principal staircase, which being fitted up with shelves and presses for books, materially adds to the actual size of the room. This apartment is the first story of the tower, and by the treatment of its inside cornices and its windows has a simple and highly artistic effect.

No. 5, is the drawing-room, a spacious, well-proportioned room, twenty-six by eighteen, exclusive of the projecting bay-window on its side.

Communicating with this is the boudoir, No. 6, fourteen by seventeen, opening by means of a large French window (as do also the drawing and dining-rooms) upon a wide veranda extending entirely along the garden or western side of the villa. Next to the boudoir is the dining-room, No. 7, eighteen feet by seventeen, attached to it being a waiters'-pantry and china-closet, No. 8. This pantry is made with a slide into the kitchen, No. 9, for the convenience of serving, but, as will be seen at a glance to the plan, does not open directly into the kitchen, and by that means no effluvia or exposure of the culinary operations would be likely to be inconveniently present.

No. 10, is the kitchen pantry, with a back vestibule leading into an inclosed yard containing every requisite to the comfort of the house, which should be within easy reach, and yet kept out of sight.

No 11, is the gentleman's dressing-room, which having a door into the passage leading by the dining-room to the kitchen, would be conveniently near the dining-room, and yet secured from sight. This room contains an inner dressing-room, No. 11, and a bath-room and water-closet—and the whole suite might be used as a sleeping-room and corresponding appurtenances, if thought preferable to the occupancy which I have designated.

No. 13, is the scullery, and as underneath the building is a large, well-lighted cellar, a cool-larder, vegetable-room, and a laundry are reached below by a flight of stairs under the back staircase which leads from the kitchen to the chambers above.

The distribution of the sleeping apartments will be seen by reference to the plan of the chamber floor.

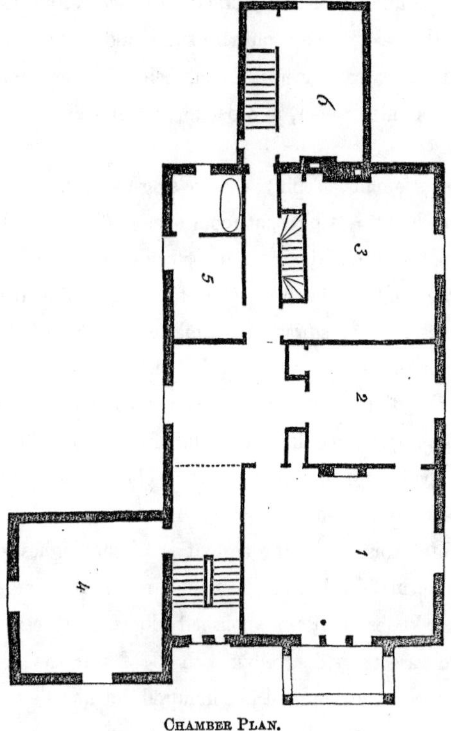


CHAMBER PLAN.

No. 1, is a large chamber, the same size as the drawing-room below; it has a pleasant balcony over the projecting southern window, and is so large as to admit readily of being divided into two rooms if thought better. It has a large closet as shown on plan, provided with deep cedar drawers for preservation of clothing from ravages of moths.

No. 2, is of the same size nearly as the boudoir below.

No. 3, a room over the dining-room, out of which is taken a space for a staircase to the attics, and for a large closet.

No. 4, a chamber over the library, provided with pleasant balconies on the eastern and southern sides, and making a well-proportioned and very cheerful room, being higher than the other chambers on this floor, in order to give sufficient elevation to the tower.

No. 5, is a small sleeping or dressing-room, with a bath attached, and No. 6 is a pleasant room over the kitchen. In the attic above is the cool and airy upper story room of the tower, and two large, well-ventilated rooms in the roof, with a space for drying clothes, and for storage of trunks, etc. The whole well lighted and protected by a very thickly framed and covered roof from the heat of the sun. Openings are constructed for the admission of properly regulated currents of air across the space, so that the dead stagnation of close atmosphere generally found in attics is entirely prevented.

The finish of this house throughout is of the highest order, more expense, in fact, having been incurred in its plate-glass, silvered door-knobs, registers, polished doors, etc., etc., than many would care to undergo, but with all of this the expense would not exceed ten thousand five hundred dollars to erect just such another building. The house is warmed and ventilated throughout by Janes' Hot-Water Apparatus, a mode of warming of such excellence, that a chapter especially to explain its principles has been thought desirable, and will be found in a more advanced portion of the book.

The grounds for such a house should be more artistically dressed than the more extended gardens of the open country, and here and there a few quiet objects of art in the way of seat, or vase, or pedestal may be scattered, giving connection to the house and grounds, and pleasant points of rest to the contemplative eye from within or during an out-door stroll.

THE "PARSONAGE"

Elevation

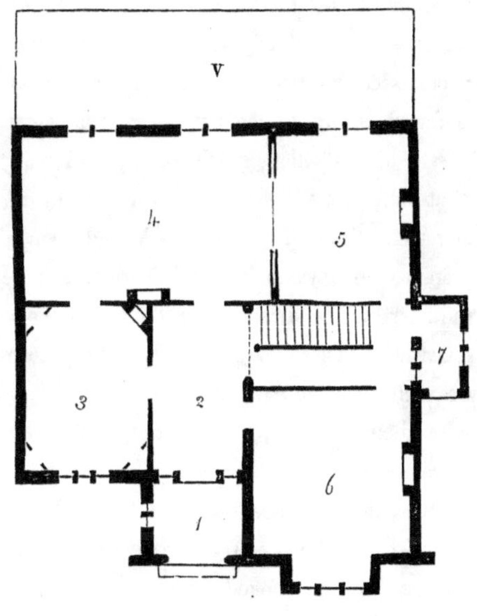


GROUND PLAN.

## CHAPTER IX.

### THE PARSONAGE HOUSE.

Many a rural village, now but a pretty assemblage of shading trees, neatly kept streets, and cleanly painted houses, might be made to contain points of absolute beauty, and be models for imitation, and vehicles for teaching the simple country folk around,—if they possessed but each one an appropriate Parsonage House. The church is ungrudgingly made as ornamental as the means and taste of the villagers will allow; and many a meeting-house that finds little favor in the eyes of the more travelled stranger passing through the place, is looked upon with a pride and a reverence no ways inferior in intensity to the feeling that swells the heart of the dweller near Trinity, or the residents of ancient Cathedral Close in church-abounding Europe. Though country churches I could say a good deal about, I must make no mention of them here; and yet are they not to many a gentle heart—rural homes?

But the glebe house, the residence for the pastor of the flock, having, in common with the houses of the residents of the village, the same necessities, and looked upon with a more domestic eye than could be its church, may easily, by its quiet, every-day appeal, draw the heart closer and closer to the person of the minister, and the church he dwells so near. No sectarian prejudices need bring into play a heap of objections to this; all sects who have a church in which to gather for assembled worship, and a settled minister among them to follow and to love, should see that the dwelling of the pastor is, as it were, a part of the church; for most sure it is that the domestic life and teaching of the man are worth more in the village annals of wavering weak ones saved, than the eloquence or the fervor of the pulpit. So the abode of that teacher, the scene of his domestic life and quiet home-teaching, should be as cheerfully made a feature in the village scene as the house of God.

Moreover, setting apart a house for especial occupancy by the minister would render a religious community more permanent and stable; for provision for the dwelling amongst them of a constant guide, as long as buildings framed by human hands can last, would be so serious and engrossingly interesting a matter, no light breath could shake the stability of the band of men who, with one heart and mind, lent themselves to the task.

Therefore will I assume that there is a want of some directions for building parsonage houses, and that, though they must, for reasons presently to be given, be more distinctive than other country dwellings, they are no less to be considered and treated as rural homes.

The parsonage house must be more distinctive in its character than other residences, because it is, in the first place, set apart for a particular and never varying occupancy, and because it is built for all time. The tastes, manners, and means of the flock may change, but only so much as necessarily influenced by such changes need parson-life vary; for stability is the vital element of religious teaching. Then, with the altered tastes and manners would come altered styles and fashions in building, so again must a distinctive character be assigned to the church's house, based on principles that, like that church's teaching, know "no change or shadow of turning." These principles, after the remarks I have made upon "the homestead," I need scarcely say, are fitness and honesty of constructive purpose. The house is wanted for the residence of a refined and intellectual man, and yet one whose family life must be regulated by strictest, yet elegant economy. To meet these wants, a plan must be contrived with no ordinary care. The showy rooms, folding doors, and divided parlors of the houses most esteemed by the villagers, must not be thought of for a moment; nor, on the other hand, must the parsonage be a mere kitchen and keeping room. The student, the teacher, the hospitable friend, the thrifty housekeeper, must be conveniently lodged—each one attribute of parson-life be recognized and provided for. So there must be the inner study for seclusion, the cheerful, roomy library for earnest talk, the ladies' parlor for livelier occupancy, the dining-room, and a shaded porch, and hospitably spacious hall. Kitchen and store room, pantry, and sleeping rooms are more matters of course, and so are less distinctive. A small expenditure is absolutely essential, and even where the church has been a costly structure, there seems no reason that the parsonage house should be other than a simple, honest building. If the house be too large, it will inevitably entail expense upon its clerical occupant; if too ornately decorated, it will be a constant source of outlay to the parish. An expenditure varying from two to five thousand dollars would probably cover all that might be requisite; and as the arrangement of the building and its distinctive character are what I would dwell upon in this chapter, I have given a design of a parsonage house suitable to almost every situation where one is required.

The building material may be of stone, brick, or timber. In the particular case for which this design has been made, stone is the material selected; but, with some slight modification of the roof on the front gable, a timber framed construction would be perfectly suitable. The cost of this building, if executed in the manner shown in the accompanying illustration, would be a little under five thousand dollars if executed in a substantial manner in stone; if of timber, and no more ornament introduced than the exterior view presents, its cost would be about three thousand.

The external character of the design is of that simple, quiet nature, that without challenging attention by any very marked or peculiar features, or by a severe attention to the restrictions of any one style, commands attention and gives pleasure to the passer by. As it would stand near the church, which, if of stone, would probably present some conformity to ancient ecclesiastical architecture, a certain congruity of outline is necessary between the soaring tendency of the lines of the church structure and those of the parsonage, so a pointed roof, a pyramidal arrangement of the whole mass seem necessary. Hence, the sharply rising front gable, which, as the rough masonry of which the house is built, would permit at no increased expense the picturesque management the design shows, instead of being covered by a projecting roof, is built in steps, behind which the roof stops. This, though perfectly permissible and productive of very good effect in stone, would be out of place in a wooden building. In the latter the roof must project beyond the face of the wall, and may be decorated with some simple and durably-made large board, or be left plain, with only a heavy roll moulding as a cornice, supported by blocks or moulded corbels placed at intervals of a foot or two apart.

The distribution of the rooms on the principal floor will be apparent upon examination of the ground plan.

No. 1, is the entrance porch, a wide and open covered space in which, on either side, should be an ample seat for hospitable resting of the caller at the house. Within is the entrance hall, No. 2, a roomy apartment, nine feet by sixteen, at right angles to which is the staircase hall, and passage way to kitchen below. In this design I have supposed the ground so to fall away as to allow the kitchen and domestic offices below, but in any other situation where such an arrangemeut would not be desirable, they can be extended in a wing from the northern side of the house.

No. 3, is a parlor or ladies' room, sixteen by thirteen, the corners of which are cut off, to form in one end a fireplace, and in the others three convenient closets.

No. 4, is a large library or principal room, both for general occupancy and for reception of parishioners, a large room of such a nature being far more desirable in a parsonage house than a showy drawing-room, or parlors divided by folding-doors. This room is sixteen feet by twenty-five, and its western French windows opening on to a large veranda, would be a very pleasant apartment. Communicating with this, in such a manner as to be thrown into it at any time, is a private study for the exclusive use of the pastor. This room is sufficiently large for such a purpose, being sixteen by thirteen feet, and the wall space is ample enough to afford room for a sufficiently large number of books, the room connected with it being also furnished with book-cases. Annexed to this is a back porch, which, as being nearest the church, would be the readiest entrance to the minister's study, and would give seclusion and private access to the room.

No. 8, is the dining-room, the door of which is immediately at the head of the stairs from the kitchen, or, if the offices be contained in a wing, a pantry could be constructed to take the place of the porch, No. 7, and thus connect with the kitchen. The dining-room is fifteen by seventeen, exclusive of the projecting window, and as its aspect is east, would be cheerful and pleasant. The arrangement of this floor, it is thought, would be found very convenient for the purposes for which the house is intended, and the space has been economised as much as possible to secure the results desired.

The sleeping-rooms are contained in the floor above, a plan of which will show their arrangement.

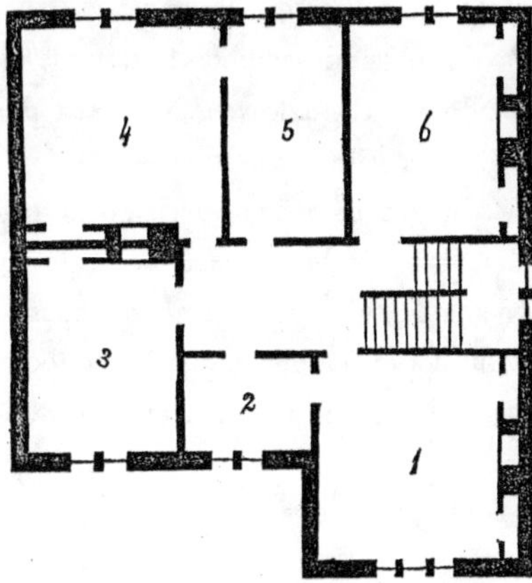


Parsonage House.—Chamber Plan.

No. 1, is a chamber over the dining-room, and of the same size; it is provided with two large closets, and attached to it is a smaller room, No. 9, over the hall, which would serve as a dressing-room, or is sufficiently large for a child's sleeping-apartment.

No. 3, is over the ladies' room below, and has in it a roomy closet.

Nos. 4, 5, and 6, are conveniently arranged sleeping-rooms over the library and study below. In the attic, formed by the high pitch of the roof, could easily be made at least two airy and good-sized sleeping-rooms, lighted and ventilated by windows in the gables at the east, west, and south.

If thought advisable, a bathing apparatus might be placed in the dressing-room, No. 2.

The accommodation comprised in this building is all that its purpose would require, or might be increased somewhat if the domestic offices were contained in a wing instead of in a basement below the main house. If in a wing, the rooms in its second story could obtain in addition to servants' sleeping-rooms a bath-room and water-closet, leaving No. 2 as a private dressing-room to the chamber with which it connects.

Other plans might be made which would give the desired accommodation, but this has seemed to me to contain all the requisites of a simple, substantial, parsonage house, and has been designed to form not only a building suited to the pastoral wants of its occupants, but to be to them and theirs, at all seasons, a rural home.

## CHAPTER X.

### SOUTHERN HOMES.

A HOME in the sunny south is a very different thing to arrange to one suited to a northern clime. Space for free ingress and egress of occasional breeze—space, too, that can be convertible into habitable apartments, is the first element. Compactness is only valuable, as securing economy in construction, and as affording convenient nearness of relation in all the constituent parts of the building. Life out of doors is not the necessity that has to be met, as affording cool retreat from summer's sun, but shaded retirement within. Therefore, what in a northern house would be an ample provision of architectural shade, in the shape of veranda, porch, and ombra, does not constitute all that has to be thought of in planning the *agremens* of a southern home.

The elements of construction, too, are widely different; the roof of the northern building has to withstand, at times, a direct pressure from the weight of accumulated snows; that of the southern has to resist lateral assaults of tornado and heavy winds. These influences exert a corresponding sway upon the material embodiment of the other parts of the design. The walls have

SOUTHERN HOUSE—adapted to a large household—elevation p, 132

to be strong, yet pierced with larger openings for doors, windows, etc.; and light—because wood, the material generally used, derives its strength from scientific framing, and with liability to sudden strains, mere weight would only tend to weaken. To give these remarks a practical bearing, I would say that a roof of high pitch is indispensable, not only on account of its slope, allowing a shingle covering, which will be lighter and cooler than one of metal or slate, but in order that its sides may not be injured by sudden and violent wind-storms, which in southern countries are of more or less frequent occurrence. The roof should project at the eaves and over the gables, the rafters being brought down and supported by struts or brackets, which, pinned into the principals or posts of the frame of the building, will lessen the thrust of the roof, and prevent its spread. The windows should be large, and above all things, should nearly occupy the entire height of the room, so that ventilation may equally be applied to the ceiling and the floor. The doors, both external and internal, should be double, one being a close-pannelled, ordinary door, and the other with slats that will open to admit a current of air, and at the same time give seclusion to the room. All the doors and windows should, for comfortable habitancy of the house, be provided with folding-frames, lightly made, and covered with netting, either of wire, gauze, or muslin, to exclude those flying torments that infest a southern home.

The internal arrangement and distribution of the rooms should be such, as that the kitchens and domestic offices may be cut off from the main dwelling, and yet be so near as to allow all the machinery of living to be fully attended to; the dining or living-room may be on the side nearest the kitchen buildings, and, connecting them together, may be an airy, well-lighted vestibule, containing on the one side a waiters'-pantry, so arranged as to open upon the sideboard in the dining-room. This pantry must farther have a direct communication with the kitchen, or with a serving-room attached thereto. The other side of the vestibule should contain spacious store, china, and glass-rooms. Below this, should be a large cellar, artificially ventilated, (of which, more anon,) in which wine, fruits, meat, and vegetables may be stored. The kitchen buildings must be much lighter, and more spacious than anything that would be contrived for a northern home;—in fact, the domestics require, as it were, a distinct house, and a separate establishment. Nothing could be made prettier than a roomy block of kitchen buildings, with the little cots of the colored servants artistically grouped around.

The house itself should have wide and spacious halls,—spacious only, however, where ventilation can be served;—otherwise, merely loss of room. Halls running across each other, their ends by sliding screens at any time convertible into separated apartments, form a good basis upon which to begin the design for the ground plan of the house.

The plan annexed shows the arrangement of the rooms. A wide and airy veranda surrounds the house, stopping at the connecting building between the main house and the domestic offices.

No. 1 is a wide hall running clear through the building and opening by means of double-doors, (provided also with Venetian blind doors within,) upon the veranda floor.

No. 2 is the library, a spacious and airy room opening *en suite* by means of double-doors with the boudoir, No. 3, and thence with the drawing-room, No. 4. The boudoir or vestibule is made with wide folding-doors shutting it out from the entrance hall, so that, as occasion needed, the entire space might be thrown open.

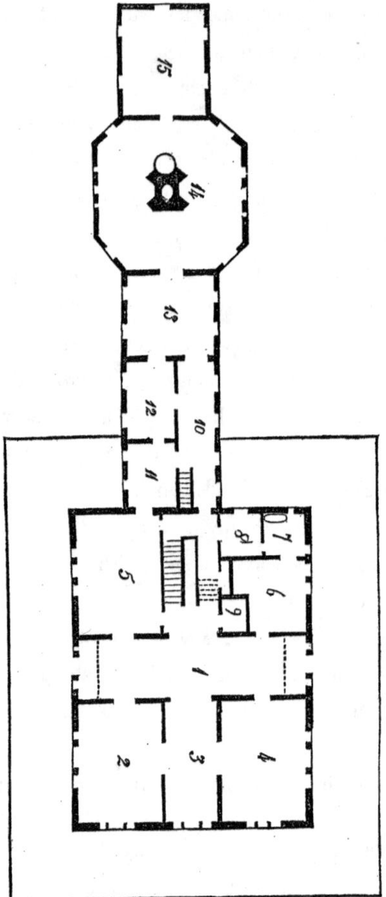


SOUTHERN HOUSE.—GROUND PLAN.

No. 5 is the dining-room, of the same large size as the library and drawing-room on the other side of the entrance hall.

No. 6 is a large chamber, eighteen by sixteen, with an alcove at its one end to contain a bed, and communicating therewith is a dressing and bath-room, No. 7.

No. 8 is a gentlemen's dressing and wash-room, opposite the dining-room door, and its entrance being under the staircase, it would be secluded and yet easily reached.

No. 9 is a large hall closet for hats, shoes, etc., and adjoining it is a smaller closet for brooms and other articles in daily use.

No. 10 is a corridor leading from the dwelling portion of the house to the kitchen buildings, and contains a back flight of stairs to the chamber floor.

No. 11, a large pantry filled with shelves, and every convenience for a waiter.

No. 12, a light and airy room, containing presses for china, glass, and such dry stores as would be desirable.

No. 13, a serving-room, whence the servants would convey the dishes to the waiters'-pantry, from which room they would be at once placed upon the sideboard or table in the dining-room.

No. 14 is a very large irregularly octagonal kitchen with the cooking apparatus in the centre, and No. 15, is a servants' hall, or outer room, connecting with which may be a laundry and such other domestic offices as southern life may need. The peculiarities of the plan are space, simplicity of arrangement, and facilities for ventilation. Independently of the natural means the arrangement of the plan would afford of securing the latter, artificial aid is offered in the following construction of the kitchen fire-places. These are shown built around a large octagonal flue, and a view of the exterior will exhibit this flue carried above the roof of the kitchen in a somewhat formidable manner. The inner flue is for purposes of ventilation; and the action of the air contained in it operated upon by the heat communicated thereto by the surrounding smoke-flues from the kitchen fire-places, could draw off with considerable force the contents of all air-ducts opening therein. The base of the tower contains a ventilator for the especial cooling and purification of the kitchen and its adjoining buildings, and its action is as simple as it would be effective. The floors and ceilings of the main portion of the house should have air-ducts leading into downward shafts connecting with the ventilating shaft, and they might be led along and concealed in the roof over the connecting building between the house and kitchen wing.

The rooms on this floor in the dwelling part of the house are fourteen feet and a half high; and in order to show the whole of the house, the plan is drawn to half the scale of other designs in this book, being to a scale of a fortieth of an inch to a foot. On the floor above would be very spacious chambers, and the plan would cut up into a great number. In the centre, the principal stairway would enter upon an upper hall ten by twelve, which, carried up into the roof, and then beyond it, as a species of tower, would give an airy and pleasant circulation to the inner atmosphere of the house. Bath rooms might be got from off the first landing of the staircase, over the dressing-rooms and bathing-rooms below, which, not needing to be higher than ten or eleven feet, would afford ample space above for these desirable means of comfort. The distribution of the chamber floor being so evidently dependent upon the partitions of the plan below, I have not given a separate plan.

This would make a house of the dimensions of seventy feet front by fifty-two deep. The roof should *hip* up all ways towards the central projection, and the chimneys of the building might easily all be so gathered as to form turrets to flank the species of tower that I suppose occupying the middle of the roof.

The material I have most frequently found used is wood. The style suitable for such a building would be one admitting greatest breadth of effect and simplicity of detail. Any one of the styles I have described in former pages could be easily modified to meet the requirements in such a case. The Italian would probably be the most appropriate. Its peculiarities and its genius would seem more in character under a southern sky and amid southern scenery than any other.

The veranda should be extended clear round the front, rear, and flank, to where the kitchen buildings join on, their projection being hidden by a thick screen of flowering shrubs. The southern veranda has already been incidentally mentioned, and the provision of one on the northern side must depend upon the peculiar situation of the house. Not being a necessity, as those on the other sides are, I do not insist upon it here.

The perfect ventilation of such a building will constitute its most habitable excellence. This can be secured by proper arrangement of doors and windows, and by artificial assistance, in the way of air-flues, discharging above the roof, and their openings into the rooms provided with the *Berrian's ventilating valve*, which has been so often referred to in previous pages. One material aid to the maintenance of a cool and equitable temperature in the house will be in the perfect ventilation of its veranda. Though it would seem, as this is always so open, that nothing more could be done, those persons who are willing to make the experiment with their thermometer will be surprised to find how much higher the temperature of the air immediately under the ceiling of the veranda is, than that at the same altitude within the rooms. This is, naturally enough, caused by refraction, and by the accumulating pressure of ascending heated air. Unless some means of escape be made for this, much of it must find its way into the rooms. This can be done by making in the veranda roof occasional openings against the wall, at such points where chamber windows do not open immediately thereon.

Provide over these apertures small projecting pent-roofs, to protect from the effects of rain; make them about six inches wide, and three to four feet long, and at intervals of ten to twelve feet.

The cost of such a building would greatly vary in different portions of the southern states; but, unless unusual difficulties in the way of procuring efficient workmen prevented, the expenditure needed to erect it in a thoroughly substantial and well finished manner would not exceed thirteen thousand dollars, and in some situations would not require more than from eleven to twelve. But this is a larger and more expensive house than is frequently needed. I will proceed, therefore, to the description of one on an entirely different scale.

The principle on which the success of a design for a small southern home will depend, appears to me to be its perfect adaptation to purposes of ventilation. Convenience of arrangement, and economical distribution of the space contained within its boundary walls, can be obtained by study of houses around; but the means of procuring satisfactory circulation of air is not so easily determined. A house on a small scale—of which, say the accommodation would be found sufficient with four principal rooms on each floor—might very economically and advantageously be arranged in the form of a cross.

The plan would, in fact, show four apartments, all radiating from a centre, that centre containing the escape flues for smoke, and the fire-places of each of the rooms, together with provision for means of artificial ventilation, of which latter I will presently speak.

But the rooms thus coming together to a centre, would require a space left from which to radiate, amounting to a cube of the width of their ends; this would waste room. I would propose, therefore, that the corners of the rooms so connecting be cut off, leaving the inner end of the form of a half octagon. The cube, then, would only be that of the straight side of the octagon; say five feet square, sufficient to contain all flues and ventiducts, and making an economical arrangement for the rooms. Passage ways would be saved by the ends thus coming together, one room opening into the other by a door placed in the sloping side. Taking this cross-form as that for the plan of the house, I will attempt a description of such a home in detail.

Take a block thirty-six feet long by fourteen feet wide; let this represent the transom of the cross; a block eighteen feet long and sixteen wide would form the lower portion of the stem, and one of similar dimensions the upper. These would intersect the transom in the middle, thus leaving the latter to project ten feet on either side. The transom points west to east, and the entrance is in its eastern end. A large parlor runs south, entered from the entrance hall through the angular side; and, jutting out west, also so communicating with the parlor, is the dining-room. On the north, connected through a pantry with the dining-room, are the kitchen and domestic offices. This comprises the general distribution of the rooms on the ground floor. I will now speak of them in detail.

On the ground-plan, No. 1 is the entrance hall; No. 2, a

large and well lighted closet; No. 3, the principal parlor; No. 4, the dining room; No. 6, a large and light pantry, with

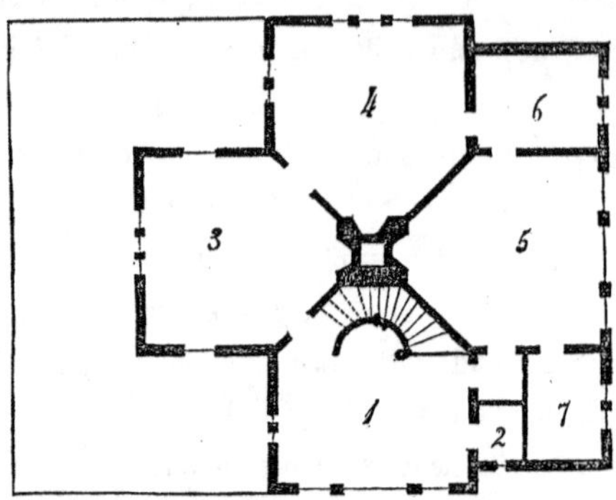


SMALL SOUTHERN HOUSE.—GROUND PLAN.

space for store and china closets; No. 5, the kitchen; No. 7, the scullery, in which, if a cellar were excavated, might be the staircase leading thereto.

In the entrance hall is situated the staircase, running up with an easy curve, concentric with the half octagon end of the apartment. Under the stairway is a large hall closet, and in the hall is an enclosed vestibule, and an entrance to the kitchen. The hall would made a pleasant third room, particularly for afternoon occupancy, the sun being entirely off its sides, and the enclosing screen forming the entrance vestibule could be made to fold back, and framed with slats, as a Venetian blind. From this projecting ten feet of the transom, a terrace floor would run round on three sides of the parlor, stopping against the corresponding projection on the west.

This terrace would be screened from the sun by a peculiarity in the construction of the roof, which I propose should run straight through from north to south—not broken out at the projecting portions east and west, but extending clear over them, and continued the necessary width all along. Thus, over those portions of the building setting back, the roof would extend ten feet or more—thirteen in fact, as the projecting ends would require at least three feet to protect them; and this projection of roof would shade the terrace below. On the southern side, where the gable of the roof would show, I would propose a floor, on the level of the chamber floor, extended over the terrace below, making a more effectual shade, and giving a pleasant walk out from the bed-room. The roof might, at the gable ends, (it would not require to project over more than three feet on the northern end,) be supported by rustic posts, with interlacing knotted limbs between, at their upper ends; the whole with the bark on, nailed with copper nails, and preserved by varnish.

In the centre, the chimneys so gathered together would allow a large flue in their midst for ventilation. The fire necessary at some portion of each day for culinary operations, would give sufficient heat to one of the brick or tile sides of this flue, to cause a radiation, and consequently an upward tendency to the column of air within the central shaft. This shaft must be made to communicate with each of the rooms by apertures above the floor, and under the ceiling of each room. In the upper one must be inserted one of the Berrian's useful little valve boxes so often alluded to; and by carrying the central shaft above the other flues, and capping it with one of Janes and Beebe's Ejecters, a rapid current will always be found therein, and the heated air and used-up gases be readily drawn off from each room.

The chamber accommodation on the floor above would comprise one large bed-room over the parlor, one over the dining-room, two over the kitchen, and a small one off the hall, the stair-case not requiring the whole of the space. If needed, additional attic rooms might easily be obtained in the roof, as the pitch necessarily made for a shingle covering would, in a house of such a span, afford considerable space within its frame for any such arrangement.

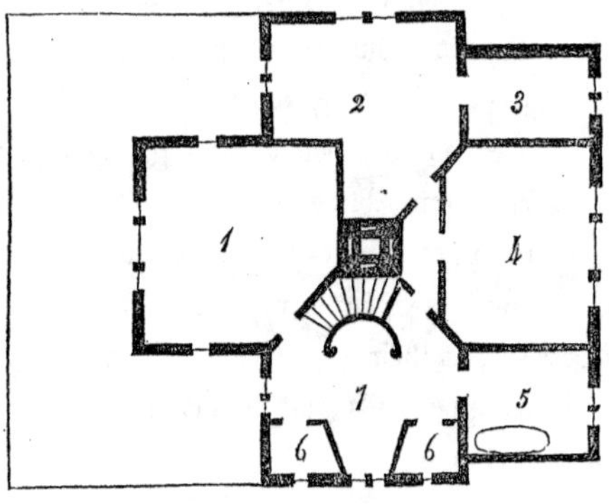


CHAMBER PLAN.

In the Chamber Plan, No. 1 is a large room over the parlor, one of its sides being left square, for the sake of forming a more convenient shape for a bed. The windows of this room would open upon the balcony floor, as would also those of chamber No. 2, and the one in the hall, No. 7.

No. 2 has a convenient recess for a bed, against the pier necessary for a chimney and ventilating shaft in the centre of the building, and connected with this room is a roomy dressing room, No. 3. No. 4 is a large and pleasant room for servants (unless the space in the attic be converted into one or two sleeping-rooms,) and is over the kitchen. No. 5 is a good sized bathing and dressing-room; Nos. 6, 6, are large and airy closets, for linen and other clothes; and No. 7 is the hall or vestibule, which, by reason of its pleasantly embayed window, would be a charming place to sit in for the lady of the house.

A home constructed upon this plan, with simple rustic posts supporting the roof and veranda floors, with the battened sides and with sharp roof, would look highly picturesque, and be of moderate cost. Here it would require an expenditure of about sixteen hundred dollars.

## CHAPTER XI.

### COTTAGES.

In that pleasantest of all country-written books—*Rural Hours*, the observant authoress dots down a series of observations upon rural architecture, so terse and pertinent, that, but for its length, I would like to quote the entire chapter. In a sketch of the several architectural eras that the history of this country could show, she defines so admirably the transition, step by step, from the *log-cabin* ;—" its very opposite, the lank and lean style, the *shallow* order, which aimed at rising far above the lowly log-cottage; proud of a tall front and two stories; proud of twice too many windows: but quite indifferent to all rules and proportions; to all appearance of comfort and snugness." Then, next in order, the "*shallow-ornate*, assuming the Grecian portico, running up sometimes one wing, sometimes two; pipe-stem columns one-fiftieth of their height in diameter, and larger, perhaps, in the centre than at either extremity, stand trembling beneath a pediment which, possibly, contains a good-sized bed-room, with a window in the apex. Such buildings are frequently surrounded with a very fanciful paling of one sort or other. One looks into the barn-yard of such a house with anxious misgivings, lest the geese should be found all neck, the cocks all tail, the pigs with longer noses, the ponies with longer ears than are usually thought becoming." Then comes the "plain straight-forward style," and succeeding to this, "new wooden cottages, which, in the anxiety of the architect to escape the shallow, err in the opposite extreme, and look oppressively heavy, as though the roof must weigh upon the spirits of those it covers." Finally, the last change that the piquant writer I am quoting sees, is the introduction of a few "Rural Gothic and Elizabethan" cottages, "which have grown rapidly into favor about the suburbs of large towns." These seem to have made great impression upon the region whence the writer dates, and before leaving the agreeable pages of this delightful volume, I would direct my reader's attention to the chapter from which I have quoted. In the large edition, illustrated, it will be found in page 380.

The expression of character in a simple country dwelling is an effect that would seem difficult to attain. In rural districts, one pervading genius always seems to have inspired the production of the whole of the buildings recently erected. One may be a little larger or differently painted than the other, but the general type appears identical. Near a railroad, particularly if one on which the stations have been made "tasty," the fashion most in vogue is a species of Gothic, thin and ineffective in reality, but pleasing to the builders from the inch-board finery and wooden insertion-work they are able to stick about. These cottages are mostly cheaply built, and will last their time; meanwhile, they do good by directing attention to the desirableness of giving a building some external character and appearance suited to the scenery amid which it stands, and as country people are beginning to learn of themselves that such houses look bald and bare without tree-shade surrounding them, and creepers festooning their fronts, a point in advance is evidently gained. Gradually may be seen stealing over, first one and then another of such cottages, changes that, although the type and prevailing characteristics are similar enough, begin to mark a difference and an individuality; so that, ere long, the features all possess in common will be so softened down and differently treated that an expression of individual character will be marked upon each.

In the smaller cottage houses this is most to be desired—larger houses are built more generally under different circumstances and in accordance with particular tastes, and hence are becoming far less uniform in treatment, but village buildings, mostly erected four or five in a batch, have too many requirements in common to be susceptible in the minds of their builders of any very great variety.

Nothing an architect can employ himself upon requires, in fact, closer attention and more careful study than a design for a cheap and simple country cottage—there is such a temptation to prettinesses, whimsicality, and the false picturesque, and yet there is no lack of examples of what a cottage home should be, and no excuse, with Mr. Downing's excellent works in such extensive circulation, in not knowing what it may be.

A cottage home should be compact, for land generally cannot be spared for a building much spread upon the ground—it should be simple in its architectural character, too much detail not only involving a large outlay at first but needing constant and expensive repairs; it should be roomy, that is, spacious by relative arrangement of the rooms rather than by their actual size; it should be naturally ventilated by certain circulation of its atmosphere within, then will it be sweet and healthy. Its walls should be protected by its roof, its windows by artificial shade in the way of some simple and inexpensive veranda, and its windows should be contrived more in reference to admission of light and fresh air, than to the old fashioned method once so fashionable, of crowding every side of a house with glazed openings. I have often been amused at the ingenuity evinced in some old, unaltered building, in filling it with windows, making it a huge lantern, or rather, in a hot summer sun, a huge forcing-house. I wonder how the sturdy Puritans of old fared in such hot-houses, and whether they found them conducive to vigorous growth; perhaps, as a friend once wittily suggested, by such means were raised the "early Christians we read about." A room filled with windows is unpleasant on account of the cross lights; uncomfortable on account of the reflected heat of so much glass; and difficult to furnish for the want of some wall spaces for table or sofa.

A cottage home suited to the neighborhood of some small country town, and indicative of refinement and taste on the part of its occupants, may be made a very pleasing feature in the landscape. The illustration given here represents such a building, and I will proceed to describe it in detail, premising that its cost being but fourteen hundred dollars, it would be found within the means of most persons desiring such a house. *(See next page.)*

The character of the exterior is architectural, partaking something of the Rural Italian. Its low walls, overshadowing roof, wide veranda, and projecting ombra in its southern front, give it an appearance of symmetry and refinement that adapts it to the occupancy of a family of elegance and taste. The material of which it may be constructed may be stone, brick, or wood. If of stone, no change may be made in its form or the nature of its details, unless perhaps making them heavier, and their marked features still more bold. If of brick, I would merely add a projecting face, one brick wide and projecting two inches round all

Elevation.—Suburban Cottage.

of the windows, and a band running horizontally below the brackets or cantilevers of the roof about a foot deep, upon which they may rest. If of wood, the covering should be clap-boarding or smooth ceiling, not battens and perpendicular planking, as the leading characteristics of the composition are horizontal lines, and would be contradicted by any other direction in the lines of the covering. The roof, of sufficiently steep a slope to carry off all water or snow, should be shingled, and the gable over the centre of the southern front be made water-tight with metal strips in the valley formed by its intersection with the slope of the main roof. The chimneys, formed of brick, rise in simple form from the ridge, and as they have no portion of the roof or building higher than themselves, need not extend above the ridge more than sufficient to ensure good proportion of height to width.

Before proceeding farther with the exterior of the building, I will describe the plan.

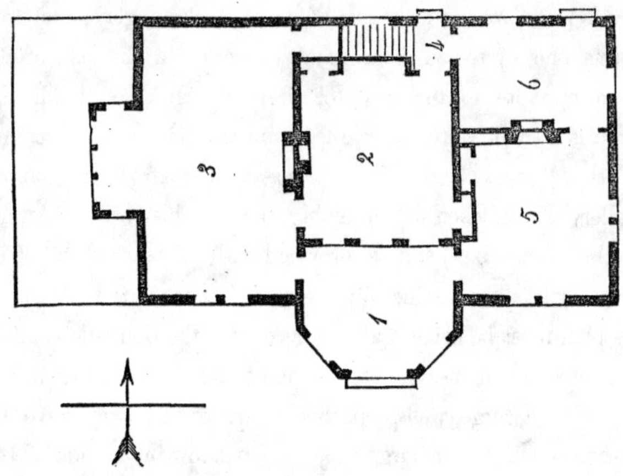


GROUND PLAN.—SUBURBAN COTTAGE.

A peculiarity in this design is in the projecting half-octagon porch or ombra, which, from its position, serves the double purpose of a delightful and cool retreat, and that of an entrance-hall —it is marked on the plan, No. 1. In the winter, its sides might be filled with windows, and the opening in front with a glass door, thus making an enclosed vestibule or porch, and rendering the dining-room a very warm and comfortable apartment. From this porch are doors into the dining-room, No. 2; the parlor or library, No. 3; and the kitchen, No. 5; and according as a visitor's business in calling was to such and such a portion of the house, a door might be opened, thus saving the internal room necessary for a hall, and yet gaining all the advantages of such a portion of the building. The dining-room is a good-sized pleasant room, fifteen feet by seventeen, with French windows opening upon the ombra or porch at one end, and a recess for sideboard underneath the stairs at the other. Attached to this room are the necessary adjuncts of china, glass, and store closets, one by the sideboard, and the other in the side of the room opposite to the stove or fireplace. Back of the dining-room is a small vestibule, five feet square, enclosed so as to shut off the staircase, and being the passage way from the pantry, scullery, and kitchen to the dining-room. This entry is marked in the plan, No. 4, and is provided with an outer door. The economy in space attained by the arrangement of this portion of the plan must be evident at a glance, and the domestic comfort and convenience ensured, seem to me to render it very desirable. No. 3 is a large, well-proportioned apartment, twenty-five by fifteen, exclusive of a large projecting window in the side of the room. This would serve as a parlor, drawing-room, or country library, as the taste of the occupants lead them to determine. The projecting window opens upon a large veranda extending along the side of the room, and from one side of this bay-window a portion of the veranda might, if thought pleasant, be enclosed, forming either a conservatory or a small summer study, attainable at very little additional cost. As this house might in many places be thought adapted for the dwelling of the clergyman of some small society, I would suggest that the room I have just described would very agreeably afford ample space for purposes of clerical use, and the small study thus attached (entered by a door from the side of the bay-window) might be provided with a flue in one of its sides, so as to be warmed by a stove in winter. Few houses of far greater pretension and expense have rooms so spacious and well-proportioned as those in this little cottage, and hence its desirableness for erection. No. 5 is a kitchen, back of which is a large scullery and wash-room, No. 6. Underneath the building, a dry and well lighted cellar (lighted from the one end and the rear side) might contain a store and flour-room, a larder, etc., with a flight of stairs leading thereto. Back of this building, I would propose an enclosed yard, containing wood-shed, and such offices as are better out of doors, and as the pleasant, occupied rooms are all on the other side of the house, the yard so enclosed might extend along its entire rear length, and being conveniently opened into by means of the enclosed vestibule at the foot of the stairs, would be easy of access from the living rooms. This enclosed yard would keep everything neat and orderly in appearance round the building, and give it a refined character in keeping with its more exposed exterior.

The height of the rooms on this floor is ten feet in the clear, the walls to be prepared for paper, and the inside finish of doors and windows of the simplest, plainest description.

The sleeping accommodation in the floor above is adequate to the comfortable use of a small family, and is arranged as follows:

No. 1 is a hall, well-lighted and roomy, containing the staircase from below, and from which open the doors into the several chambers.

No. 2 is a large room over the dining-room and extending clear to a line with the front of the house, the recessed portion below being floored over. From this room a window opens upon a large balcony, No. 3, over the truncated projection of the porch below. The room is provided with a large closet for clothes, and a flue for a stove or fire-place.

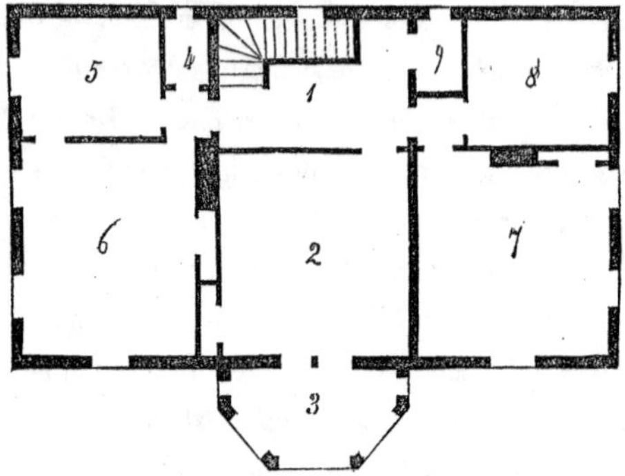


CHAMBER PLAN.—SUBURBAN COTTAGE.

No. 4 is a large linen-closet, well-lighted, and formed by the small entry from the upper hall leading to rooms Nos. 5 and 6.

No. 5 is a small chamber or dressing-room, in which might be a bathing apparatus, and serving either as a separate single room, a child's sleeping-room, or a dressing-room connected with the larger chamber, No. 6, which is over the library or parlor below, and is provided with a spacious clothes-closet and a flue for a stove or fire-place.

No. 7 is over the kitchen, and has also a large closet and a fire-place, and No. 8 is a servants' sleeping-room. This room is shut off from the other chambers by an entry similar to that on the other side of the hall, and is sufficiently large for the purpose and is well-lighted and ventilated.

No. 9 is a large store-room, well-lighted and airy—completing the accommodation provided on this floor, and the compactness and convenience of the plan must, I think, favorably recommend itself.

The rooms on this floor extend partly into the roof. The walls are seven feet high to the under side of the plate, and the ceiling follows the slope of the roof sufficiently far to allow the rooms to be ten feet in the clear. The roof is so framed as to admit this, and by such an arrangement greater internal height and airiness are obtained, with more modest lowliness of the exterior. The sloping sides of the ceiling should be firred down so as to leave a space of dead air (the most perfect non-conductor) between the lathing and the covering of the roof; by this means the rooms will be always cool and the additional height gained be very valuable. The room over the dining-room having a gable over its ceiling would be a higher and more symmetrical apartment than the others, and hence might be reserved as the guest-chamber, its large balcony making it a very pleasant sitting place for ladies with their books or needle-work.

The furniture and finish of such a house as this should be very simple. The dining-room being as it were a hall, and consequently frequently seen, should be neatly and appropriately arranged. In the summer, its floor covered with Indian matting; removed in the winter for a carpet of one of those pretty, warm-looking patterns that one sometimes sees in churches. Few colors should be in its composition, a mosaic work of deep purple and orange, or crimson and brown or black, interwoven in small patterns and without any contrasted spots of brighter colors. The tables and chairs of oak, maple, or birch, the table shut up into small form and standing in the centre of the room, its additional leaves stored away in a recess left purposely for them at the side of the side-board. This latter should as it were be a portion of the room (in this case) not a distinct piece of furniture. With a heavy wooden slab at the top, drawers and a lock-up cupboard below; and above the slat at top, in the recess again another recess under the risers of the stairs for the urn, or such other somewhat ornamental portion of the dinner or breakfast equipage as would properly fill it. The back of this recess, on either side of this central inner one, might, if wished, be formed of mirrors set into the wall, without any frame, but a narrow moulding of the same wood as the sideboard and furniture, and the top of the recess should finish in a low, three centred flat arch, with merely a bead moulding on its edge, its side or soffit being papered like the rest of the room. The walls papered in oak or maple, with no cornice other than just a bead an inch and a half deep to break the corner formed by the right angle between wall and ceiling; and the woodwork if not left as the natural wood, oiled and varnished, should be grained oak or black walnut, though the latter might perhaps be too dark, as the rooms are low and the projection of the ombra would somewhat quench the light.

An open Franklin stove set in an arched recess would serve for heating this room, and as it would be removed in the summer, would be perhaps better than a fireplace, the width of the room leaving nothing to spare for projection of chimney breast.

The parlor, whether library or drawing-room, would be treated in a very similar manner. If of use, bookcases should be built in the walls; simple shelves with an arched finish at top, and a drawer or two with a couple of low folding-doors enclosing a small lock-up cupboard at the bottom, and without doors; a curtain meeting in the middle and running on rods across the top, made of silk chintz or some light material, would look more cheerful and gay, and be less expensive. For the rest, the carpet, when the days for matting were over, should be lighter in color and more variety, but to my taste of small pattern, and of that indescribable mosaic that, whether floral or geometric, never offends the eye by its imitation of flower or foliage, or by its stiffness and harshness of outline. The paper of oak pattern or some other one-toned character, the furniture of light-colored wood, the mirrors void of gilding. Around the bay or projecting

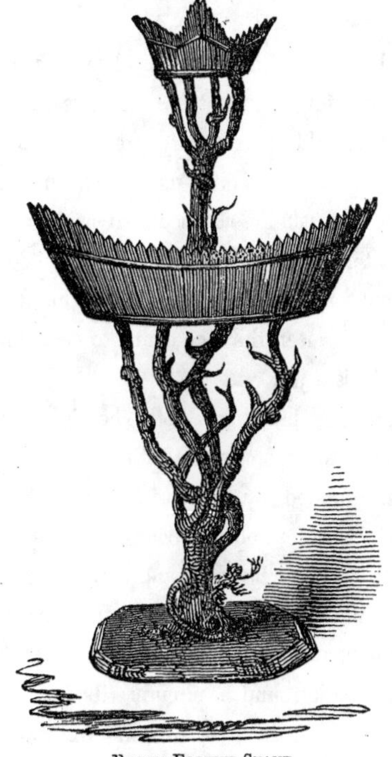

Rustic Flower-Stand.

window, a low chintz-covered seat, excepting where the windows open to the veranda floor, or the door (if there be one), leads into the study or conservatory, and as the space would be large, its centre might prettily be occupied by a light and elegant work-table, or by a rustic flower-stand or jardiniere. The foregoing cut shows a pretty rustic flower-stand just suited to such a situation, and as it is inexpensive and can easily be procured, I have given its representation. It is made of bark finished neatly and varnished, and can be got at the Berrians.

The staircase is wide, roomy, easy of access, and is well-lighted, and, excepting on the upper floor, would need no balusters.

The external character of the house has been before spoken of. The porch or ombra in front has an appearance of massive simplicity which should be carefully preserved in executing a building after this design. It is not by any means expensive, and as the building itself has been drawn at large, specification prepared, and a tender made by a respectable builder to contract to erect the same for a little under fourteen hundred dollars, it will be satisfactorily seen that the claim to economical expenditure of the means is a just one.

The color of such a building should be light—whatever the general aspect and tone of coloring of the objects around—that let it be. If surrounded by trees, with a leafy background, its coloring should be warm and approach the cream; if standing more alone, with rocky foreground and bold crags near enough to be seen in outline and color, quench the warmth somewhat by deepening the cream to a light, cool brown; if other buildings are near, and the background be circumscribed, give the building relief and its features distinctness by using more than one color thereon—covering the main block with a warm, light tint and deepening the prominent portions, as window frames, cornices, brackets, doors, veranda posts, and ombra or porch. Here one word respecting a contrary mode sometimes suggested: It has been said that in such a case the building should be the dark tint, the details light, and at first thought this would seem correct, but, on after reflection will come the fact that the details being such small portions of the general mass—spots or lines as it were upon its bulk—their hue would be merged into that of the rest if made lighter, as we see delicate pearl green is lost amid dark foliage, but would stand boldly out in evident form and distinctness if of darker hue, like the pines and dark evergreens of a more tenderly tinted plantation, or the dark eyebrows and eyelashes of a Spanish face.

Sanding paint, or mixing sand therewith, besides assisting in its preservation, takes away from the oily glare and glisten of ordinary pigments, and by lessening the refracting power, gives to the surface of the building a softer and more pleasant tone of coloring. But I do not recommend this process in all cases, believing in no universal rule that admits not of exception; frequently where the detail is minute, the roughened appearance imparted by the use of sand gives a clumsy aspect to the part, and in all cases where sharpness of outline is sought to be obtained by any particular decoration of the construction, the use of sand would be perfectly inadmissible. By using the last coat of oil color thick and smooth, without boiled oil, or any fatty, or resinous substance, a flat, unshining surface may be obtained, more durable than a brighter, reflecting coat would be, and more pleasing in effect.

The approach to such a house, where the size of its ground-plot would permit, should be directly from in front, straight from point to point, but should be by means of an easy curve, sweeping round a clump of evergreen shrubbery in front, a small grassy mound, or some such central feature, and returning either to the same gate, or, perhaps, if the space widened sufficiently, to a second gate a little farther on. The end containing the kitchen, etc., in a line with one side of the enclosing back-yard, should be planted out, and screened by trees. The other end, towards the veranda and bay-window, should be laid out as a pleasant lawn or flower-garden, and left as open as space will permit; its extremity, where perhaps a neighbor's land joins on, planted in such a manner as to hide the wall or fence, screen from observation, and at the same time appear to connect with the land beyond, (if there be any worth conveying such an idea) so that ownership may seemingly be suggested therewith, and the apparent extent of the grounds increased. How this may be done has been explained in a previous chapter.

Perchance the building may have to stand upon a corner lot; in that case its appearance could not fail to please, as the bold projection of the porch or ombra on the side, and the simple and well-proportioned outline of either end would be seen to great advantage. The fences around it, if enclosing a tolerably large area, may either be wooden palings, within which a privet hedge might be tried, (I say tried, because its growth is not always certain, but its pretty effect worth trying for,) or an iron railing of simple pattern and inexpensive character might possibly be decided on. Frequently an iron fence proves the cheapest in the end, though its first cost may be more than one of another description. I hear a great deal of a woven iron fence which is greatly extolled, but having had no personal opportunity of trying it, I can merely mention its existence here. It is called

"Wickersham's Wire Fencing," is patented, and is advertised in most country and city papers, and claims to be less than half the cost of cast iron railing. Sometimes posts strongly made and deeply sunk in the ground, the corners chamfered off, and the tops protected by pointed rooflets over, answer the purpose very well if set at intervals of ten to twelve feet apart, and iron wire drawn through holes every fifteen inches up. This wire made of galvanized iron, and the posts painted, will make a cheap and durable fencing at very little expense, one, too, possessing a good deal of character, and of very pleasing appearance.

The rooms in this suburban cottage should be ventilated by means of Berrian's valves opening into the chimneys of each; the sleeping-rooms especially should be so provided, as the windows being less than the height of the centre of the rooms, the air would require to be drawn off from the space above their opening. This may be done by inserting a valve in the flue within the room a few inches below the line of the straight ceiling. The windows must *all* be so made as to open at the top, whether dropping as in ordinary weight, hung sashes, or French windows with sashes hung with hinges. The importance of this will be thoroughly estimated by those who in hot weather have been condemned to sleep in rooms, the windows of which only are capable of being opened in their lower half.

A house built in the manner above described, and in accordance with the illustrations given, would form a really comfortable, economical, and elegant cottage home, and would be adapted to most situations in which one would probably be placed.

A still smaller and cheaper building is often needed. Some that have been intended for erection at sums varying from six to twelve hundred dollars, have, however, proved in actual execution to cost much more. I find that country builders are generally very sceptical when a plan professing to represent a house constructed on such a scale is presented to them. To avoid this in every case, I will here give an actual representation of a small cottage built from my designs in two places, the cost of which in neither instance exceeded eleven hundred dollars,

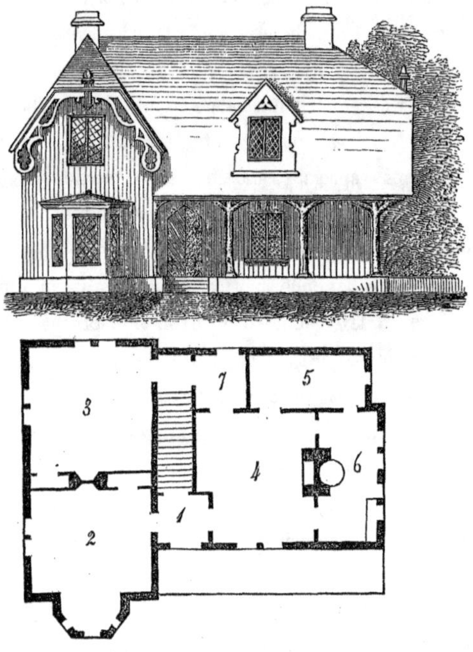


Small Cottage.—Elevation and Plan.

and as there was nothing peculiarly favorable in the circumstances of erection, but on the contrary, material and labor were both very high, there is every reason to believe that in many situations the house could be built for even less.

It is built of wood, covered with perpendicular plank and battens, and the interior lined with brick, thus making a warm and comfortable building.

Its external appearance is pleasing and picturesque. The walls are low, the roof steep and projecting in such a manner as to afford sufficient shade. The side of it is brought down so low as to form a covering in front over a veranda floor, making a protected entrance and a pleasant place for out-door sitting and rest.

The accommodation is sufficient for a family of moderate size. On the ground floor the space is thus distributed.

From under the projecting eave of roof on the front is the entrance into a small vestibule, No. 1, containing the staircase, and opening on one side into a best parlor, No. 2, thirteen feet six inches by fourteen feet, exclusive of a projecting bay-window at one end. This room contains a fire-place and a large closet, and is a pretty and cheerful apartment.

Back of this is the living room or dining-room, entered by means of an entry under the stairs, and conveniently placed for access from the kitchen and pantry. This room is of the same size as the parlor, and like it is provided with fire-place and large closet. The kitchen, No. 4, occupies the centre of the house and is a good-sized, well-lighted room. Back of the fire-place is a wash and sink-room, No. 6, containing a boiler heated by the kitchen range or cooking stove. No. 5 is a large pantry communicating with the kitchen and wash-room. No. 7, a back entry furnished with shelves and used also as a milk-room.

In one instance, the cottage built after this design had the distribution of the domestic offices somewhat changed. The kitchen fire-place was put against the pantry partition, No. 5, and that apartment made the wash-room, the latter occupying the place marked on the plan, No. 6. This change involved no variation in the expense, and either arrangement might with perfect propriety be adopted as seemed best.

Underneath the whole is a good, airy, well-lighted cellar, seven feet high in the clear, and entered by a flight of stairs under those shown on the plan.

The rooms on this floor are nine feet six inches high; in one of the houses they are finished with tempered walls, in the other are prettily papered in imitation wood, and the doors and other wood-work stained and polished to match. The floor of the veranda in the latter is made of hexagonal blocks of yellow pine nicely fitted in, and producing a pretty effect. This, where mill-power is at hand, would be but of trifling cost, and would assist in imparting character to the building.

The sleeping-rooms are contained in the floor above, and as the partitions are the same as those below, a separate plan has not been thought necessary.

The staircase lands over the entry, No. 1, and a small bulk-head is taken out of the front chamber to form the entrance to that in the rear over the dining-room. Each of these rooms has a large closet, and can be warmed by a small stove if necessary. The space over the kitchen allows of one large chamber and a smaller inner room over the wash-room. The roof dipping down over the part below, containing Nos. 5 and 7, the space above is only available for large, low closets, one of which is reached from the sleeping-room over the dining-room, and there is also one to each of the rooms over the kitchen and wash-room.

This arrangement affords in all one small and three large bedrooms, and a large closet on each side of the upper landing of the staircase over the entry, No. 1. The roof is made double, that is, a space is left betwen the rafters and the lathing on which the ceiling is plastered. By this means no heat is transmitted from the roof, and the temperature of the sleeping-rooms is easily maintained as cool as that of the rooms below.

The useful articles of furniture required for this little cottage, if simply and strongly made, would, in their places, be sure to look well. The parlor might have a pretty carpet of small and cheerful pattern, and a small book-case, hanging book-shelves, or cabinet, made of oak, maple, or brick, or even common pine stained or painted; these, with chairs of simple form, a centre folding-table, a few cut flowers in the summer, and dried grasses in the winter, in a rustic stand or in vases over the mantel, a settee covered with chintz, and curtains of material and pattern to match, would be all that would be needed to decorate and furnish the room. The kitchen, with a cleanly kept white wood dresser opposite the fireplace, (a wall unobstructed by doors is left for its reception), with a wooden mantel supported over the chimney opening by wooden or iron brackets, with a rack for plates, and a shelf or two, would, with the never-failing Yankee clock, be sufficiently and inexpensively complete. To these (with the chairs and tables that are matters of course), might be added a folding settee ironing-table. This is made so as to be used as a settee with a high back, or as an ironing table, and taking but little room and costing but from four to six dollars, is well adapted to a cottage kitchen. The top, forming when not in use the back of the seat, turns upon wooden pegs inserted in the arm-chair-like ends of the settle; when shut down for

KITCHEN SETTEE TABLE.

use as an ironing board, two other pegs are dropped into holes made for the purpose, securing it in its place, and making a firm and steady table. The seat itself is made to lift up, and is enclosed at the bottom, back, and ends, so as to form a locker or chest, useful for clothes and a variety of purposes. Made of common pine and left unpainted, this simple piece of furniture could be procured from any handy carpenter, or can be found for sale in New York.

The general form and appearance of the building is in execution pleasingly simple and modest. In one case the hipped roof has been changed for the ordinary gable, but the effect is not nearly so satisfactory, the sloping back line of the hip keeping the building down, and giving a more pyramidical and artistic outline to the general map.

The dipping eaves of the front forming the veranda are supported in one building by rustic posts, formed by cypress trunks with the bark retained, and in the other they are made of studs put cross-wise, four together, and the edges chamfered with a moulding breaking round top and foot to form cap and base, and strengthened and enriched by cut brackets. Of the two I prefer the rustic treatment as more in harmony with the character of the design.

The verge framing under the hipped roofs is of heavy plank cut out to the proper outline and chamfered. The drops are moulded, and so is likewise the ridge pin or pinnacle. The dormer window on the front has its gable enriched by a simple cut and chamfered barge-board, the sashes being made to swing open from within. These sashes are frequently fastened in a very imperfect and unhandy manner; the stiles being narrow, and in so small a window no room being left for a standing mullion against which to bolt them, the fastening, whatever it may be, has but slight hold, and requires to be very strongly and thoroughly made.

I have given a representation of an ingenious and effective fastening adapted to such a window, and also to blinds, for which latter purpose it is principally sold, but with thumb bolts above and below is admirably adapted to such a small dormer window as is here represented.

This is made in iron, brass, plate, or bronze, and is simple and effective, and like all the other ironmongery I have occasion to describe, is kept for sale by Baldwin & Many of New York.

Blind or Dormer Window Fastening.

The color that such a cottage should be tinted, would depend upon its situation and the remarks made in the former portion of this chapter, in reference to the larger example given of a cottage house, would apply equally well to this.

This building would look well in stone where that material is plentiful and cheap, but the bay window would require to be made heavier to be in keeping, though not necessarily constructed of stone, as a character could easily be imparted which would render the cheaper and more easily worked material in harmony with the rough rubble walls. Or the window might project as a simple parallelogram, the sides not being truncated to form a half octagon, in which case, particularly if windows were dispensed with in its sides, and an opening only left in front, it could readily be built of the same material as the rest of the house, and would look bold and sturdily honest.

A small garden patch in front, an inclosed yard in the rear, screened by light trellis work, garnished and rendered still more impervious by flowering creepers, a neatly kept gravel approach, a simple fence and unassuming gate, would be all in the way of adjunct necessary to complete the rural, comfortable character of this cottage home. Cheaply and durably built, easily kept in repair without, and snug and comfortable within, unpretending, and yet not without a modest beauty of its own, such should be the small homestead of the honest mechanic or small farmer.

An even smaller and less extensive cottage could be described, but the cheaper building is one that to do it justice requires study *on* the spot and *with* the builder, or a pretty plan would be found to cost a pretty price. And for this reason very few houses are executed from books or printed descriptions *exactly* as there detailed. Changes, that to the eye and reason of the amateur appear quite unimportant, and entailing no extra cost, are decided on and introduced; then he finds that somehow when he begins these changes, the parts don't fit, don't dovetail in so nicely as they do in the professionally studied plan. One change involves another, and with a semblance of the model, a house is finished ostensibly like it, and complained of because costing perhaps half as much again as the example that it was intended to follow. So especially is this the danger in a small house, where every fraction of expenditure has been closely and thoughtfully studied, and in the design for which so nicely has every part been weighed, and so cunningly has every contrivance been brought to bear upon it that could possibly be taken advantage of to reduce the cost of its embodiment, that any deviation made will inevitably jeopardize the whole, and entail unforeseen and incalculably expensive extras.

Comfortable, effective, and carefully designed cottages have been built for even five hundred dollars; and yet it is true that many architects could multiply instances where a design especially made for a certain situation and to meet particular wants, and which had there been executed for the small sum named, in other places where the attempt had been made to copy the same building, the cost frequently had been nearly double. This can only be explained by reference to the temptation to introduce changes, which, seemingly trifling and unattended with increased expense in themselves, nevertheless result in a very perceptible swelling of the builder's account of cost.

A small cottage comprising three rooms on ground floor, with a cellar underneath and a back lean-to, containing a sink and wash room, the plan of the form of an L, and the roof extended down over one side in a somewhat similar manner to the last design, has been executed under my direction for four hundred and sixty dollars. The rooms are of good size, and the building is well and substantially built. This of course could be done again and again; but as the sum mentioned would have to be so carefully subdivided through every item of material and labor, I have not thought it best to give an example, for fear it might mislead. If any one needs such a house, the plans can be furnished to them modified by the statement made of circumstances that might influence the design.

Before concluding this chapter, I would say a word or two upon the common practice of placing unsightly buildings around cottage homes. Outhouses are necessary of course, and must be provided, but they need not be so prominently introduced to the notice of every passer-by. A neatly inclosed yard in the rear, containing every out-door office necessary to comfort, wood-shed, well, piggery, and the like, with space enough left in the centre for a green sward to dry clothes, would really cost less, because the sides, or back, or roof of one building could be made available to another; space of course would be saved, and a more healthy and far more agreeable result be obtained.

Not only however are those things which ought to be kept in

the background thrust, unsheltered by tree or fence, frequently into the very centre of the small cottage lot, but they are constantly seen so tricked up with some kind of fantastic carpentry as to challenge observation in the most peremptory manner. We will put them back, if you please; and in so doing, gain a prettier patch for sweet-smelling flowers, and more ample room for a little lawn or useful garden.

What a healthy, refining, useful thing might be a cottage garden; and how sad it is to see the many ostentatious and vulgar looking little boxes that have usurped the place of the home, so many barren, weed-fringed wastes that have stolen away from some village or suburb its brightest ornament—the neatly kept garden. What stores of simple pleasures a little lot of fifty feet square might accumulate; what cheerful occupation, useful, purest teachings, might it afford. The busy man morning or evening might find half an hour's toil a real recreation, aye, and a profitable investment therein; the children be early taught that most refining and heavenly of all tastes, a love for flowers, and learn lessons of order and diligence prettily and pleasantly from the operations and loved cares of the flower garden. I cannot do better than conclude with a quotation from the heart-speaking book that has before enriched the opening pages of this chapter:—

"But another common instance of the good effect of gardening may be mentioned: it naturally inclines one to be open-handed. The bountiful returns which are bestowed, year after year, upon our feeble labors, shame us into liberality. Among all the misers who have lived on earth, probably few have been gardeners. Some cross-grained churl may set out, perhaps, with a determination to be niggardly with the fruits and flowers of his portion; but gradually his feelings soften, his views change, and before he has housed the fruits of many summers, he sees that these good things are but the free gifts of Providence to himself, and he learns at last that it is a pleasure as well as a duty to give. This head of cabbage shall be sent to a poor neighbor; that basket of refreshing fruit is reserved for the sick; he has pretty nosegays for his female friends; he has apples or peaches for little people; nay, perhaps in the course of years, he at length achieves the highest act of generosity—he bestows on some friendly rival a portion of his rarest seed, a shoot from his most precious root! Such deeds are done by gardeners."

# CHAPTER XII.

## MEANS OF ARTIFICIALLY WARMING—HOT-WATER APPARATUS—THE BATHING-ROOM.

ONE of the very first things to be thought of—before commencing even the foundations of a house, is,—what means shall be used to warm it? In an early chapter, I devoted as much space as could be spared to the subject of ventilation, and therein incidentally alluded to the most reliable methods of obtaining artificial heat.

The importance of a timely consideration of this first element of comfort in a rural home will appear when it is stated that any system to be thoroughly efficacious should be commenced in and with the foundation walls. The flues, air-ducts, calorific chambers, should and must be embraced in the arrangements of the plan, and if not, not only will a great expense be incurred by making provision for them at a later day, but the working of the apparatus will probably be not nearly so satisfactory.

Generally speaking, the house and all its parts are determined on and the building commenced without any definite idea as to how the temperature in winter is to be moderated, the owner trusting to some one of the thousand furnaces, or hot-air stoves, or other health-destroying machines advertised to supply the means required. Yet, whatever the apparatus adopted may be, if its parts were incorporated into the building from the first, and reference made to its working in the laying of every floor, or the placing of every flue, a house more easily warmed and more economically contrived might undoubtedly be obtained.

The importance of recognising some system of ventilation in connection with the means of obtaining artificial heat must be apparent to all. And yet, in not one instance in a hundred is this necessity ever met. In the smallest cottage, equally as in the costliest public building, an adequate and consistent ventilation should be arranged, and whether the rooms be warmed by air-tight stove, open fire-place, or the most exquisitely contrived heating apparatus, it can be secured by the very same means by which the artificial warmth is imparted.

This principle must, in fact, be made the basis of all the systems of ventilation. Doors and windows are pleasant auxiliaries at such seasons as they can be used, without causing inconvenient draughts—chimney caps of this or that patented shape assist sometimes under certain conditions of the wind—but the only constantly acting and reliable method of purifying the air of a room, drawing off its foul gases, and introducing a flow of fresh and pure oxygen, is obtained by the heat that raises its temperature.

This can be done in various ways. In the simple cottage where a stove is used, an air chamber of sheet iron in the chimney back through which the stove-pipe may pass, and provided with a register to be increased in opening at pleasure, will effect this thoroughly, as will also the surrounding of the stove with an outer case or cylinder, the openings at the bottom of which will draw off the foul air within the room. In each of these methods, the chimney valve so often alluded to at the top of the room is indispensable.

Other methods of warming will admit of the application of different apparatus for ventilating, but the recognized principle of them all is the same, viz., the imparting motion to the air by rarefaction, which, properly applied will draw off the impurities, and afford a vacuum into which the pure air from the hot-air chest in winter, or from outside the building in summer, may rush.

This would seem very simple, and the necessity for the provision of such an apparatus apparent; and yet, one house is built after another, its basement filled up with a huge furnace, and its furniture blistered with the blasts of heated, vitiated air that its pipes throw up, and no improved means are ever resorted to of obtaining heat and health at the same time.

Dr. Bell of the McLean Asylum, a department of the Massachusetts General Hospital, has endeavored in a series of cogent reasonings embodied in a condensed form, to draw the public attention to the necessity of some serious action on the part of all those having any influence on society, in view of enforcing the introduction of reliable and simple means of improving healthiness of internal atmosphere in all buildings occupied as dwellings.

In the annual address before the Massachusetts Medical Society in 1848, he says (in relation to the mysteries of ventilation, sewerage, and water supply):

"The 'ghastly bills of mortality,' as they have been termed by an English statistician (under some overlooked or mistaken modifying circumstances perhaps) of one of our new cities, the prevailing impression of the unhealthiness already of our lately populated manufacturing towns, call aloud to the medical profession to look the growing evils of hygienic neglect full in the face, and if they require a plenary and decided remedy, however costly, it will not be long in being found.

"It might not be out of place, were it of any probable utility, to inquire into the causes of this want of advance generally in an art so universally admitted, in language, to be important. We scarcely ever read the description of a new assembly room, or theatre, or hospital, or penitentiary, in which we do not find laudatory and congratulatory notices of the excellent provision for ventilation. This provision, of course, in ninety-nine cases out of a hundred, is nothing more than some small holes left in the ceiling, the inefficiency of which has been notorious for a hundred years. Still, such a general recognition is sufficient to prove a general necessity.

"Our inefficiency cannot be from want of acquaintance with what has been done in other countries more advanced in the art of living, since the books detailing the necessities and the modes of meeting them, in the most authoritative manner of investigation, are known to every scientific inquirer, and are to be found in every considerable library. We must rather ascribe our backwardness to the same general causes which have kept architecture, both as a useful and an ornamental art, at so low an ebb throughout our country. One of these is, that for the moderate capital we have to devote to such purposes, we have an undue desire, a morbid ambition to produce more of splendor and show, than is compatible with permanence, completeness of interior arrangement, or regard to hygienic considerations. Anything out of sight, like the deep and enduring concrete foundation, the inverted arches of support, designed to meet the possible failures of succeeding centuries, or the concealed arrangements needful for a thorough and universal ventilation, which must commence almost at the corner stone and be kept in continuous design until the last finish, would be struck out, in a vast majority of instances, from the architect's specification, (if he dared to suggest them) as an expense which might be saved without being felt. On the other hand, the dome, the spire, the columns, the pilasters and balconies, some of which, as mere ornamental appendages, could be added at any time, now, or a century hence, when funds might be more abundant, or never, would be adhered to as essentials, as indispensable.

"Despite the science and mature experience of a thousand European attempts fully and exactly detailed in the unmistakable language of description and pictorial representation, our building committees would, assuredly, after making their personal enquiries among the hundred interested patentees or dealers in new furnaces, chimney-tops, revolving turn-caps, and the like, conclude that, amongst so many *practical men*, promising in their advertisements and circulars so many cheap and effectual methods of doing that which the Old World artists consider so difficult and expensive, some ready measures would turn up, when their part of the duty was finished.

"The most costly edifice in the Northern States, just finished with eternal granite, on foundations based in the ocean, at a cost of a million of dollars, is an illustration, an abundance more of which could be easily adduced were not the task an invidious one. Proposals for heating and ventilating were advertised for after the building was finished."

Presently he goes on to say:

"Our present demand for internal ventilation as a domestic necessity, has also been strongly influenced by the change in the modes of heating within a few years. The roaring fire-place, built with an open-mouthed immensity of voracity, as if the struggle were in getting rid of the primeval forest, has been replaced by furnaces, stoves, air-tights, of all forms and shapes which caprice or ingenuity has invented. The sweeping flood of air which carried with it in its course the most liberal indraughts of the pure breath of heaven, compensating for the abduction so largely of the warmed air itself by the radiated caloric of the blazing pile, has been dammed up, and that almost entirely. The re-respired, roasted, ill-conditioned air of the dwellings even of the rich, is the result of a parsimonious economy which strangely and absurdly exists as to this, in a thousand instances, where comfort and luxury make no other sacrifices to saving. *Fuel saving* is one of the cardinal virtues in the housekeeper's creed, while provision saving, or pure water economy, would be scouted as the height of meanness or uncalled for self-denial."

Dr. Bell has himself matured a system of warming and ventilating the buildings committed to his charge, so perfect in its working, and so triumphantly demonstrative in its results of the advantage to be gained by attention to these sister sciences, that his opinions and directions have enforced weight which they could independently, however, have had from their philosophical lucidity, and the zeal and honest heartiness with which they are given in the little work containing the address from which the above have been quoted.*

* "The Practical Methods of Ventilating Buildings, being the Annual

In private houses where other heat than that obtained from stove or fire-place is necessary, the means usually adopted is, to have constructed in the cellar either a hot-air furnace, a steam, or a hot-water apparatus. Of the first there are several kinds in use, and the objection to nearly all of them is, that they vitiate the air whose temperature they raise. This objection can only be moderated by increasing the radiating surface against which the air is brought in contact; and in selecting a hot-air furnace, the principle that should govern a choice would be this. But loss of heat is thought by furnace makers so serious an evil that the attempt generally has been, not how large an area of moderately-heated metal they can present to the passage of the air for its absorption of caloric, but how intensely they can heat an iron pot without cracking, against which the air may scorch and burn, and be shot into the room above, red-hot and stifling, on the principle, in fact, of "making a little go a great way."

The coal-pan or pot of a furnace should be broad and shallow, not deep and narrow, experience and scientific test having shown that the heat is obtained more healthfully, more regularly, and with increased economy from the former. The radiator should be large, and the more the air is twisted and drawn within and around its coils, the more easily will its temperature be raised. The air to be warmed should be drawn from a pure and undefiled source from without the building. That, too, from an

Address before the Massachusetts Medical Society, May 31, 1848. With an appendix on heating by steam and hot water. By Luther V. Bell, M.D., LL.D. Honorary Member of the New York State Medical Society, etc., Physician and Superintendent of the McLean Asylum for the Insane, a department of the Massachusetts General Hospital. Boston; Dickinson Printing Establishment; Damrell and Moore, 1848."

elevation, if possible, or at all events, from such a point where it is not contaminated by contiguity to cesspool or drain, for, if there be any aromatically offensive or unhealthy particles held in suspension in the air, then their existence and effects will be rendered very palpable after it has been heated.

The waste or smoke-pipe should be made a means of ventilation by running within a shaft communicating with the rooms, and, in addition to this, the foul air from all or any of them may be gathered into one duct and burnt in the furnace itself by making the duct connect with its mouth, and no other means of feeding the fire being provided, its combustion will draw off the vitiated gases that are presented to it, in return restoring pure and freshly-warmed air—like a great lung, the arteries will be fed and emptied, and the body be kept healthy, and its veins filled with life-giving fluid. These remarks will equally apply to all systems of warming.

Warming by means of circulating hot water throughout the building, though pleasant and mild, is not very efficacious or reliable, and is costly. The difficulties are in keeping the fluid at a temperature, that, without throwing off steam (thereby risking an explosion), shall be sufficient to radiate enough heat within the rooms; and in concentrating the mechanism in such a manner as to avoid the necessity of any great length of pipe. Where that is unavoidable, the water has become so cooled before it reaches the extremities of the pipes that its radiating power is too weak to be of any use. In the many instances where this system of circulating water has been tried as a means of imparting heat, after a tedious endurance of disasters and failures, the plan has generally been abandoned. Still, in a small house, and where only an auxiliary increase of temperature is required, with a boiler and pipes of large size, this mode of obtaining heat might be trusted to, particularly as the air is soft and pleasantly warmed thereby.

The circulation of pipes charged with steam in and about the rooms of a dwelling is a more reliable method. Where great heat is needed, as in a forcing-house, a large and lofty hall, the doors of which are frequently opened, and for manufactories and public buildings, this agent can advantageously be used. It requires care, however, in its management, and seems difficult with the present apparatus in use to control a small supply. This mode has but little favor with house-keepers. I will therefore pass on to heating by means of air warmed by hot water.

This is the most perfect of all the systems now in use, and cannot fail to become universal when its application and advantages are thoroughly known. Its principle is this: A boiler fed with a supply of fuel smaller per diem than is needed by an ordinary kitchen range, keeps at a proper temperature a certain quantity of water which, circulated through many hundred feet of pipe contained in a metal chest, returns to the boiler to be again and again passed on, its waste compensated by a supply from a self-acting cistern in connection with the boiler; this cistern so placed as to be itself kept at a moderate temperature, so that its water when the evaporation of that within the boiler requires replenishing may not too suddenly cool it down and retard the action. To still farther ensure the regularity of its working, (as dependent on uniform temperature,) the apparatus is furnished with two boilers, one within the other, the circulating pipes being freshly fed from the one, and discharging into the other in such a manner as that by the time

A SMALL HOUSE—for a small Family—Elevation p. 180

the supply is again returned to the boiler, the quantity previously discharged has become so restored in temperature as to be ready to take its place.

These pipes, all packed into a metal chest, with spaces between, and each extremity firmly attached into a distributing box at one end, and a union box at the other, for the supply and return of the heated water, radiate and give out heat to the air within the chest or air chamber. This chamber is fed with cold air from outside the building, which circulating all around the heated surfaces of the pipes, is conducted up a wide shaft into the chambers to be warmed. The advantages of this method are great. They are, first, equable temperature and purity of the air; freedom from trouble or expense in attending, for the fire once lighted, the boiler feeds itself, and the cistern may be supplied from the roof, whilst the consumption of fuel is very small; softness and elasticity in the warmed air, by which even highly polished furniture is never cracked or injured as by ordinary hot-air furnaces. And last, and this the most important, admission of air, moderately, but always sufficiently warmed, which is undeprived of even the minutest atom of its vitality, and is circulated through the room as fresh and as invigorating in its oxygen as it can be found in the open air. The expense of this admirable heating apparatus is not greater than that of any *satisfactory machine* in vogue, and its action is certain. In selecting one, a large size should be chosen, as the advantage of a large flow of moderately-warmed air over a condensed draught of atmosphere highly raised in temperature is very great. The registers or openings into the rooms should also be large, at least twice or even four times the area usually seen. The mild genial breeze flowing from such an enlarged opening is truly

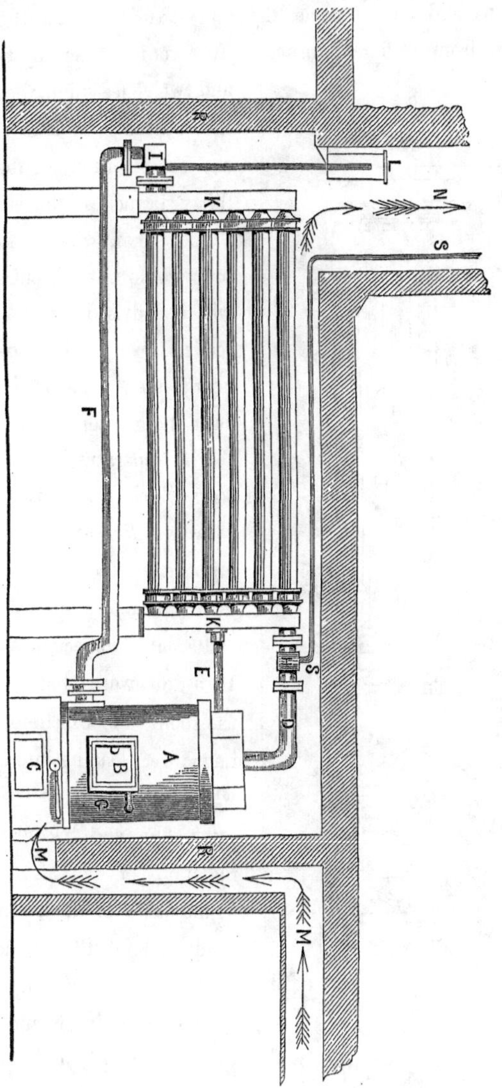


JANES'S HOT-WATER APPARATUS.—SIDE VIEW.

delicious, and far more healthy and luxurious than the fiery current from a hot-air furnace. In a room sixteen by twenty, and twelve feet high, the size of the warming register should not be less than eighteen by thirty-six inches; this is larger I know than what a furnace man would put up, but if you will be advised by me, dear readers, you will choose the liberal area I have given or even one greater.

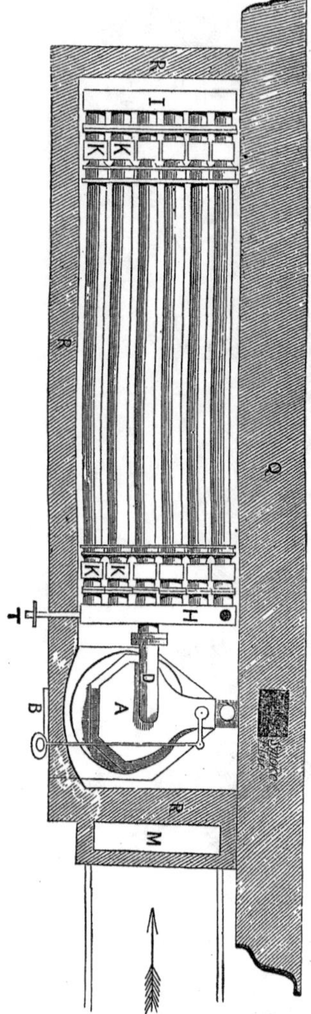

JANES'S HOT-WATER APPARATUS.—PLAN.

The apparatus is for sale in New York, and is called "*Janes's Patent Hot-Water Apparatus, for Warming and Ventilating Buildings.*"

Its latter object is secured by a downward shaft from all the rooms into which hot-air is introduced, leading into a duct which is drawn up into the smoke-flue, and by means of radiation of heat from the metal waste or smoke-pipe is conducted up the shaft and discharged at its opening. This is both simple and effective, and greatly adds to the practical value of the apparatus.

A representation is given, both in elevation and plan.

The various parts of the apparatus may be understood by reference to the letters thereon and to the accompanying description.

*A*, boiler. *B*, furnace door. *C*, ash-pit. *D*, flow pipe from boiler. *E*, return pipe to inside boiler (*not shown*). *F*, Return pipe to outside boiler from union box, *I*. *G*, connecting pipe between outside and inside boilers. *H*, distributing box. *I*, union box. *K*, *K*, gang-ends. *L*, supply cistern. *M*, *M*, cold air duct. *N*, hot air duct. *O*, smoke pipe. *P*, damper rod. *Q*, wall of house or partition. *R*, *R*, wall of hot chamber. *S*, *S*, air pipe. *T*, gauge cock.

This will suffice to make this desirable method of warming a house intelligible. It has been in use several years in the cities and in country houses in various parts of the States, and has never failed, as I have been assured, in giving satisfaction. As a healthy, manageable, and economic apparatus, it has very great merit, and is rapidly superseding all other modes of warming where its excellencies are at all known.

There are a few general directions that may advantageously be offered as applicable to all warming apparatus.

The cold air to supply the rooms when heated should be drawn from outside the building, (as before stated,) and in such a pipe or duct as can readily be preserved air-tight, so that none of the impure air in the cellar can become commingled with it, the furnace should lead at once into the escape or smoke-flue, as where a long, horizontal pipe has to be resorted to, to connect therewith, loss of power, loss of heat, and a vitiated air within the cellar, and possibly upward escape into the house, are the consequences. The hot air-conducting pipes should be large, and should increase in diameter as they increase in length; they should if possible be so arranged as that when cut off from any one room the valve may be shut quite closely to the furnace, to ensure which a crank and wire might be attached, leading into the room and closing a flap or valve in the pipe at the point where it leads immediately to the chamber.

I have before alluded to the increased size of the registers within the room—if the air could be broken up into several ducts before discharging itself, the effect would be still more desirable.

The cornice of all ornamental rooms could contain a tube, the two ends of which would open into the ventilating shaft so often described, this tube furnished with openings here and there in area a little more in all than that of the shaft, and the cornice perforated in such a manner as very many ornamental designs permit, would secure a perfect and even ventilation of the apartment. A valve in sight could not then be necessary, but should be made within a box where the two ends of the tube could be inserted, and then communicate with the discharging shaft. By this means all risk of downward current would be removed. I would here say that Janes, Beebe & Co., the inventors and manufacturers of the warming apparatus that bears the name of the first in the firm, and which I have described, have made ventilation on the principles above detailed their especial study; those building would find it greatly to their advantage to intrust so important a means of comfort in a home to their skill and control.

---

The proper arrangement of water conveniences in a house should receive notice here, as certainly a home can be neither perfect nor comfortable without their adequate provision. In such parts of the country where water is easily obtained at a superior elevation or is forced up by a ram, the most perfect arrangements can easily be suggested; but where neither of these advantages can be enjoyed, and a pump and manual labor or a rain cistern in the roof are all that can be relied upon, considerable ingenuity is required to make the free use of the pure element attainable with ease and economy.

A bathing-room to be really useful—useful, too, every morning and evening, (as it should be,) must be on the chamber floor, hence its supply is difficult and troublesome where the water has to be raised or carried. A large cistern in the roof is not always desirable, and as a constantly filled reservoir is scarcely ever so. Warm water heated to boiling point is only needed in very small quantity for bathing purposes and is not difficult to raise, but a supply of cold sufficient to reduce to the temperature necessary for bathing requires some other means than the simple hydrostatic principle that will force the heated water from the boiler below.

Perhaps the simplest is to have a small cistern above the bathing-room supplied by a force pump from below. This is easily done, the only objection being the manual labor required to fill it. Various contrivances have been made to obviate this difficulty; one house that I know of has a windmill which works a small pump that supplies the chamber floor, and as in thirty minutes a supply equal to the consumption of forty-eight hours can by this means be obtained, the use of this capricious force is really not so liable to objection as might at first sight appear. Another method I have seen has been by the turning of a small water-wheel sunk to the level of the spring which supplies the well; this has power enough to work a small force-pump which draws off the overflow into a cistern or reservoir dug by the side of the well and conveys it up into a cistern as before. In another instance, the stable has been made a means of obtaining the necessary motive power, a horse being used to turn a tread-wheel attached to the floor of his stall, and which communicating with a pump and cistern as the other contrivances, has answered the purpose.

But perhaps the handiest and easiest way is to have in the scullery or sink-room one of *Streever's Double-Action Pumps*, the action of which is so easy, and the stream so continuous and so readily forced to even a very considerable elevation, that no domestic could reasonably object to the ten minutes' labor every day necessary to keep the cistern full. This pump is both a lift and a force-pump, and is double-actioned, that is, produces its stream at both an upward and a downward stroke, is thus more steadily and easily worked, and has a leverage so powerful that a child's arm could use one of the largest size made for domestic purposes. One pump would thus suffice for all wants; it could be made to connect with the well and with the rain water cistern, and also with the boiler; could conduct to and from the upper cistern and the bathing-rooms, and by shutting off the taps of pipes not required could be worked as an ordinary lift-pump for domestic uses, or be converted by opening them again and shutting off the spout into a forcing-pump, with ease and dispatch. A flexible hose could, if thought desirable, be provided, which might be attached and lead up to the cistern when required, thus obviating the necessity for permanently fixed plumbers' work, saving expense, removing danger from frost, and, moreover, affording a valuable aid in case of fire.

These hints may suffice to show that the luxury of daily use of pure water is attainable at moderate cost even in the country where Croton pipes do not liberally lead the fluid over the dwelling.

It is necessary that the bathing-room be effectually ventilated —still more necessarily the water-closets. These latter may be most thoroughly kept free from impure air by having an air-duct leading from *below the seat* into the discharging ventilating shaft. By this means the draught is downwards and through the apparatus—hence no unpleasant air can rise from the soil-pipe, and all impurity is drawn away. This plan has been adopted with entire success in the McLean Asylum.

Bathing-rooms require ventilating apertures near the ceiling, as the air being heated would rise, but they must also have means of supply of pure air into the lower part of the room to produce a circulation.

Such simple means as those detailed in this and in the previous chapter on ventilation, will be found to render warm and sweet the interior of a rural home. It is hoped that the inattention that has allowed amateurs and professional men too long to leave these important qualities to the hands of this and that advertising quack is passing away, and that the houses of the next half century will show that Americans are not unmindful of the almost peculiar purity and elasticity of the atmosphere that circles their country homes, and that its admission will be courted and welcomed, and its purity preserved intact, instead of shutting it out and charring and poisoning it as now.

In conclusion, I would simply call my readers' attention to a novel method of warming and lighting a room by the fire-grate, which has been carried out in England. The grate is set into a reflecting speculum. of polished metal, and the light, from the combustion of the coal refracted into the room.

REFLECTING GRATE.

One of great elegance of design is here shown, and may serve to give my readers some idea of the appearance such a "reflecting grate" would have. At present, I am not aware of its being manufactured in this country; but if the demand were made, there is spirit enough among iron-workers to supply the new want.

# CHAPTER XIII.

## SUMMER FURNITURE—CANE-WORK—ENAMELED WARE.

A HOME in the country requires furniture in its way more difficult to select than to choose between this and that costly article, offered by Baudouine or others, for town use. It is doubtful whether, as yet, the true ideal has been nearly reached in country furniture. The painted ware, that finds favor with many, has some grave objections to its universal use, in the great temptation with which its makers are assailed to lavish gilding and decoration, and which has rendered, in too many instances, this style of furniture gaudy and *bizarre*. The true way to treat such furniture seems to be, not in imitation of rosewood, buhl, or inlaid work, nor by gilding or bronzing; but by giving the set a quiet, smooth tint, with the parts picked out in flat, carefully contrasted or harmonized lines of other colors; here and there medallions may be advantageously introduced, and the projecting knobs, scroll-work, feet, etc., may be enriched with more elaborately-finished decoration, in which, however, an effect more truly in unison with good taste may be secured by carefully avoiding all shading, or, as it is technically called, "relief."

As articles made and finished in this manner can be economically afforded, and from their light and gay appearance are in very general use, a description of rural homes would not be complete without some detailed directions as to the selection and arrangement of pieces of enameled ware; in the latter portion of this chapter I shall return to its consideration, preferring to dwell upon the simpler and more peculiar styles first.

In most cases, cottage furniture, of a simple kind, would look best if left in the natural wood, unpainted and unadorned; its surface carefully rubbed down, oiled, and dead varnished. I have often seen such furniture, that has not only been very pleasing in appearance when new, but after standing the wear and tear of ten or twelve years, has looked far better at the end of that time than any painted ware would have done. It is, in fact, a recommendation to articles of furniture treated in this manner, that they improve in color and smoothness of surface with use; and with the aid of a little cold linseed oil rubbed in by means of a flannel cloth every month or two, their gloss and tone of coloring become richer every day.

Miss Bremer makes frequent pleasant mention of the cherry and walnut furniture, in her "Neighbors" and her "Home," and evidently would, were she to write on such a subject, point her pen against French polish and upholstery for country use.

For the hall, a settle, either of heavy wood, with carved claw and high back, or one of the light, easy bamboo seats, the Berrians delight in presenting in such variety of form and size; a chair or two, of comfortable form, and of lightness such as may be carried out upon the veranda, when an extra seat is wanted; Indian matting upon the floor, an iron hat and umbrella-stand, a bracket or two for flower-vases, a folding bracket-table against the wall for occasional use, a thermometer and a weather-glass, with perhaps a cabinet of dried grasses, or other little museum curiosities, will be all that can be needed to render that portion of the house home-like, characteristic, and comfortable.

The library, with its book-cases framed in recesses of the walls purposely left in building, the books protected with doors of latticed wire-work, and glass or curtain behind, as taste may suggest, with a good, large, open fire-place, and a quaint old chimney-piece above, on which may stand a clock to mark the flight of time that the books beguile; the walls papered probably with a quiet oak-colored paper, the furniture (such that is heavy enough to require other than cane for its material) of black walnut, un-French-polished, and with a few pictures or engravings hung up, or in portfolio-stands about the room, an easy chair, and some vases of cut flowers, can readily be made as cosy a place as any heart could desire, without seeking furniture other than country handicraft can supply.

The parlor, drawing-room, or whatever it may be called, will permit of only greater variety, not any greater splendor, in its plenishing; little knick-knacks, if curious or beautiful, may be strewed here and there, and a richly-wrought armoire, or cabinet, perhaps a gem of an inlaid table, or a glorious old "*moyen-âge*" clock upon the mantel, may show that the wealth is not absent that might fill the room with costly furniture, only the restraining good taste is also in equal plenty. Lounges, conversation-chairs, and ottomans may (if needed) be there, but the fairy fingers of lady workers can better render them beautiful than the most cunning of fashionable upholsterers. Suspended baskets for flowers are pretty embellishments to a drawing-room, particularly to any recess, as for instance, that of a bay-window; and the little "Fisher Boy," so truthfully suggestive of quiet home life, may deservedly find a niche somewhere in the apartment.

Some exquisitely designed specimens of Wedgewood-ware have recently found their way over here; two of them so truly beautiful, I am tempted to give in this connection illustrations; they were made from the articles themselves, and I have lately seen them at various stores in New York. These were purchased at Collamore's, 477 Broadway, and I presume there are more like them.

FLOWER VASE.

The beauty and delicacy of this design are very great, the taller one is equally elegant but of different character.

Recesses left in building the walls, may serve as simple cabinets for a few choice books, some old, time-honored china, or other articles of *vertu*, valued more from association than from intrinsic cost, and the mirror that custom seems to demand a place for, should be simply let into the wall without frame or gilding, serving only as a reflecting face to image the objects of

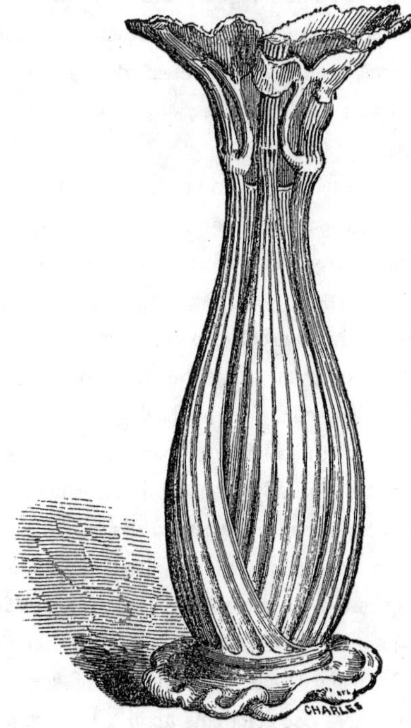


FLOWER VASE.

interest in the room and out, making thus a home picture, not a gaudy show.

If the floor be carpeted, a pattern of small figures, with cheerful colors, in which *green* bears but a small proportion, (for if *green* be used, *red* must greatly preponderate to kill it,) and in which the chromatic effect is that of a mosaic, rather than of any specifically detailed design, should be chosen. A large pattern destroys the apparent size of the room, and dwarfs all other colored embellishments in the apartment. Carefully shaded flowers, wreaths, and other vegetative decoration always appear out of place upon the floor to be trodden on: crushing living flowers under foot, even to inhale their odor, is a barbarity, but to tread on worsted ones, odorless, and without form, certainly seems senseless.

The walls, if papered, may be prettily and gaily decorated by using what is called encaustic paper. This paper is one color, and without any pattern, its surface exactly resembling the finest painted wall.

It may very easily be used in such a manner, as at small cost to produce all the effect of an artistic fresco or oil painting. A proper tint being selected for the back-ground, and the whole wall covered therewith, portions of paper in another color may be placed upon it, either only in simple lines, or in larger surfaces in accordance with some pre-arranged design. By this means panels (using no artifice however to give shaded, and sunk or raised surfaces thereto—a tricky abomination in great favor with most "fresco-painters") and compartments may be made upon the wall, and by using fine, thread-like lines of very bright color upon the edge where one color cuts upon the other, a very beautiful and truly artistic effect may be produced. In a boudoir or drawing-room or in the guest-chamber, medallions here and there, at the corners and in the centre of the compartments, containing a landscape or some floral decoration, will impart a rich and dressy finish to the rooms. Medallions of any prettily painted subjects, treated after the manner of Watteau, may be procured where the encaustic paper is obtained, and the colors matched therewith.

But the prettiest and most simply elegant effect is produced by only using two colors. Mr. Pugin, the great English architect and colorist, has shown how pleasingly this can be done, as have also Owen Jones (the chromal decorator of the Crystal Palace), and many who have sought to raise the character of internal colored decoration with increased economy and good taste. The inexpensive nature of the materials, and the elegant results that may be obtained, recommend this method of covering the walls to all about completing their country homes; the ladies might find interesting and pleasant occupation in designing and supervising the process, and as when done the work is very durable and the paper will bear scrubbing. I suppose housekeepers will not object to making the experiment.

The colors to be selected for the walls must depend upon the use, the nature of the light, size, style, and furniture of the room. In a dining-room, particularly if its walls are to be embellished with pictures in gilded frames, the color may be a sage green, or that which goes by the name of "fallen leaf." These colors just so much tinted as that their hue shows only by contrast with a sheet of purely white paper. The baseboard, doors, and other woodwork of the room should be dark oak or black walnut, and just under the cornice (if there be any) and two inches from the woodwork should be a fine riband-like line cut out of paper of a pure and bright primary red about one sixth of an inch in width. If the wood-work be maple, light oak, or white, between the green and it should be a margin of about four inches wide of pearly green of the same tone as the walls, but many degrees lighter; on the centre of this, a fine line not more than the eighth of an inch wide of pure red, and on the edges of the light and darker green, a line rather wider, say one sixth of an inch, of pure blue. The corners may be enriched by giving to the lines some curving knot or rectangular fret; a little ingenuity and a sharp pair of scissors will produce them as fast as wanted.

In a library, where but very little of the wall space is left uncovered by bookcases, cabinets, or pictures, a very rich and quaint appearance may be given by *diapering* the walls in two or more colors. If the bookcases, etc. be of dark wood, let the ground-work be a rich, deep blue, on this, in finest lines, work a net-work of brilliant red or orange in some lace-like pattern that a lady-fancy will easily suggest: or a cold diaper may be made by using blue as before and letting the net-work or pattern thereon be of very much lighter tint of the same. Rosettes or small cut patterns placed in conformity with some set design upon the ground tint of the walls will produce the same effect, only care must be used that they do not appear too "spotty."

Drawing-rooms, boudoirs, etc. that require a more elaborate decoration need some specific design especially adapted to the particular room. Enough has been said, I trust, to hint how cheaply and with what perfect taste, a novel and elegant effect may be produced by the use of "encaustic" or one-colored paper.

A material now in very general use in this country, the rattan or cane of the East Indies, affords an immense variety of articles of furniture, so strong, light, and inexpensive, that it seems peculiarly adapted to general introduction in rural homes.

Its manufacture is now becoming so important as to furnish employment to a very large number of persons. In the House of Refuge alone, there are between three and four hundred boys at work upon cane seats, and at several places in Bloomingdale and in the suburbs of New York are a number of Germans who have in their employment at least two thousand girls occupied in this manufacture.

CANE FURNITURE.

Sofa, Arm Chair, Arm Chair with Rockers, and Foot Bench.

The Messrs. Berrian, in Broadway, are the most extensive manufacturers of this article; they have, in fact, created the trade and with it a name for themselves. The articles of furniture I have selected to illustrate the use of this strong and light material can all be procured at their warerooms, where an immense variety is kept.

The wood of which the frames for the chairs, etc. are made is white oak or hickory, and is, in the first instance, selected with great care so that the grain may be straight. After being steamed to soften it, it is bent into the required forms and allowed to dry, so that it may not shrink or start out of shape after it has been made up.

The cane itself (*rattan*, as it is properly called) is split, where it is bound on the frame-work—some pieces of furniture show the wood in its undivided state. As yet, the manufacturers in this country have to trust to Dutch vessels to bring the rattan *via* Antwerp, Bremen, and Rotterdam, but in the increasing demand for it as an article of commerce, no doubt facilities will be found for obtaining it more direct.

The principal excellencies of cane as a material for chairs, sofas, baskets, etc., etc., are its durability, elasticity, and great facility of being turned and twisted into an almost endless variety of shapes; hence in chairs there is every assistance given by it in obtaining that greatest of all luxuries—an easy seat and a springy back.

The articles grouped together in our illustration exhibit a sofa, arm-chair, rocking-chair, and foot-bench; the sofa, from the pointed termination of its curves approaching to the Gothic principle of construction, and hence suitable to a building in that style; and the other pieces, from their symmetrical and rectilinear and spherical lines, adapted to an Italian or any other description of finish but the strictly Gothic.

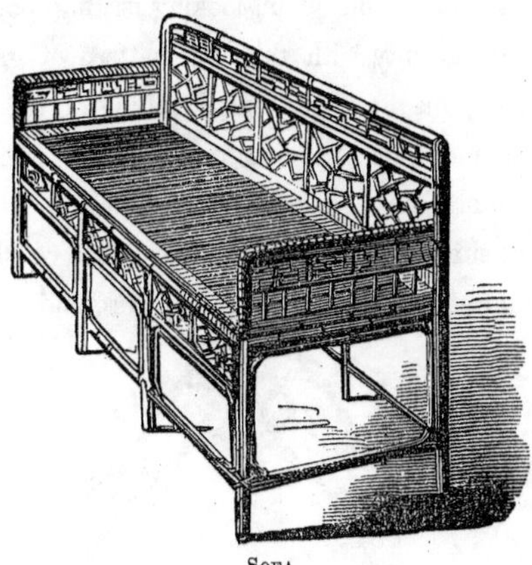

SOFA.

Another style of sofa or settee is shown, which, from its peculiar Chinese character, is very pleasing. It is made of the cane

CHAIR.

in its solid form—in such a shape generally styled "bamboo"—and is originally a pattern of Chinese manufacture. For a hall or an old-fashioned and quaint-looking sitting-room it is very suitable. In congruity with this is a pattern of great elegance and character; this has a pleasing blending of the curved and angular lines, and appears to me to show a very successful treatment of the material.

Somewhat similar in design to this is a crib or standard bedstead for children. The lightness, sweetness, and coolness of the

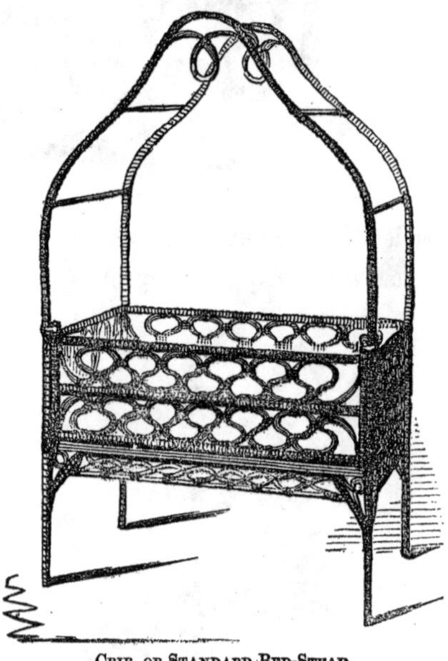

CRIB, OR STANDARD BED-STEAD.

article, particularly adapted as it is to ventilation, must greatly recommend it. A very graceful use of the material is seen in the firm and delicate braid-work that is wrought upon some of the chairs and other articles.

CHAIR.

FIRE-SRREEN.

The chair shown (p. 201) is an example, the braidwork running over the top and forming arms. It is very elegant and light.

The old-fashioned, heavy fire-screens, and the lighter but clumsy-looking basket-work used as a substitute, are now entirely superseded by the articles made for the purpose in this material.

In the accompanying illustration a very pretty effect may be given by the lining, which, either made of one color, or of colors in stripes (their widths adjusted to the pattern work of the screen), embellished with embroidery worked upon the ground of the lining so as to come in the centre of each opening of the frame, will afford an opportunity for the fingers and skill of the lady decorators of the house.

A great variety of other articles are made, some of great

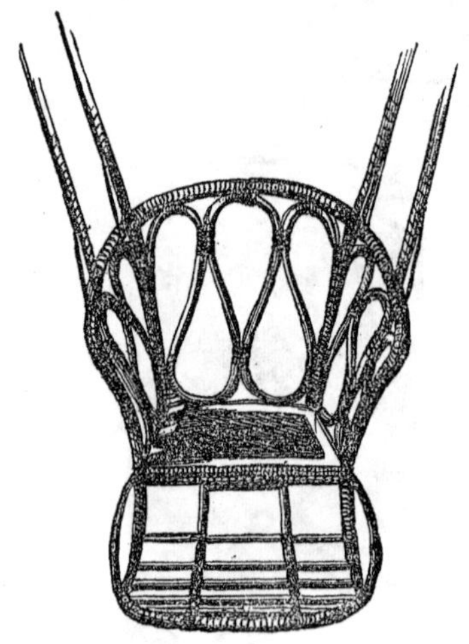

SWING-SEAT.

strength, and for purposes requiring considerable wear and tear. Of these, one of the most desirable is a swing-seat, for trees, verandas, or summer-houses, an illustration of which is given. This, from its firmness, elasticity, and absence of sharp corners, is peculiarly adapted to the purpose. There is a place for the feet, and the back is at such a slope as to assist in preserving the balance of the little pendulums that use it.

Of light, fanciful, and ornamental things within the house, the

PAPER-BASKET.

infinite variety the material will permit precludes a description; for the library, a paper basket, such as the illustration shows;

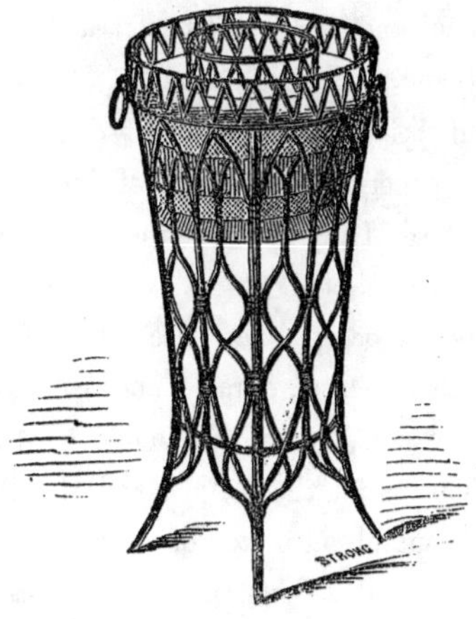


WORK-STAND.

for the boudoir, or ladies' room, a work-stand (p. 203) of which an example that may prettily be lined with rose, blue, or orange silk, is here given.

For the drawing-room, the ombra, or bay-window, a flower-stand, within which is a metal lining for holding water or wet sand.

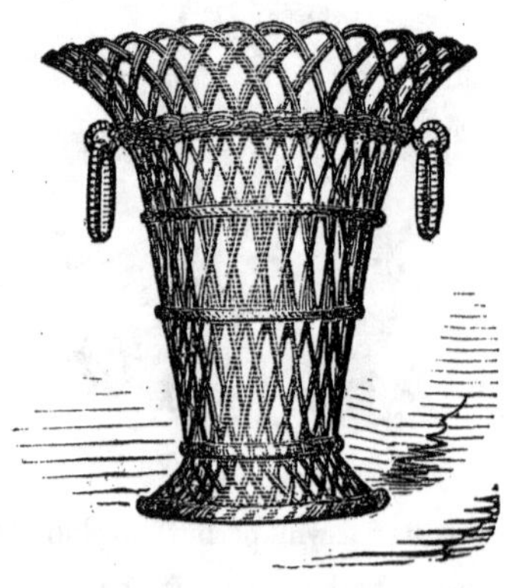

FLOWER-STAND.

These are all substantial in construction, and by no means the fragile, easily broken articles they may look, the material though slender and light, being tough and very strong.

With an open paper-basket (p. 205) of simple pattern, and of very convenient form, I will conclude the number of illustrations of cane-work, I have selected.

I have ventured to occupy the space I have done with them from a thought that a cheap, durable, and satisfactory article for summer use could not but prove valuable to the dwellers in a rural home. The useful, the simple, and the elegant in form are the most beautiful attributes of every accessory of inner finishing; anything that like cane-work ministers to these, deserves more than a passing glance, and the introduction of its description will not appear trivial to those who reflect upon what

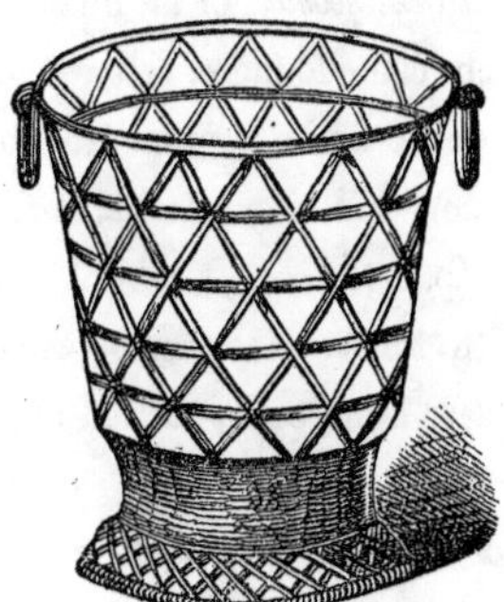

PAPER-BASKET.

small and inexpensive articles the impress of character and good taste in a furnished room, frequently depends. I would rather

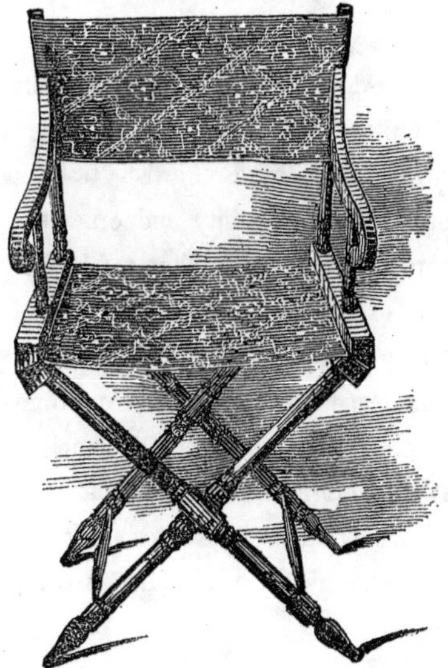

FOLDING-SEAT.

indeed, show how a chair costing but a dollar or two may be shaped into an elegant and graceful form, than elaborate a design for a costly *Louis Quatorze seance*, or an inlaid *tête-à-tête.*

On a veranda, such cane lounges, settees, and chairs being light and easily removed would be appropriate; but of all articles made for such an use none are more desirable than the webbing or carpet folding-seats (p. 205.)

These are made with the seats either of canvas, webbing, or Brussels carpet; they are light, easily carried about, and pleasant to sit in.

The natural color of cane-work is a light yellow; it is stained sometimes black, and sometimes left parti-colored, producing a pretty effect.

---

*Iron* is made into a great variety of light and useful articles suitable to in and out-door life. The Berlin workers of Europe (the name of the place has given a title to the ware it once solely excelled in), have employed an artistic taste upon the production of various objects of utility and ornament, which has furnished specimens of manufacture almost fairy-like in fineness and texture, and exquisite in design. Many of the most strikingly beautiful patterns have been reproduced with entire success here. Some specimens lately shown to me, made by Janes, Beebe & Co., I have had the opportunity to compare with the trans-Atlantic originals, and as a matter of interest in art, pride must be felt by all who have been able to examine the works so far perfected, which justly challenge comparison with the foreign specimens.

Of the larger articles made are some vases supported by

stag's head and antlers, of great beauty and freedom of design, suitable for a hall, or for a recess in a large library.

Flower-stands, hat-stands, bed-steads, etc., etc., are easily made in this facile material, and frequently can be found in stores devoted to their sale, of great beauty.

A great mistake is made sometimes in painting this metal; graining it oak is an absurdity, for wood never could be used in the manner that it aims at showing; imitation marble or other stone is as bad; bronzing or gilding are allowable, because not suggestive of a different material, only a different or higher quality. But of all colors chosen, none are so suitable for large articles, as vases, tazzas, etc., as the dead, unshining black that the ware has when it comes over here. This is given to it by oil (united, I believe, with some pigment) put on thinly and rubbed in so as to dry without any gloss, leaving only a smooth evenness of surface, admirably adapted to the gravity of the material, and giving a greater appearance of finish and richness than the most elaborated painting. Fountains, out-door vases, and seats, are frequently seen painted dead white; the coldness and baldness of this coloring on iron is to my eye very objectionable; the black would be more suitable, and have the additional advantage of not soiling, whilst in a fountain, nothing could surely be prettier than the contrast of diamond and jet—the sparkling water and smooth black iron would afford.

White, on iron, always seems a mask; there is a translucency about marble which the white is supposed to imitate, that paint can never reach, and beneath the white-lead colored iron, the solemn, black influence seems felt, and *will* cloud the mocking, garish hue that is every way so dissimilar.

The heavy, chocolate brown color (that looks like rust, only it has not its variety of tint) that iron is sometimes painted is nearly as bad; the paint always dries rough and coarse-looking, and there is a clumsy, unfinished appearance about iron work so painted, always suggesting the idea that it is only primed over, and that one of these days the painter will come with his pumice-stone and paint brush, and finish the job. Black or bronze are the coverings for iron—the grave, honest, strengthy old substance will only be contented with sober, unchanging negation of gaiety in hue.

Sometimes one sees iron sanded in imitation of stone;—many area railings in New York are so finished,—he would be a cunning mason who could cut such splinters of Connecticut brown-stone!

---

*Painted Furniture*, or enamelled ware, as its best manufacture is now specifically called, might be more cheaply furnished than it is. The gaudy, show-loving spirit of the age has caused cabinet-makers to gild and bedizen plain pine in such a manner, that the painting costs a great deal more than the article itself. In fact, many articles of painted ware—a handsome wardrobe for instance—are in certain collections as costly as one of rosewood or mahogany. The lower priced articles that are sold are little better than trash, and at present there is no medium between a gaudily bedecked set, costing more than thrice what it should, and a cheap imitative furniture just as gaudy, and of course, not being so carefully finished, looking more tawdry.

The fault rests with the *buyers*, not the *makers;* if on going to select a set of enamelled ware, the lady purchaser were uniformly to say "this is all too elaborately and showily finished; I want a set just as well made as this one, but painted only one color, with a simple line of a lighter or darker tint as the case may be, but no gilding or ornamental painting—for what will you make me a set ?"

This constantly done, furniture manufacturers would find it to their interest to supply the improved demand, and the price of the ware would quickly settle down into a regular and far lower rate, by which this cleanly and characteristic work could be placed within the reach of all furnishing their country houses.

Furniture such as I recommend can be seen and procured in New York; many recently furnished hotels show it in their sleeping-rooms. McGraw, in Broadway, has made some of the character suggested, and though to supply the taste of his customers the showier sorts are more abundant, purchasers will find no difficulty in procuring exactly the style described, made in the best possible manner, and at reasonable rates.

A bed-room with the larger pieces of furuiture made as fixtures may be easily ornamented in this manner, the doors and fronts only requiring to be enamelled. The wardrobe in a recess; the bureau treated in the same manner; the wash-stand, simply a marble slab in an alcove, with folding-doors below, and the sides and back of the recess panelled above in the same style, would require merely the bed-stead and chairs to be moveable. With the walls papered in encaustic, and the enamelled ware of a tint in harmony therewith, the room would admit of great embellishment and possess a character and interest that could not fail to please.

---

*Porcelain*, as a finish to ornamental articles of hardware used in buildings, is now in very general use. As a cleanly, cheerful, and durable material, it is highly recommended, and for all such articles as project, door-knobs, bell-pulls, etc., is very suitable. It requires no cleaning like metal, and does not soil the hand.

For country houses, where glare and glitter are out of place, and cleanly, labor-saving finishings are most required, the various articles made in this material are particularly suitable.

Here are specimens of a set of hardware finishings for a room, in which this material is used.

BELL-PULL.

This cut represents a bell-pull or lever; the knob on the handle and the boss in the centre are of porcelain, the mounting and other metal work being of silver, plate, or bronze, and the porcelain work may either be pure white or embellished with colored decoration. If upon a papered wall of two colors as before described, the painting of the porcelain may correspond, the body of it being the tint of the wall and a fine line of the hue that is used thereon traced on the knob and boss.

The curtain-band here represented is of similar materials, and its design is in the same character as the last. The head is of

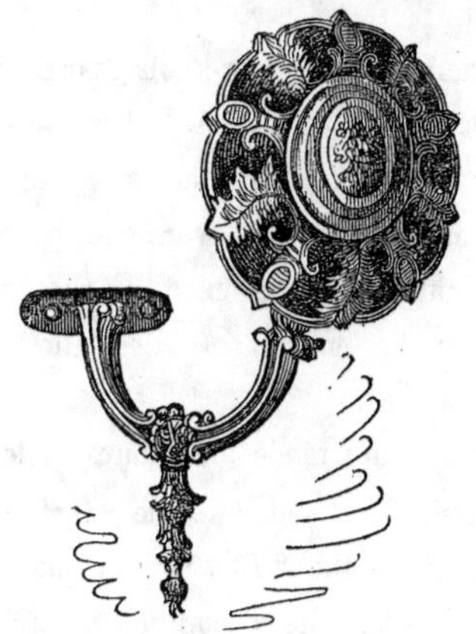

CURTAIN-BAND.

porcelain, painted to order, and the metal work silvered or bronzed.

A useful addition to a bell is found in a speaking-tube communicating with the servants' apartment; the mouth-piece of this, which may be just above or below the bell-lever, is susceptible of ornamental treatment in this material. One advantage it has over metal is in its pleasant feeling to the lips and its greater purity.

SPEAKING-TUBE.

The design here given is of one to match the other finishings, and may be of pure white with floral decoration, or of the same tints as the walls.

For the manufacture of door-knobs, porcelain is, of all the various materials that have been tried, the most suited. Clean—strong—easily attached to the handle, and susceptible of great embellishment, it is much in favor, and, as by an improved method of fastening the knob on to the shoulder all danger of its becoming loose is entirely obviated, the only objection to such knobs is removed.

The patterns that are made are innumerable. The one here shown is of a design best suited to the set of other articles. It is called by the trade the "Elizabethan pattern," I presume, from a resemblance in its decoration to the detail of that period.

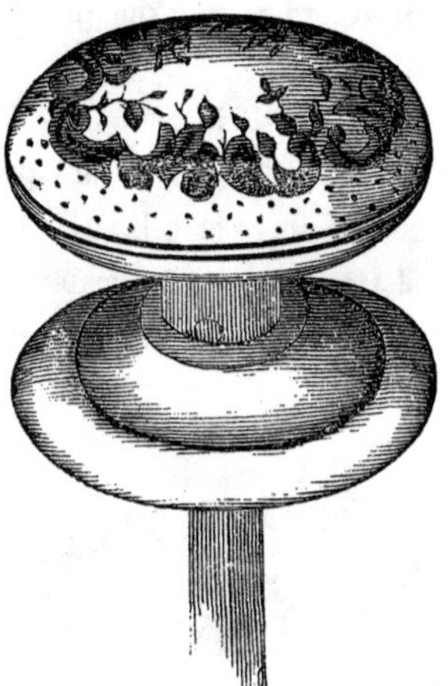

Elizabethan Knob.

The centre of the knob is white, with the outer edge buff,

and the figure of maroon. The buff is powdered with gold, and the combination of coloring is rich and well suited to a dark or black walnut door.

The other door furniture, consisting of escutcheons and drops, is also made in porcelain. The patterns that would best match with the others are, too, here given. One of them is called the "tulip pattern," and the other the "English pattern."

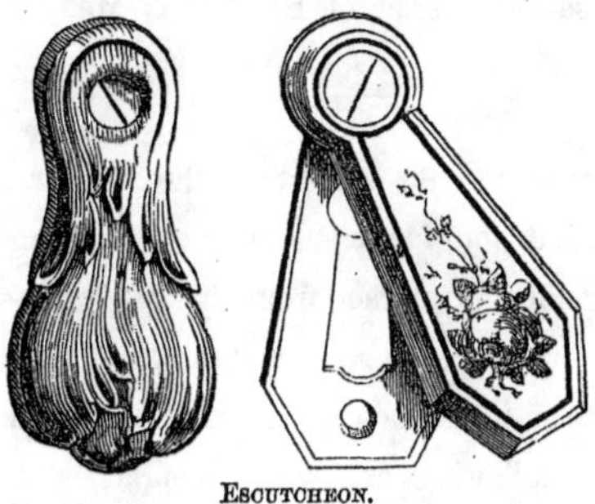

ESCUTCHEON.

A very ingenious use is made of the article in clothes, hat, and coat-hooks. For entries and halls, and for the walls of bed-rooms they are very well adapted. Especially suitable

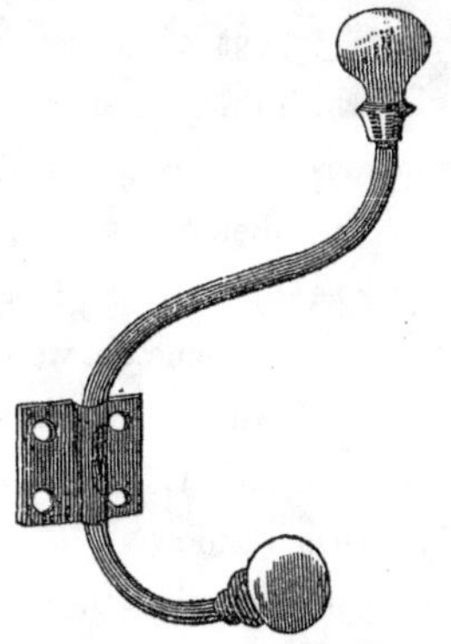

HAT AND COAT HOOK.

would they be to a bathing-room, where the steam and wet would have no effect upon them.

A hat and coat-hook, with a shield through which to screw it upon the wall, is here shown, and will give an idea of the innumerable useful purposes in the way of pegs and hooks, to which this material is capable of being applied.

These articles can be procured, together with a vast number of others in the same material, of Baldwin & Many, New York.

---

This much by way of directing how the interior of a house may be embellished and furnished at small cost, and in good taste. With a delightful extract from the graphic pen of Mrs. Kirkland, I will bring the present chapter to a close. The fair writer, in an article in Sartain's Magazine about the World's Fair, makes the following remarks, so practically useful in themselves, and so graceful a testimony from an American traveller to the home-charm of English country houses, that I present them to my readers.

"We have not yet learned, in this extravagant country of ours, how much may be got out of modest means, or how various are the modes by which the requisitions of circumstance may be met. All our notions of must-haves and may-haves are stereotyped; as we furnish our houses, so we regulate our way of living and managing, one by another, dreading originality like pestilence. It is to be hoped some old-world secrets of life may be picked up by those who go abroad this summer, a fair return for the many new notions which the English will undoubtedly acquire from their visitors.

"By the way, every American who has the opportunity

should be sure to visit an English country residence. They are the perfection of beauty, comfort, and refinement; often on a small scale, which requires that every inch should be made the most of, which is done so cunningly, that one forgets to wish them larger. One thing they never lack, viz.: a library, deemed a superfluity in so many of our best houses; and this library is the magnetic gathering-place of a thousand tasteful trifles,—relics, specimens, objects of art, curiosities, suggestive nothings—which serve to make talk independent of politics, dress, fashions, and scandal. Then the grounds are laid out with so much judgment, and kept in such perfect order, that they add, in effect, several drawing-rooms to the villa, since they are delightful for conversation or strolling. These residences form a happy medium between too much rusticity for city habits, and a cold, showy splendor, which insults nature by hiding her as much as possible under a town disguise. They look domestic, and like the home of many accomplishments."

# CHAPTER XIV.

## ADJUNCTS TO A HOUSE—THE ENTRANCE LODGE—OUT-BUILDINGS.

The country home consists of more than the dwelling. The out-buildings, such as barn, granary, stable, coach, and wagon house, etc., are all important features, and require equally careful consideration as the house itself. A good and convenient house will be rendered still more home-like by the proper arrangement and position of the out-buildings—the charm which probably constitutes the acknowledged excellence of an English country-house being found in the adaptation of the offices to the house.

Of these, in an English home, the gateway or entrance-lodge is generally the most prettily treated and effective. In this country such buildings are, as yet, by no means common, though, in consequence of the increased and park-like extent of many of the best American homes, they will be found presently as their convenience becomes apparent.

Most houses of more than very moderate character and extent require a small cottage, wherein may reside a farm servant, assistant gardener, or hand of some sort, whose occasional duty it will be to open the entrance gates for a visitor, and to answer such inquiries as may be made and responded to, without immediate reference to headquarters. Such a cottage, seen as it must be from the travelled road, should indicate the character of the place within, and be simply picturesque, or quietly ornate, as the circumstances may seem to require.

The *Entrance Lodge*, regulated in its design by strict adherence to the same rules that have been insisted upon for the larger structure, may be more finished and elaborate in detail than would be admissible in a building on a grander scale, that is, its parts may be more fancifully ornate and the construction more minutely wrought up for effective appearance. Many of those found so plentifully in England are too *pètite* and fantastic for satisfactory adoption here, yet, in their way, they are exquisite little gems of rural art, and seem less out of place there, in unison with the richly dressed lawns and shrubberies and general smoothness of landscape, than they would if transplanted as features in the broader, bolder scenery of this country.

It is not necessary that the lodge should be of the same character as the dwelling; the material to be used, and very probably the nature of the precise locality in which it is to be placed, may suggest a different mode of treatment than had in the former been determined on. This rule, however, must be insisted upon: that in no case should the lodge possess a greater severity of style than the larger edifice. That is to say—supposing the style chosen for the mansion be that described as the rustic Italian, the lodge must not, on any account, show a more classical treatment of the same elements of design. The necessity, however, that the smaller building should be freer and less in accordance with symmetrical architectural rule seems obvious, and yet the recollection of the effect produced by its violation leads me to insist upon it here. In the neighborhood of this city is a lodge of the model of a severely finished miniature Doric temple, and the house within a modern bracketted Italian building; the two are seen together, and the effect is repugnant to good taste.

The home side of the lodge should be that away from the road; the entrance will best be at the end nearest to the gates; the other end would be protected by an enclosed yard; with the walls or fences sufficiently high to allow culinary mysteries and domestic lavations to go on unexposed to public view. This hint is a necessary one; for I have often thought how unfittingly a shrubbery looked, spotted here and there with snowy mantles undergoing process of drying.

The internal arrangements may conveniently be considered as consisting of three rooms on the principal floor; one an evening and holiday sitting-room; a kitchen, with a scullery, etc., next the yard; and a third room, either used as a sleeping apartment, or, if the lodge be occupied by the gardener, as a seed-room or dried plant cabinet; whilst in the roof above, three other good-sized sleeping-rooms might be finished off if necessary. The inner side of the building should be sheltered by a rustic veranda, or by the dipping down of the rafters of the house roof; in either case supported by cedar or other timber posts, retaining the bark, and instead of any moulded cornice above, using bark and crooked limbs of trees for tracery and fascia, which may easily be so wrought as to cheaply produce a very pretty effect.

The roof, whatever may be its character, must project so as to shelter and cover in the walls, the wider the projection, in reason, the more home-like and rustic will be the feeling and expression of the building. The general effect must be carefully considered, so as not to appear *high*—a lofty, stuck-up cottage rearing its pert head beside the entrance gate being very objectionable. The structure should be low, spread out upon the ground, and if large, the shape should be irregular.

A smaller lodge than this, consisting of two rooms on each floor, or of three on one floor and one in the roof above, will often be all that is needed. Even the small cubical box, that economy would suggest as the most easily contrived form for a two or three roomed cottage, may, by means of a projecting roof, a rustic porch, and a due regard to proportion, be made to look admirably well. As buildings of this description may be infinitely varied, and their external appearance is dependent upon so many circumstances, instead of dwelling thereon, before describing the design that illustrates this chapter, I will endeavor to direct attention to the points of most importance within.

---

A great mistake is generally committed in forgetting that these lodges are places of residence, provision not always being made for the daily necessities of their inmates. There is a show parlor and a show kitchen, but the one is too fine, and the other often too small for use. Country people, too, such as would be placed in a lodge, are, in a measure, obstinate, and opposed to all "new-fangled notions," as they term the, what you consider really excellent and convenient arrangements made for them, in the culinary and other departments. So long as they have space about their kitchen stove, a convenient closet or two, a

THE ENTRANCE LODGE—Suitable also for a Cottage Residence. p. 221.

roomy dresser, and a wood-shed covered over in the yard, they would be perfectly contented, and feel much more at home than if you provided them with one of "Beebe's" best ranges, or planned their kitchen after one of Soyer's own designs. But, there are many little things you can give them in spite of themselves. You can provide an efficient and self-acting mode of constant ventilation; can place the copious use of water within their hourly reach, even to the extent of a simply contrived bathing-tub and shower-bath in the chamber above; and all these things may be done at little expense and be productive of great comfort. I have often noticed, too, that the windows in the pretty little toy-houses erected by the side of the entrance gates, are continual sources of trouble. The only safe way to construct is to make them ordinary windows, hung with weights, and opened in the usual way; any ornamental or characteristic tracery required being outside, and considered as decorated support of the head of the opening.

The sleeping-rooms are frequently too low and hot for comfortable habitancy. The desire to keep the building down, and the facility a high, pointed Gothic roof affords for cheaply obtaining rooms within its frame produce this effect. Its evils may be avoided by always framing the roof double (as has before been remarked), or by firring out so as to leave a space of dead air—not a space open at the ends, but a space hermetically sealed air-tight—between the ceiling and the framing of the roof. By this means, the confined air—the best non-conductor of heat known, will prevent the transmission of hot air from the roof, and will thus aid in keeping the chambers cool. Windows in the gables, their heads as near the ceiling as can be made, with another window somewhere under the eaves at the side of the

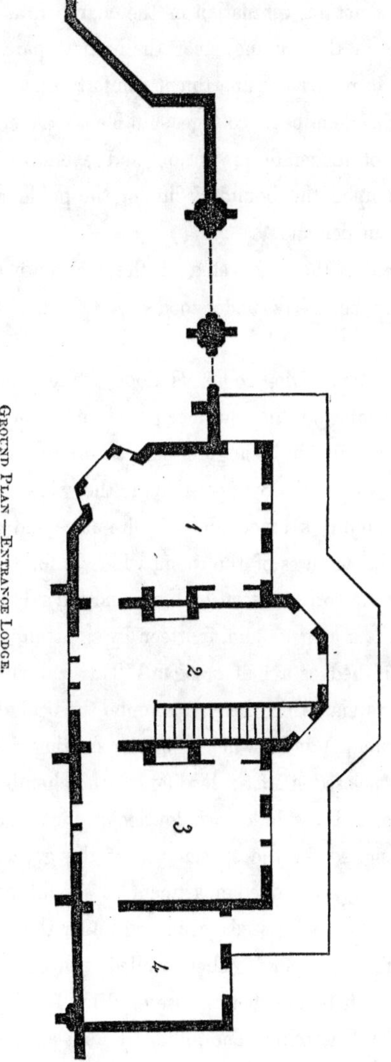


Ground Plan.—Entrance Lodge.

room will secure a natural ventilation in the chamber, and this, with an opening in the chimney near the highest part of the room, will suffice to render the apartment comfortable.

I will proceed to describe a cottage suitable as an entrance lodge to a home of moderate pretension and extent. I have supposed it built upon the boundary line of the public road, a situation in frequent demand.

The arrangement is that suggested in the first part of this chapter, and may be easily understood by reference to the ground plan.

No. 1 is the general living room, its door opening under a veranda roof, extending to the entrance gate; this room has a pleasant hanging window in its angular side, affording a view up the road, and its other window opens upon the wide veranda that shelters the building's inner side. A fire-place and a large closet, complete the features of the room, which is fourteen feet square, excepting the corner cut off by the truncated side nearest the gate. No. 2 is a longer room, fourteen by eighteen, one end projecting and finished as a half octogan. This end contains a door on to the veranda (which here runs round the octagon, and forms a pleasant shade,) and a window in each slanting side. In the room is an enclosed staircase leading to the chamber floor above, a fire-place, and a wide low window looking into the road. This room is designed for the special use of the gardener; a pleasant and tastefully arranged apartment it should be, with drawers and places for choice seeds, contrived under the partition of the stairs—with a few hanging shelves filled with books, upon his rural pursuits—here and there a case of dried ferns, grapes, or other horticultural curiosities, and all neatly kept and ordered.

No. 3 is the kitchen, fourteen feet square, and connecting with a scullery. No. 4, twelve feet square. This latter is a lean-to building and enclosed in a yard which runs in a line with the road, and comprises a sufficient area for drying clothes, and for the wood-shed, out-house, and such other offices as are very necessary in themselves, but best kept out of sight. In the kitchen, one of the useful "ironing settles," described in a previous chapter, would be very appropriate, and occupy but little space. Above, are three good sized sleeping-rooms, the same dimensions as the apartments below. The landing of the stairs would be toward the road, and a hall, four feet wide, running off over the end of room No. 2, would afford a means of entrance to each of the end chambers, and to that in the centre which might either be finished with the half octagon, as in the room below, or be square, the octagon being discontinued and roofed over to this point.

The accommodation contained in this lodge might, perhaps, be more than that generally needed, but as an example of a building on a thorough scale of finish, and comfortable means of living, it may be offered as a study of this pretty adjunct to a rural home.

The entrance gateway is recessed from the road in the manner shown in the plan. The piers, the walls, and buttresses, are of stone, which as it comes so closely before the eye upon a public road, must be more symmetrically laid than would be necessary were the building more removed. The angle stones or quoins, the masonry round the windows, the caps and bases of the piers, the weathering and plinth of the buttresses, should all be of cut stone, not too finely dressed, but yet smoothly and sharply finished. The main body of the walls, themselves, may be of rough rubble work; this, indeed, will give greater value to the parts that are cut, and will impart a rustic and quaint appearance to the whole, thoroughly in keeping with the character of the design. The projecting window in the angular end, is to be framed of wood, heavily and simply, and then painted in the same manner as the framing of the gables and roof. It is true that the wood-work should all be of oak, or at least yellow pine, and oiled and varnished, but as the material may prove in many cases too costly, I will suppose pine painted, to be decided upon. The roof gable over the centre of the road point, is supported by a framing, projecting from the face of the walls. This should be heavy and look real. The finial at the top and the drops at the springing of the gable, may be moulded and carved in the manner shown; the former may, however, be changed for a turned ball, resting on a moulded cap, if the carving cannot be conveniently procured.

The window frames should also be heavy, and on their outer faces show a chamfered or splayed edge.

The chimney caps may be of cut stone, or, if the builder likes to risk the winter's frost, of "Garnkirk clay." This latter material is made into chimney caps, vases, &c., and an innumerable variety of architectural forms, and is imported from Scotland, and kept for sale in this country; opinion is so varied, however, and testimony so conflicting, as to its adaptation, to the severities of winter here, that I can scarcely venture unqualifiedly to recommend its use. I know, however, of instances where it has been used for four or five years in different parts of Connecticut, and shows no ill effects from frost. Farther than this I have had no opportunity of judging if there be any well founded objection to the material.

The gates should certainly (if possible) be of oak left unpainted, and studded together with cut nail heads; they ought not to be too heavy, a light gate is more durable and less liable to injury than one very ponderous, and of course is less costly. The frame may be three inches by eight, and the planking not over seven-eighths of an inch thick. The hinges made of iron, flat and broad, should show; and cutting them into gracefully curving forms, will greatly assist in imparting character and beauty to the gates.

The inside finish of such a building should be characteristic, and the directions previously given in the chapter about cottages will equally apply.

The cost would vary considerably in different neighborhoods, according to the quality and expense of working the stone. Where the material has to be brought from some distance, and is hard and difficult to work, the entire cost of the lodge, its gates and enclosing fence walls, would not fall short of three thousand dollars, and might be three thousand five hundred. On the North river, with stone on or near the site, of an average quality, and not unusually hard to work, the cost would be from twenty-five to twenty-eight hundred dollars. In Pennsylvania the sum required would not exceed twenty-five hundred dollars, and a builder from Bridgeport, Connecticut, has recently examined the plans and expressed his willingness to contract for twenty-three hundred and fifty. In wood, if that material were selected, (in which case the character of the piers, fence wall, and buttresses, should be changed,) the estimates would of course be much less; fifteen to eighteen hundred dollars would finish it in the most thorough manner, and many an economical builder would erect it for considerably less.

On a prettily wooded estate, the road undulating, and green-sward edging its sides, the lodge as depicted would look well; it should be backed up with forest trees, and the open gates afford a peep upon a gay and neatly kept little flower-garden before the rustic veranda of the inner front.

These remarks will suffice for the guidance of my readers in setting about the construction of an entrance lodge. I will now proceed to discuss the other adjuncts to a rural home.

There is scarcely a country residence that has not out-buildings so large that they might, if properly comprehended at first in the general design, be made to contribute very greatly to the beauty and picturesque appearance of the home, and where from any reason it might seem desirable to keep the offices at a great distance from the dwelling, there can scarcely be a situation in which, from some points of view at least, they are not seen together, and should therefore be made parts of the same whole.

A house on a small and economical scale, with outbuildings merely of such capacity as are absolutely needed, and of simple character and materials, may, by careful grouping together, make a really imposing and home-like appearance.

A farm-house indeed requires the outbuildings conveniently near, so that every operation may be carried on under the immediate eye of the farmer. Hence, we see the E-shaped plans that are so common in the old country, and not unfrequent in this; the house stretching widely out as the upright portion of the letter, the porch the central projection, and the stables, cow-houses, granaries, etc., forming the wings as the arms, and from each of these a substantial fence and gates stretched across, build up the quadrangle, so favorite a ground plan with the architects of the olden time.

There can scarcely be any situation in which an artistic

grouping of the house and its offices is not perfectly attainable. They need not of necessity be close together. On the contrary, the outbuildings may be removed as far as may seem desirable, and yet connection with the main building be given them by their treatment and character. This may be done by reproducing some of the marked features that the house possesses—by similarity of detail—or by general resemblance of outline; but if the house has any very distinctive and strongly-marked feature—as, for instance, a lofty tower, or look-out, with the rest of the building flat-roofed and comparatively low—the outbuildings must be carefully kept subordinate. The same flatness and projection of roof, and, though less ornate, the same character of detail, will sufficiently mark the connection; and their position on the ground should be such that they are, from no point of sight, so seen as to appear of greater elevation than the main dwelling. They should be made lower, being, in fact, the first step from the ground, the house being the second, and the tower the third, or highest. Frequently, a tower or turret, containing a clock and surmounted with a vane, is a very desirable addition to a range of stabling and farm-buildings. The clock itself is a useful feature, and I would like to call attention to the light and inexpensive time-keepers made by Sperry & Byram, of Sag Harbor. It is strange that in this proverbially clock-making country, there are so few *good* out-door clocks; but lately, Mr. Byram has succeeded in producing some admirably adapted for a gentleman's out-buildings.

The particular form to be given to the out-buildings must depend upon circumstances almost too varied to discuss. Many persons just now are strongly in favor of a circular, hexagonal, or octagonal plan for the stables; and certainly a very economical distribution of room may be made, and the purposes of feeding are admirably met; and, also, there is, to me, another advantage in such a form—that of easy ventilation. The central portion, from which the divisions forming the stalls radiate, may contain a large air-flue, carried above the roof, and terminating with such a ventilating-cap, or other apparatus, as may be approved; and immediately above the floor, and, again, just under the ceiling, should be apertures, (the upper one supplied with a valve, to prevent downward draft,) for the passage upwards of foul and heated air.

If the farming or cattle-feeding operations of the establishment be upon so large a scale as to require a boiling-house, the flue from that may be carried underground, and discharge upwards through this air-drain, so as to increase the upward current, and consequently afford a means of forced ventilation. The loft for feed would be in the roof above, and the advantages such a mode of ventilation would give in drying and sweetening wet-made hay, must be apparent. The chaise, harness, wagon and tool house, in a building of lower elevation, would form a wing on one side, and the cow-stable, root-house, etc., a corresponding wing on the other. A very convenient and economical cow-stable may be made by forming the divisions between the stalls of double folding swing-gates. The cows are brought in, one by one, at one end, the first admitted being led up to the farthest stall, and the gate closed; so on, each stall is filled, and no room is lost. The stalls are ten feet long, and five feet wide—the gates folding in the middle, exactly against the stall end, when open. An alley-way, three feet and a half wide, is left in front of the animals' heads, for the purpose of feeding, and the whole space occupied is but fourteen feet in width. Some farmers prefer a less width than five feet for the stalls; in which case, all that will be necessary to be done is to make the gates fold into three instead of two folds, and to strengthen them by a bar dropped through staples on each gate—which bar would stand upright when not in use.

The most effectual method of ventilating such a building would be as follows:—It would probably be covered with a lean-to sloping roof;—ceil across about four feet straight, leaving a triangular space inclosed. In the under side insert gratings of open wood or iron work, three feet long by two feet wide, one over each stall. At each end of the building cut openings corresponding to the triangular space under roof, and protect from the weather by a sloping board or iron pent roof over; or, if the two ends of the building abut upon other buildings, so as to prevent such openings, or there be a loft above, then frame an air-shaft, leading upwards from each end of the drain, enclosed as directed, and carry one about two feet above the roof, terminating it with one of Janes's Injectors, (which, in such a situation, would answer admirably well,) and extend the other at least six feet higher, and cover it with any cap that will prevent down-draught.

This, with a good-sized drain under the cow-stable, and a large grating leading thereto from each stall, will thoroughly ventilate the interior of the building; and were cattle-feeders aware how all important to the well-being of their stock fresh and pure air is, they would take means always to secure as abundant a supply as they do of food. In fact, an animal well supplied with plenty of cool, pure air, will thrive on a moderate quantity of food, where another, more bountifully fed, will pine for want of the breath of heaven to refresh him.

A great deal of character may be given to a place by its gates and fences. A very light and pretty gate, suitable rather to the cottage than the farm-house, may be made of a frame of seasoned timber one inch and a half thick, and covered with split-oak, or cedar, or cypress stems, nailed up and down, and leaving the bark on. The posts may be trunks of similar wood, with the bark made to adhere by copper tacks here and there through it, and protected by a varnish. The upper portion of the gate may be curved downwards, or made of any other outline that taste may suggest. A sturdy timber-framed gate, with the edges chamfered, and with heavy, rough posts spurred to the ground, is suitable to a farm, and, if properly made, will last as long as the house. A thoroughly good soaking of linseed oil will be found to protect its timbers better than paint, which it is impossible to prevent blistering and scaling off with the heat of the sun.

A useful gate for farm purposes may be made by framing two halves so that they may meet in the middle, and instead of hanging them to a post on hinges, putting up two light standards on either side and passing a *pin* through them and the lower end of each half. To open, all that will be necessary is to lift them up and let each half fall back between the standards. These standards should be placed within the wall, rail, or stone fence, and the gate made very light (the lighter the better), and when opened, protected from injury by being against the wall. These are an excellent substitute for lifting bars, and are cheaply and easily made. They can be fastened by a bolt and staples on each half of the gate.

In almost all country places, the size of the orchard or fruit garden demands a fruit room, either in a building by itself or in some portion of the house or offices. A very excellent room for such a purpose is described by Mr. Barry, in his useful work *The Fruit Garden.* and in the following words;—

"*Fruit Rooms.*—A fruit room is a structure set apart exclusively for the preservation of fruit. Its great requisites are, perfect security from moisture or dampness, exclusion from light, and an uniform temperature. If these points are obtained, no matter where, how, or of what material the fruit-room be constructed. It may be built of stone, brick, clay, or wood, above or below ground, as circumstances or taste may dictate.

"A good, dry, and cool cellar, is as good a place for keeping fruit in as can be provided; but the great objection to cellars used for other purposes is, that currents of air are frequently admitted, and too much light, by which the temperature is changed, decay promoted, or the fruits dried and shrivelled. There are, also, other objects that unavoidably saturate the air more or less with moisture.

"Where a fruit room is built on the surface of the ground, it should be on the ice-house principle of double walls and doors, to prevent access of either heat or cold from without. A good cellar or cave, built in a dry, sandy, or gravelly bank, or side hill, will answer every purpose. The walls may be of stone, brick, or timber; the roof should be thick, with a slope sufficient to throw off water freely, and the earth about should be so graded that water will flow away as fast as it falls. Provision may be made for lighting and ventilating in the roof, and the door or doors should be double.

"The interior should be filled up with shelves and binns,

with places for barrels or other articles, in which fruits are packed."*

The complete *drainage* of a yard and of the offices therein is a point of the utmost importance. One of the chief excellencies of a system of drainage consists in such a plan being chosen as will render the drains as little liable as possible to get out of order, and will permit the reinstatement of the materials first used, after they have been disturbed, by the necessity of removal, for purposes of cleansing.

The plan that has the greatest reason to recommend it, is one by which the common cess-pool is omitted, and a tank for the reception of liquefied manure substituted. This tank, made either entirely below the ground, or placed in such a situation as will allow of any accidental fall in levels to be taken advantage of, and thus leave an easy means of access to the bottom, should be so built as to be easily emptied, flushed with water, and cleaned. It should be built of brick or stone, and laid in cement, made of course water-tight, and covered over at the top either with a brick arch or with a stone slab. The refuse from the drains of the house, the contents of the sewers from the barns, &c., may all flow into this; and below it should be a larger tank, filled to a depth of three feet or more with small straw, dead leaves, &c., and the contents of the soil-tank be allowed to discharge, either constantly or at will, thereon. A very valuable and cheaply procured compost or manure will thus be gained—useful to the farmer as well as to the gardener.

The rain-water tank or cistern should be removed from this,

* See "*The Fruit Garden*," page 359, by P. Barry, of the Mount Hope Nurseries, Rochester, New York; published by C. Scribner, New York.

but its overflow-pipe may communicate, furnished with a trap, to prevent rising of foul air into the cistern. The waste from the well and sink, and all surplus water should also be run into the soil-tank, as well as the water necessary to flush the drains and sewers. All main drains that are of any area exceeding one foot by eighteen inches, should be formed with concave bottoms, to allow the water, however small in quantity, passing along with the solid matter, to act with the greatest possible effect; they should have a fall of not less than one inch in every thirty feet. These should have, if possible, a constant flow of water through them, or powerful flushes admitted every now and then.

Where drains lead from the cellar of a house, or where their mouths are anywhere near to the building, it is very necessary that they should be ventilated. The gratings that are over them at intervals assist in doing this, and may be made a most effectual mode of so acting, if attention is given to the principle upon which all drains must be purified. Fresh air must enter them from a low level, and the foul and heated air be drawn from them at as high a level as possible. If the drains in a house, gathered together, as they might easily be, into one distributing mouth, had over them a covering into which an air-duct from the nearest secondary chimney could lead, the foul and heated air would pass away up this passage and be discharged by the flue into the air above the roof. By this means (not forgetting to provide a grating into the drain at the lowest possible point, at some distance from the house) the drains would be perfectly ventilated, and all impure and noxious gases prevented from escaping into the dwelling.

The floors of the various offices and out-buildings, when not of wood, may be formed in a great variety of ways; the most economical are, lime-ash, concrete, stone-pan, and brick.

*Lime-ash floors* may be cheaply made in the following manner:—Mix sand, after it has been well washed and freed from earthy particles, with lime-ashes, in the proportion of two-thirds sand, to one-third lime-ashes. Let it remain mixed two or three days, screened from the weather; at the end of that time temper the mixture with water, and lay it on the surface to be floored, to the depth of three inches. In three days at farthest it will have become sufficiently set to bear the foot; it should then be beaten all over with a wooden mallet, or a plank with a raking handle and a heavy stone or two laid on it, pushed backward and forward by the hand. It will rapidly become hard, and when so, will be very durable and will last a great number of years without repair. If it hardens unequally or too fast in places to finish smoothly, use a little water and a trowel.

*Concrete floors* are formed first of all by providing a hard and well beaten foundation of broken stones, bricks, or hard pan, and on this, putting a concrete composed of gravel, sand, lime and tar, covering with a cement of one part Hadsell's cement to three parts sand, to a depth of two inches, the surface carefully floated and trowelled. This floor is economical and very durable, and has a great advantage to recommend it in the fact that the lime-dust never rises, and it is always clean and sweet.

*Stone-pan* is formed in a similar manner to the lime-ash floor, only using finely broken stone, in equal quantities with the sand. It is a cheap and solid floor, but cannot be so smoothly finished as either the lime-ash or the concrete.

*Brick floors* are too commonly seen to need description, they are best mode when placed on edge.

*Asphalte* is not used so much now as it was when first introduced. For some purposes it might, however, very advantageously be employed; for instance, for granaries, store-rooms, and for all floors not trodden on by cattle, or passed over by wheels.

Dr. Ure directs an artificial asphalte " equal in every respect to the natural, to be made by mixing boiled coal-tar with powdered bricks." This is somewhat different to the asphalte usually made and probably the nature of the brick-dust would cause a more perfect incorporation with the tar, and the mixture be hard and durable.

Thatch in England is frequently seen as a covering to the roof of out-buildings; it is there pleasing in effect, though the objection there is to its use from danger of fire, and the harboring of insects, precludes more than its occasional adoption here. Shingles are commonly used, are light, cheap, and easily procured. They may be used even as a means of decoration, by giving to the end exposed some definite form that may work in one shingle with the other, and by the outlines form a pattern upon the roof. For the more ornamented portions of the outbuildings this may be done, and only cost the additional labor of cutting.

The Dairy might be often made a very effective and pleasant feature in a rural home. Built in some sheltered and secluded spot, and with low walls, deeply projecting roof, small recessed windows, low door, and tile or stone flooring, it affords opportunity for a display of a good deal of taste, without necessarily involving expense. It may sometimes advantageously be placed over the ice-house, or a spring may be sufficiently near to give coolness to its air, and it may be, water to form a little rustic fountain in its porch, or even within the dairy.

There are many such buildings in England, generally formed upon a Swiss model, and pretty and cool places they are with their Dutch-tile covered walls, their marble slabs, encaustic floors, and white wood ceilings. In this country these prettinesses would be thought too expensive, nor are they, I think, in very good taste. On the floors clean, smooth tiles, or marble slabs—the shelves of native marble, supported by piers of the same, or by iron or wooden brackets; the walls thick, if of brick—double, if of wood, filled in with brick, and the windows wide rather than high, and latticed in diamond form in lead, with the glass enamelled, so as to soften the light; the ceiling of four and a half-inch boards plowed, tongued, and beaded, and the walls rough-cast and of a pure pearly white; the wood unpainted and of good hard quality; these are all easily procured and inexpensive, and properly disposed, will make the dairy a pretty and consistent building, and as such, a pleasant feature to a rural home.

# CHAPTER XV.

## PRACTICAL DIRECTIONS TO AMATEURS BEFORE PROCEEDING TO BUILD—FORM FOR A SIMPLE CONTRACT AND SPECIFICATION FOR THOSE ACTING AS "THEIR OWN ARCHITECT."

I REMEMBER to have heard of a man, who, before his builder could give him any intelligible idea of the plans presented to him, had to see the walls of the first floor built up in brick (without mortar), so as to comprehend where came the doors and windows, and how the rooms were arranged. In such a case, a person about to commence for himself a house, is sorely puzzled by the drawings or sketches presented to him, and finds, the more he examines, the more bewildered he becomes. His only way of proceeding is, himself to make with a pen or pencil a rough outline of the plan, which he perfectly comprehending, a competent adviser can very soon shape into the requisite form. In fact, in every case, even before consulting an architect, the amateur who is desirous of a home, should endeavor to embody his own ideas and requirements in some way, no matter how roughly, upon paper. By this means he will (particularly if he attempts to draw his plan by a scale of inches to the foot), acquire a tolerable idea of how one part affects the other, and be better prepared to comprehend and profit by the practical advice and remarks of his professional guide.

Before concluding this little treatise on rural homes, I would wish to give some few and simple directions, how the amateur may himself proceed to provide himself with a plan, not that I would be understood to advise him to be his own architect, (you know the Italian proverb—*chi s'insegna, ha un pazzo per maestro*), but that I think it would prove profitable to *both* were the client somewhat acquainted with the mechanical part of the architect's profession.

Architectural drawings are called geometrical and perspective, that is, linear and pictorial. The geometrical drawings are the plans, sections, and elevations; the perspective are views of the exterior or interior of the building in which the actual appearance as seen from a certain point of sight, not blank opposite, would be represented. These last require skill and artistic practice to make, and are not necessary for the amateur.

These drawings are made to some diminished scale, by which every part has its proper proportion given to it, and admits of its dimensions being measured off as accurately as if from the executed work. A convenient scale is obtained by dividing an inch into eight parts, each division representing one foot; one of these parts may be subdivided into four, representing three, six, and nine inches, smaller divisions into single inches not being necessary for such a drawing. A larger scale, as for instance a quarter or half of an inch representing a foot, may be used; but as an easy and sufficiently distinct scale to work by, the eighth scale will be found convenient. The only instruments required will be a T square, as it is called, that is a straight rule, with a stock at one end set cross-ways, and which, held firmly against the drawing-board, will always give lines true and at right angles; a pair of dividers; a small compass with shifting leg for pen and pencil, in order to strike curves; and a drawing-board, the edges of which must be true to each other, forming a perfect parallelogram.

Wafer down a piece of drawing-paper on the board and first block out the plan. Do so in the following manner: Sketch first roughly on a loose paper the number and the distribution of the rooms, and figure—about—their dimensions in each; then add them together in such a manner as you may get the distances from external point to point on each side, and thus ascertain the area of the whole block. Include thicknesses of walls and partitions in doing this, to ascertain which, in a stone house, put down the external walls as two feet, and the wooden partitions as eight inches. In a wooden house, suppose the outer walls as fourteen inches, and the partitions six. These dimensions will allow for studding, firring out, and plastering, and will leave the rooms the size you mean them to be *in the clear*. A finished house often disappoints in the dimensions of its rooms from the fact that the owner directs the size on the ground to be so and so, not thinking of the diminution the walls, etc. will make; it is to avoid this that I direct the walls to be thought of at first.

Then, having some idea of the size of the main block of the house, set it out from the scale upon the paper, using the square at the side for those lines across the paper, and from the bottom for those up and down.

Having disposed the rooms, and seen that the dimensions

work in rightly, the next thing to be thought of is the staircase. This should be arranged at once, as its proper position and size are very important. Say that the principal floor is to be eleven feet high; you have therefore twelve feet to get up (one foot added for the joists and flooring), to the chamber level above. This must be divided by the height each riser is to be, which we will say is seven inches, and will give the number of steps required, which we will take as twenty-one. The treads of each step should be eleven inches; so that if the stairs went directly up in one unbroken flight, they would require a space on the plan of nineteen feet by whatever their width was made. But such a flight of stairs would seldom be wished in one straight ascent—a landing and a turn would be made, the landing most probably at such a height as would come to a level with the chamber floor, over the secondary or servants' part of the house, and which would not be so high as eleven feet. Take this at nine, and say there is a a turning on the staircase—the space it would occupy would be about fifteen feet, and its width, eight.

Under the stairs, where doors or passage ways were needed, calculation must be made that there is sufficient *headway;* which can be done by counting the number of steps to the place, and then, if at seven inches each, they made a height not less than seven or eight feet, the headway would be sufficient.

The next thing to be done is to determine the position of doors, windows, and fire-places. Allow four feet for each door, which will prevent any crowding in actual execution, and the same for each window; the fire-places, if merely for flues and stoves, need not be very large, nor need they be set out, only as securing a proper place for them that does not interfere with doors or other openings. If for chimney pieces and grates, four to five feet must be left by eighteen inches deep.

Then see how the chamber floor is best divided; try and make the partitions come over those below, keeping an eye also upon the position of windows, that they also may be in line with those on the ground floor, or if otherwise placed, that they may not mar the symmetry of the elevation.

Nothing more is needed in the plans than to show where the verandas, the porch or ombra are to be; and those points settled, and a generous width left for the veranda floors (never less than eleven or twelve feet), some attempt may be made upon the elevation.

This should first be roughly sketched, the heights of the rooms calculated, so as to show the actual skeleton of the building, and lines drawn lightly across, to show the range of top and sill of the windows in each floor. These should be never more than two feet four inches from the ground on the principal, nor more than two feet six on the chamber floor, and should extend to a height not above ten inches of the ceiling, nor lower than eighteen. Then set out the roof line; if a gable, find its centre and set its pitch, marking the projection of its eaves (never less than twenty inches,) on the side. Then, with the line drawn for the veranda cornice, the level of its floor and its height above the ground determined, all the points of the elevation are obtained and its general form can be seen in mass. The character and the detail no rules are needed to obtain; whatever the style chosen is to be, such the treatment. And here I would not recommend the amateur to proceed further, unless he has sufficiently studied the subject to be able to develope the character of his structure in detail.

General arrangement of the plan, the height, and leading outlines of his building he can, with great pleasure and profit to himself, set forth, but the practical part—that his builder must have drawn understandingly to be able to carry out. He had better not attempt this, or he will be led into trouble. If no architect is at hand to supply him with a set of working drawings, he had better let his builder draw out from the plans he has made, the elevation and some details, and possibly he may be able, from them, to suggest to the mechanic what alterations he would have made, and between them, may concoct a very satisfactory dwelling, and if all I have said before this has been carefully read, I would hint, they cannot go very far astray in making the structure worthy of the name of a rural home.

But to make the wishes of the owner intelligible to the builder, and to designate the character of the finishing, and of the various works necessary to the house, a written description of them will be requisite. This is called a specification, and is of great use where no regular drawings are made.

Where an architect is employed, it is not so necessary, as if the drawings are properly prepared, there can be no opportunity for the builder to evade his contract. With these, and a few memoranda of finishings, there is less room for litigation and cavil upon settlement after completion, and no specification would be so fully drawn out, as not to admit of evasion, if the builder were tricky, and desirous to run up a bill of extras. The best way is always to employ a respectable man, who has a character to lose; even preferring to pay a little more in the first contract price, than to select the well-looking, but frequently deceptive, cheap tender, of some speculating carpenter.

The simplest form of specification is the best. It should be always more a series of general directions, with any especial or peculiar features of the house explained in detail, than an itemizing particular schedule of works, in which it is scarcely possible not to omit the enumeration of something. I was once made a referee in a case of a contested bill, in which the contractors claimed a considerable amount over their tendered price, and defended it on the grounds that the works and materials charged had not appeared in the specification. The building was a church, and the committee had tied the contractors down in a very stringent agreement, by which "the specification, the whole specification, and nothing but the specification," was to be acted on. This had been drawn up by some over zealous architect, who had enumerated the number and weight of such articles as screws, nails, latches and hinges to pew doors, etc., and metal covering on roof. In the bill were charges for something like more than thirty times the weight of the nails directed to be used, and the same to the other things. These, of course, were necessary, and had particular mention of them (more than a description of their quality) been omitted in the specification, the builders would have had no ground upon which to rest their charge of extras. As a caution on this head, I introduce this little reminiscence, adding that the charge was deemed a just one, and allowed to the contractors.

The following specification is intended to apply generally to stone, or frame, or brick country houses of moderate size, and will serve to show the nature of the materials and workmanship employed. It must, however, be considered as the frame-work upon which a specification should be constructed, rather than as a model of an instrument of this kind :—

---

Specificaton of Works required to be done in erecting a dwelling house, for to be situated on a lot of ground owned by him in the Township of State of

The house on the ground to be feet from East to West, and feet from North to South, in the clear, the offsets to be measured from the plan, (or are to be in manner as described.)—

The heights of stories to be as follows :—

The level of cellar floor to be feet below ground line, the cellar to finish feet in the clear, and the veranda floor to be feet above ground line, and one step of seven inches below the level of principal floor of house.

The first story to be feet in the clear.

The second to be feet in the clear.

The walls to be carried up feet above the ceiling of chamber floor, to the under side of wall-plate.

The rooms in the wing are to be feet in the clear, in the first story, and feet in the second, the walls to be feet, thence to underside of plate.

(If there are any peculiar features as tower or observatory of additional height,—here mention them).

*Excavator.* The ground is to be excavated for the construction of the foundations, drains, tanks, cess-pools, and all the other works so needed, and to be filled in again and leveled about foundations, and the superfluous earth and rubbish carted away, as directed, leaving the ground and house perfectly clear at the conclusion of the works.

*Mason and Brick-layer.* (If the walls be of stone.) The walls are to be built of stone from the          Quarry, laid in the natural bed and with headers, or bonders, passing through every six-feet in length, and three in height. To be laid in mortar, compounded of one-third, by measure, of well burnt stone-lime, and two-thirds of clean, sharp, fresh sand, well beaten and worked up together.

The sills, lintels, weathering of water-table, and all portions so indicated by the drawings, to be cut to the requisite splay or mouldings and to be carefully bedded in the walls. The face of the walls to be hammer-dressed after laying, and each course of stone not to exceed ten inches in height. (If the walls are to be in dressed, regular masonry, in breaking bond, they must be differently described, as follows: The stone to be laid in regular courses not exceeding          inches in height, and no stone to be more than two feet four inches in length, to be carefully squared and cut, and the mortar worked into the courses and lined.)

To provide and lay hearth-stones in all the rooms and chambers so directed (they should be enumerated). To put to the external door-ways stone steps where so directed, solid and tooled, and of good quality stone.

To build up, core, and parget the chimney flues.

To put to each fire-place a inch brick-trimmer, and a chimney-bar of wrought iron.

To thoroughly bed in mortar all the wall plates, wood-bricks, lintels, bond-timber, and to bed in and point round with lime and hair mortar, all the door and window frames.

To properly set with fire-bricks the grates and copper.

To construct an oven with brick domed over and lined with fire-brick, furnished with an iron plate door.

(If needed in any of the offices.) To pave the with hard, sound, well-burnt bricks laid on on edge in mortar upon a dry, hard floor of broken rubbish and stone.

To pave the with stone flagging laid in cement upon dry, hard floor.

To build all drains, cesspools, and water-tanks directed laid in hydraulic cement (or otherwise), and the cesspool steined round with brick-work and covered with a stone cover.

To dig and stein in a well twenty-five feet (or otherwise) deep, and furnish with carriage, sheaves, pulley, and bucket of approved quality.

*Carpenter and Joiner.* All timber and deals to be free from sap, shakes, large loose and dead knots, and every other defect.

All the timbers to be of full scantlings, and any not enumerated to be taken as of the quality and scantlings requisite in houses of first class.

Ground floor joists to be inches by plates inches by ; upper floor joists to be inches by ; on plates inches by ; trimmer and trimmer joists to be ½ inch thicker.

Frame quarter partitions of heads and sills inches by inches; door-posts, side-posts, plates above doors, and braces inches by inches.

The roof to be as follows:

Wall-plates inches by inches; purlines inches by inches; collar-beam inches by inches; rafters inches by inches; ceiling-joists inches by inches; ridge-piece inches by inches.

Lean-to roofs (if any), including verandas to be wall-plates inches by inches; rafters inches by inches.

(N.B. These should be given to the builder to be filled up with the scantlings he proposes to adopt; and then, if thought best, submitted to some other practical and disinterested party for examination; it is impossible to give any guide here, as their scantlings would so much vary with the different bearings required for various dimensions of rooms.)

*Carpenter and Joiner.* *Floors* to be laid in best manner, with straight joint (if to be deafened, that is, if to have mortar laid between, so as to prevent transmission of sound, so direct here and under head of "Mason"). To construct the *stairs* of twelve inch deal treads projecting one inch, and finished with rounded nosings; treads six and a quarter to seven and a quarter inches high, framed into string bearers, with newel, newel-post and balusters, two on each step, and moulded hand-rail. Balusters, post and hand-rail to be according to drawing or to an approved pattern, determined upon before completion of contract.

*Doors.*—Outside doors to be as follows: Front door in entrance to be double-folding doors, each half two feet three inches wide, four paneled, two and a half inch, eight feet four inches high; (or otherwise—if to be glazed, describe the panels to be left open for glass;) other external doors to be two inch six panel doors, seven feet six inches high and three feet three inches wide. The back door or doors of out-buildings to be one and three-quarter inch, formed with vertical ledges, rebated and beaded joints, nailed to jack braces.

To fit up all the internal doorways with six (or eight) panel doors, one inch and seven-eighths thick, for the principal doors, (enumerate the rooms,) and one and a half inches thick for the secondary doorways. Door casings, skirting board, and other inside finish, to be as represented by the drawing, or as agreed upon before completion of the contract.

*Windows.*—To fit to the openings deal-cased window frames, with oak sunk sills, to have sashes double hung with weights, axle pulley, lines and fastenings; or, (for French and casement windows,) to fit to the window openings rough rebated and beaded frames, with oak sunk sills, and two and a quarter casements, filled in with cross bars or other sash-lights, hung with butt-hinges and provided with proper fastenings (see presently, under the head of "trimmings").

Closet doors to be the same finish as room doors on their outer sides, and finished flush within. Closets to be provided with shelves, as directed, not less than one shelf to every sixteen inches in height.

To put up in the kitchen (or elsewhere) a dresser seven (to nine) feet long, three (to four) feet wide, with two long drawers, each half the length of the top, and two small drawers, one at each end; long drawers to be eight inches deep, the two small ones five inches deep and one foot wide, same length as the width of dresser. Back of dresser to be shelved with one shelf every sixteen inches of height, fourteen inches wide, and inch and a half thick. Under side of dresser to be provided with inch square framed doors, hung with butt hinges.

The sink (or sinks) to be inclosed with doors below. Water-closet to be made with mahogany (or other wood) seat and riser. (Describe the rest of the work necessary here, under the head of "Plumber.")

Outside blinds, and inside blinds and shutters. (These must be described, where requisite, severally in manner as follows.) Outside blinds to be made with slats, framed into inch and a quarter frames three inches wide, hung with hinges and trimmed with proper fastenings; inside blinds to be seven-eighths thick, made with turning slats in frames to fold, to be of pine (or better of hard wood), to be carefully made. Shutters to be inch and a quarter paneled, to match with other finish. To fold as required, hung with hinges and trimmed.

*Plasterer.* To lath, plaster, set and whiten all ceilings and partitions (mention any not to be so treated); to render and set the walls, (firring out and lathing if required) the same to be left hard finish; or, to be colored twice with a good stone color, (and afterwards finished in color as directed) or, prepared for paper.

Cellar walls and such outbuildings as so described, to be lime-whited inside.

(If any plaster cornices inside are to be used, describe them here.)

*Smith.* To provide and fix grates in the several fire-places directed, or—to fix grates provided by the proprietor where directed. Same to boiler and coppers.

To provide and fix a bar to each window (if the walls be of stone or brick.)

To provide and fix cast iron air-gratings in the external walls, and grating to drains, cesspools, and cellar windows as directed.

To provide and fix all other requisite iron-work—including lightning-rods.

(N. B. If a furnace be used for heating, the metal-work that the contractor is to do connected therewith, should here be specified.)

To cover the roofs (metal) with tin, and to provide and fix eaves-gutters and leaders as required. (If the roof be shingled, insert under head of "carpenter," to be covered with shingles, nailed on with copper nails, using at least two to each shingle.)

*Metal-Trimmings.* The locks, bolts, fastenings, pulleys, weights, &c., all to be provided, where requisite, by the contractor, and are to be of the best qualities of their respective kinds. The bells, cranks, and wire to be also provided and set as directed. (Here enumerate the rooms to be furnished with bells.) The front door-post to be furnished with an escutcheon plate, and bell-handle, (plated or bronze, as directed) to be of best quality and of an approved pattern. (The annexed illustration shows a suitable design for the purpose.)

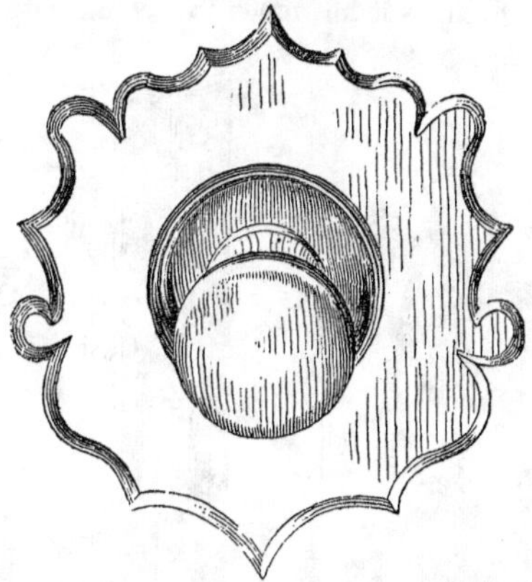

Silver Plated Gothic Front Door Bell-Pull.

The trimming of doors, shutters, blinds and windows to be of best quality, the French windows to be

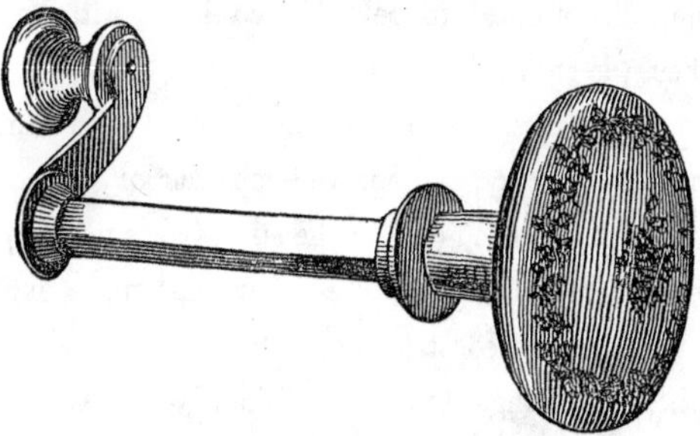

Crank Handle and Porcelain Knob.

furnished with crank, handle, and knob of porcelain, and of approved design. (Here is an illustration of one of the best.)

The hinges of French windows to be double fold or right angle plates. (There is a new hinge, lately introduced by Baldwin & Many for this purpose, a cut of which is given, as it has much to recommend it.)

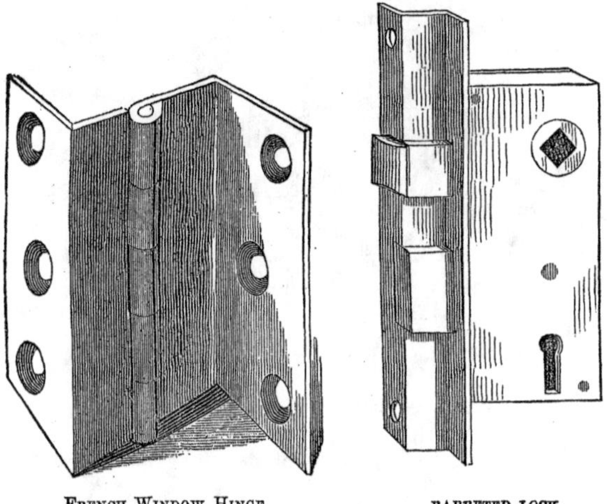

FRENCH WINDOW HINGE. RABBETED LOCK.

The locks of ditto, to be rabbeted locks, with handle and key, (as shown in this illustration.)

Sliding blinds, windows, or shutters (where used) to be trimmed with brass sheaves and way, of approved construction, and to be furnished with Astragal Latch (where the stile is very narrow), or with crank-handle latch). (Cuts of each are shown, to explain the forms of those of best construction).

Other trimmings to be furnished where requisite. (If ventilating valves, registers, and any other apparatus for the purpose of securing passage of air, be used, they must be specified here; I would particularly advise that

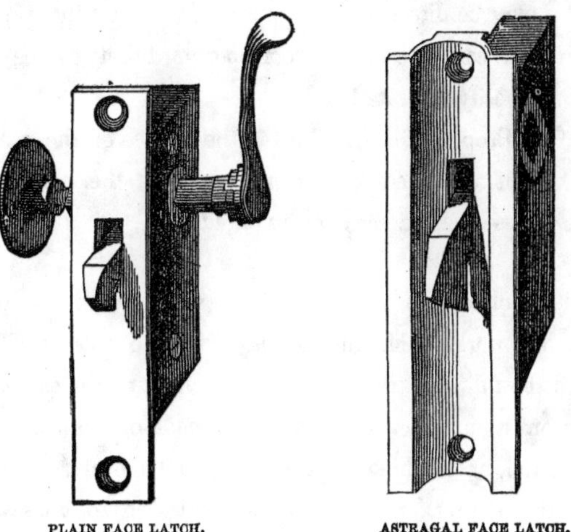

PLAIN FACE LATCH. ASTRAGAL FACE LATCH.

one of the ventilating valves so often spoken of, be placed near the ceiling in the smoke flue of every room.)

*Painter.* To properly prepare and paint the whole of the wood, (and other work required), four times with good oil color, finishing such tints as directed.

Or,—to stain and twice varnish the wood-work.

(If sand is to be used, specify to that effect).

*Plumber.* To provide and fix all leaden pipe required, to furnish and fix apparatus agreed on for the water closet and bathing-room.

*Glazier.* To glaze all the windows with clear good glass of the qualities determined, properly bedded and back-puttied. Stained glass where used to be put in with lead bandings and secured with iron rods and staples.

*Paper hanger.* To prepare properly, and hang the whole of the plastered sides of such rooms, halls, entries, and partitions as may be directed, with paper selected by the proprietor at a certain cost each room per yard that may be agreed. (specify the rate here).

*Yard. and enclosing wall,* Properly form and level the surface of the yard, and put up fences or external walls of the height, thicknesses, and description required.

The whole of the works are to be executed and finished in a good and workmanlike manner, according to this specification, and to the full and true intent and meaning of the same. And if any omission appears to have been made of work to be done, or material, or finishing, or trimming, to be provided, which is evidently an omission, and is usually supplied to houses of the class, extent, and character of this, then the contractor (or builder) is to perform the same as if fully detailed in this specification.

No extra works are to be charged for, but such as are agreed upon at the time, and an order in writing given to the contractor (or builder).

## FORM OF A CONTRACT TO BE APPENDED TO A SPECIFICATION.

In consideration of the sum of dollars to be paid to me by of and in manner following, that is to say:

Twenty-five per cent. upon laying of second floor joists;

Twenty-five per cent. upon roofing in;

Twenty-five per cent. upon rendering up the building; and the remainder within six months therefrom; I hereby agree to perform all the works described in the foregoing specification and illustrated in the drawings attached thereto, subject to all the conditions therein contained, and to be finished on or before the day of in penalty of a sum not exceeding fifty dollars per week for every week after that period they shall remain incomplete; and I farther agree to execute said works in the best and most workmanlike manner, using materials of the best quality of their several kinds, and supplying everything not specially referred to or described in the specification and drawings, but usually considered requisite in a house of this class. And I agree to abide by the decision of the architect (if there be any, if not some disinterested referee) in all contested points, and to accept his opinion as final.

In witness whereof (here follow form of signature and witness.)

The specification and form for contract here given, are simple and comprehensive, and without multiplying words, are such as a contractor or builder would find it hard to evade, supposing he were disposed to litigation. But if the proprietor be so unfortunate as to fall into the hands of a tricky builder, none but the shrewdest lawyer can help in preventing a bill of extras, and even he would not be able to control every item ; I hope, however, that the very few such men there are, may not have the erection of any of these rural homes entrusted to them, as though seemingly so cheap at first, they are dearly bought bargains before done with.

Where no architect is employed, it would be well for the gentleman who is building, from time to time, to inform himself of the market price of materials and labor, and compare the information he has gathered with the charges made him by his builder. If any one has recently finished a good house in the vicinity, occasional inspection of portions of it, and a few questions asked of its owner will be of great advantage, as his experience will be valuable, and I believe no one would, under the circumstances, refuse to give it. I would particularly caution against the introduction of frequent changes in the plan of the house, as, independently of causing increased cost, they are apt to involve the design, and if the owner is not acting under an architect's advice, the house, however promising in appearance at first, may be spoiled from want of caution in introducing changes. Let the plans be deliberated upon as thoroughly as needs be at first; it were well if a winter's study was spent upon them ; but once matured and the owner satisfied with them, they should be carried out without deviation.

Before commencing the building, an accurate estimate of its cost should be procured from the builder, and any changes economy may then suggest taken advantage of. The estimates should be made so as to show the quantities of the several materials to be used and the prices annexed; these any builder can accurately figure out, although he may be mistaken in his time and labor estimate. A very safe allowance may be made after the cost of materials delivered on the ground has been obtained, by adding that sum and one-third more as the price for time, labor, and builder's profit. This will give sufficiently near for safe guidance the probable expense of the finished building, and is a test I would advise the owner to apply, my own experience having shown it to be a very safe one. Thus, suppose the builder's estimate of cost of materials to be three thousand dollars, the cost of the house would be seven thousand. Another way of approximating the cost of a house is by averaging with the expense of previously constructed buidings; thus, an architect's experience has shown him that houses of a certain class have cost so much per square of one hundred feet, or so much per cubic foot. For instance, a building on plan forty feet square, of usual height, finish, and quality, would be taken as worth two hundred dollars a square, and as there are sixteen squares in the house, the cost would by such a rule be thirty-two hundred dollars. Another, and seemingly more accurate way, is to base the calculations on the cube of the building, multiplying the square of the dimensions of its plan by the height, and allowing a certain sum per cubic foot. Thus, in a house forty feet square and thirty-five feet high, from the cellar or foundation level to the underside of the wall-plate, would contain one hundred and twelve thousand cubic feet. Previous calculation of the expense of other buildings of supposed similar finish and average cost has shown that three cents per cubic foot would be a fair estimate, thus making its total three thousand, three hundred, and thirty-six dollars. Such calculations as these, however, can by no means implicitly be depended upon, but an architect, or any one who has frequently been in the habit of building, soon acquires experience in determining the value of work, and generally, by adopting some such formula, arrives at a very reliable estimate of its total cost. In a building costing nearly sixty thousand dollars, my estimates of its cost, based upon a somewhat similar system of calculations, proved to be but three hundred dollars different from the accepted tender and contract, nor did the finished work, so far as the architect had control, vary from the first expenditure determined on.

An experiment has recently been tried of building in a still cheaper and more economical manner than heretofore ; of course any attempt towards a result so desirable, is interesting. It consists in the use of a different material to any I have as yet spoken of for the walls, and a change in the framing of the interior. The walls are built of earth—not mud walls as were once used, and though the system is no novelty on the other side of the Atlantic, is but of recent origin here. Having recently had an opportunity of examining some economical houses so constructed, before bringing this chapter to a close, I will describe the process and manner of building. The foundation of the walling is formed of stone or brick-work rising six inches or a foot above the surface of the ground, and about twenty inches thick. On this should be a layer of broken stone or slate laid in hydraulic cement, to prevent the rising of the damp. The foundation being completed, frames of plank of any convenient length are laid upon the edges of the stone or brick-work, and secured at the bottom by stout iron wire drawn through from side to side and fastened by a nut, the upper part being kept open by blocks of the requisite width every two or three feet in the length. Drop ends are also made to this plank box, and complete the whole of the machinery required. The holes through which the wire is drawn are made with slits downwards, so that the frame may be lifted up leaving the wire remaining in the walls. Into this frame the earth, prepared in either one of the following methods, is filled in. The earth is either a loamy gravel, made as dry as possible, mixed with stones, and then, without any cement, compressed in the frame. It is held together by the force of adhesion alone, and walling of this description which is so durable as to have stood the test of more than two centuries' wear and tear in Europe, is called *Pisé.* Another method is to mix loam or clay with straw and moisten it with water, then leaving it in the frame some time to dry and become consolidated before another course is added. A third method is to fill the frame with clay lumps previously well beaten, and mixed with old, short straw, and saturated with as much water as the clay will absorb. In either of these latter methods, all stones must be carefully picked out, and the walling allowed considerable time to dry, hence buildings so constructed are tediously long in hand.

The pisé walls are proceeded with as follows: After the frame is filled (it may be three or four feet high, and as long as convenient for the openings of doors and windows) the lower wires acting as bolts are cut off and the blocks at top loosened, the sides of the frame are then raised so that the lower holes come to a line with the top, fresh wires are then drawn through and the blocks keyed up. One course may be raised upon another, as thus described, immediately it is finished, but it will be found more convenient to carry on the courses horizontally, keeping all of an equal height. As the work proceeds the tops of the walling are covered with board to screen from the weather, and the roof should be put on as soon as the walls are carried the requisite height. The usual manner of finishing the space left for the doors and windows is by placing partition boards, fastened to the framework, upright and horizontally as required, and stopping the filling in against them, inserting here and there pieces of timber two or three inches thick for attaching the door-posts and window-frames to. On the second story, sleepers or plates are laid on the inner side of the walls, as in the ordinary manner, for the floor joists to rest upon.

As an improvement, I would advise building the sides of all openings for doors, windows, etc., in brick-work, filling the walling up against it, and leaving the brick-work in alternate courses so as to bond with the walling. This method would make the walling solid and durable in the extreme, and if, in addition, the corners of the buiding were protected with stone or brick in the same manner, the structure would no doubt last as long here as similar ones have in Europe. In Devonshire and some other of the southern and western counties of England, are still standing houses so built, which the title-deeds show to be more than two centuries old, nor, as yet, do they show any signs of decay.

The internal construction may be greatly lessened in expense by a more saving use of materials. The floors, instead of being laid upon joists at right angles to their bearing, will be equally strong and require far less timber if supported by diagonal bearers laid from corner to corner, intersected again by similar bearers from the centre of each side where the size of the room requires. The diagonal principle of construction so beautifully and advantageously adopted in the frame bridges of this country, might with great benefit be incorporated by carpenters into their partitions and frames, and with the scientific reasons that exist for the change in principle and the ecomonic arguments of lessened cost, it is strange that as yet no steps have been taken to investigate the advantages diagonal bearing would secure. In the railroad bridges designed and patented by T. Willis Pratt, this principle has been recognised, and the saving in weight and material thereby effected is so considerable, it becomes a matter of regret that engineers have not been encouraged to attempt the elucidation of a new system of framing in general carpentry.

# CHAPTER XVI.

RURAL ARCHITECTURE AS A FINE ART—ITS INFLUENCE ON THE MIND, HEART, AND SOCIAL VIRTUES—WHAT AN AMERICAN VILLAGE MIGHT BE—CONCLUSION.

CONSTRUCTIVE skill in building and ingenious adaptation of mechanical contrivances to meet the wants of domestic life, are the grand distinctive excellencies of this age; in no period of artistic history have we evidences of construction being so well understood, or of the use of materials so various and so scientifically adapted to their several purposes, as at the present time. It is the knowledge of the principles of design—the *art* of architecture—that seems wanting; and now that I have given examples of its application, there appears to me a fitting opportunity before bidding the reader farewell, of offering a few remarks upon the principles upon which architectural beauty depends, and in so doing, necessarily to recapitulate much of what I have previously observed.

Lovers of ancient art claim for it a superiority in effect upon the mind of the beholder, and a sublimity beyond the reach of modern effort. This must be granted them by all who have studied the wonderful conceptions of the giant imaginings of old, but at this point the superiority ends, for the genius of the present day is as far beyond that of the "golden past" in mechanical appliances and constructive skill, as progress in well-doing could have made it. But the said lovers claim a superiority often for constructive skill also,—pointing to the Pyramids and the Pronaoi of Egypt as structures beyond the building resources of the present day—how absurdly this claim must appear, when with these certainly stupendous works are contrasted the lofty, airy pinnacles of the late Christian spire, or the still more modern aqueducts, bridges, tunnels, docks, and every useful and vast erection of this present flourishing age of commerce! The Greeks and Romans had but little knowledge of carpentry or joinery in the present sense of the words; of this we have constant proof in the vestiges of their building left; for example, in the frequent use of brick arches where wooden constructions would have been much better. Even the middle age architects, skilful as they were, had but little theoretical knowledge, and but small amount of skill in delicate constructive operations, (as in joinery, for instance,) and certainly could not have built many of the great works of modern times, even had they possessed the materials. But with all this they attained effects we with all our advanced skill and mechanical means cannot reach. A simple ruin, merely—apart from its influences derived from suggestive associations—has power to fill the mind even of the most callous with emotion. The wrecks of ancient splendor saved from the waves of time at Karnak and at Luksor, in their crumbling, perishing grandeur, have a sublimity no modern structure can present; and yet four thousand years have rolled on and accumulated treasures of skill and learning—all too powerless to frame one such building as the forgotten, almost exterminated Egyptians, reared in boundless profusion.

What the conclusion?—That architecture, as a fine art, was better understood then than now!

Again, where have we traces in modern buildings of the majestic simplicity and perfect refinement of the fanes of Greece? Those glorious embodiments of everything grand and beautiful in design, and harmonious and delicate in detail; where, even after the perfect building had been elaborated into the most exquisite completeness ingenuity and artistic handicraft could effect, the optical deceptions of distance were corrected, and the entasis of the column given it, to produce an effect of graceful and perfect diminution to the eye which before it did to the scale; the leading lines of mouldings were gone over again to secure the same result, and so careful was the scrutiny that would leave no minutiæ of detail untouched, that such exquisite manœuvres were practised as at the Temple of Minerva, in which the lions' heads terminating the enrichment of the pediment are *turned slightly outwards*, so that cutting against the clear sky instead of being in relief against the mass of shadowed moulding behind, they might not appear to recede from the plane they occupied elsewhere. These perfecting touches given too, only when the building had been deemed complete (as the researches of all travellers have shown), evince a refinement which can only be traced to the finest taste guided by the most matured judgment. Perhaps this may assist in explaining why modern copies of ancient art as seen in public buildings scattered all over the country, appear so frigid. The parts and proportions *may* be classically correct (they not often are), but the evidence of the want of careful, final scrutiny is very apparent.

It may, however, be said that all such refinements are only useful where the design is in every other respect complete. It is the last master-stroke upon a perfect work.

Where amongst modern imitations can be discovered a Gothic edifice approaching in graceful outline, harmony of purpose, and perfection of detail, the almost inspired structures of old! Where an interior like Lincoln, so gloriously replete with unearthly beauty as to be called (more from that cause than from the enshrined sculpturings within) the *Angels Choir*. Where amongst the multitude of this age's attempts can be found the faintest approach to the matchless proportions of Old England's noblest prize—the Abbey Church of Westminster? Where in any modern building are evidences of architectural genius and forethought like such as can be seen evinced in every part of this majestic abbey? I will give an instance that will prove how carefully art was brought into play then to produce an effect which we, with all our improved appliances, would be slow to bring about now. The stone shafts which run up from the floor against the walls to support the ribs of the roof above, are composed of two small ones next the wall, and one larger one in front, clustered together, and united top and bottom by continuously foliated cap and moulded base. Why was this arrangement of triple, engaged columns necessary? The object to be attained by the shaft itself was to bring down the line formed by the ribs of the roof to the floor and so to connect them therewith (for connection of parts is an important element of beauty), and give greater apparent support to the roof. This could only harmoniously be accomplished by a column proportioned to the size of the rib; but had it been but *one shaft* only, its large size would have struck the eye too violently as a single object. To avoid this, it was necessary to break it up; two columns together of the same size would have looked flat, and the rib moulded to agree with them would have had the effect of a band; three all of the same size would have still farther increased the difficulty; but by using one shaft large and bold enough to bring the line down and gather the irregular mouldings of the rib together, concentrating them, as it were, into one regular and consolidated mass; and at its side two smaller ones to connect this larger one with the wall, all is accomplished with the most perfect art. This fine, perfected conception of the beautiful is not interfered with by the horizontal string-course which runs all round the building immediately under the triforium, and which no doubt, in more vulgar hands, would have either been broken around each member of the clustered shaft, and thus have cut its entire height in two, or else have been stopped against it, and so have weakened the whole effect by depriving apparently the more slender shafts of all connection with the wall. The consummately skilful architect attained his object by stopping the string-course at the smaller columns, but carrying it round the larger one, and thus gave the connection with the wall, banded all together, and achieved the accomplishment of a difficult problem in the most perfect way. This unrivalled structure, indeed, teems with such instances, and it is by this extreme delicacy of perception which constitutes architectural genius, that the claims of superiority of ancient art can best be supported, and the insensibility to which draws the impassable line between the efforts of mere talent and the consolidated, never-wavering attention which marked the unrivalled works of the great masters of olden art.

In fairness, however, one great cause of the inferiority in effect of modern buildings may be attributed to the inartistic treatment of the decorative parts. No mere workman can carve a capital or a string of flowers, any more than a mere workman can paint a picture or sculpture a statue. Once mighty artists thought it not beneath them to attend to such details; and surely when Grinling Gibbons chiselled; when a Royal Academician climbed the scaffolding, and carved the keystones at Somerset House; and when Lorenzo Ghiberti sculptured and Raphael drew, none need now be ashamed, however high their talents may have placed them on the artist-pedestal, to do likewise. But mere beauty of workmanship again, and delicacy of detail, are not the only excellences wanting to produce a perfect modern work; Thom carved with most exquisite feeling and wonderful skill a Christian temple in modern New York, and yet even he could not by his matchless labors more than enrich. The meed of praise that posterity will assign to Trinity Church will be dealt out by the effect created by its outlines, and if they produce not the impression of beauty and sublimity, the worker will only be pitied for having had a lifeless, expressionless statue to adorn, instead of a soul-filled creation.

I could multiply instances, derived not merely from the larger and public buildings, but from the domestic architecture (of which we have memorials as distinct); but I have said enough to make good the conclusion before arrived at—that architecture, as a fine art, was better understood once, than now. Yet we have constructive superiority on our side; we have better tools to work with; more varied materials; scientific and reliable calculations upon which to base their proportions for purposes of strength and resistance, and the examples of by-gone beauty to work upon—surely, with all these advantages, it cannot be that the dawn of a better intelligence will be long withheld! My sincere hope and firm belief, as I have before said, are in rural architecture proving the leading step to an eminence of artistic success presently to be reached, as glorious and as grand as that of any now inapproachable epoch of the past. In olden times, those great results that now fill the world with admiring wonder, were brought about by concentrated expression of the pervading sentiment; the genius of the people stamped its impress upon the productions of the age. All know what the religious sentiment of the middle ages has achieved. The analytical sentiment of this age will, before very long, lead it to reject all that has not a purpose and a use—a purpose of utility, a use in aiding harmony of effect; beauty only will be valued—it will only be considered as such when so produced, and out of this sturdy determination to throw aside all not marking a meaning and intention, will result a grand, united, all-pervading influence, which at no very distant time will develope itself into a form and style. How—the Giver of Genius best can show! But it will come, depend upon it; nor will silly, tricksied imitations, and obstinate adherence to unmeaning forms, long delay it.

A work of rural art, whether a simple little cottage, or a wealthy family's homestead, as an object of beauty is susceptible of three degrees of appreciation—the simple, the suggestive, and the intellectual. These three degrees are synonymous with the admirable definitions of Mr. Ruskin in the "Modern Painters," and there classed as capable of suggesting ideas of *natural beauty*, of *relation*, and of *power*. Simple beauty is the effect of the object *per se* upon the mind of the spectator, without any reference to its destination, utility, or other extrinsic quality; suggestive, when to this is added an evident appropriateness to the object for which it was built, suggesting its purposes and its use; the intellectual, when to these two degrees is superadded an evidence of skill and *power* in the legitimate use of materials or application of principles of construction to attain the desired end by the conquering of some accidental difficulty. I will give an instance of the application of these degrees of appreciation. Take a common stone building, say, for example, the parsonage design in this book; the outlines of the building are pleasing, its proportions harmonious, and its contemplation would give an emotion of simple satisfaction to the beholder; ask him why? He would say it pleased him, or filled his eye, or use some such phrase that showed merely its natural beauty, its beauty *per se*, had been appreciated. If, however, he replied, that its beauty pleased him because he deemed the building appropriate to its purpose, that its character harmonized with that of the adjacent church, that its open, roomy porch gave evidence of ready reception and cheerful hospitality within, and its secluded study and separated entrance told to him the tale of its two-fold nature and purpose of habitancy; then the sentiment had been increased to an appreciation of suggestive beauty. If still farther to all this was added the reply, that it pleased because he thought the material had been appropriately used, and it looked real, honest, and enduring; or he admired the skill with which the outlines of the parts had been marked by the blocked stone quoins and masonry round the windows, and the simplicity that had preserved the natural treatment of the general walling, which, by its unobtrusive character, served as a background on which the dressed work showed so advantageously; then the appreciation has mounted to the highest degree, and the sentiment of intellectual perception been awakened.

Limits far transcending those now left me would be required to follow out these general principles. I can here do no more than state their existence and define their meaning.

But I can fancy some reader to exclaim, tastes are so various; who is to define in the first place in what simple, or as you call it, natural beauty, consists? That tastes are so various, I, of course, do not deny—their very variety has originated a proverb, and yet, though it may seem a paradox, this very variety is an evidence of the truth.

In almost every object that can be contemplated, there *must* exist some beauty that will produce pleasure, so, for the variety of tastes to be influenced by it, some food can be found to satisfy the cravings more or less urgent of human inner perception of the beautiful. Whether all its beauties, or whether the particular beauties that render it perfect, have been appreciated, is not the question; it may be even, that those be admired which in themselves are beautiful, but lose their charm by wrong application in this individual instance; even then this is but an evidence of taste perverted; the innate perception is there, but the knowledge to apply it has not come.

Taste is like conscience; all have it; but they may blunt it; drown its voice, and finally so deaden themselves to its power as to pervert its warnings and warp its influence; it becomes strengthened by use, and the more it is listened to, the stronger and more correct it will become, so as finally to be to the heart what the sound judgment is to the mind. I have shown that *degrees* of beauty can be estimated; in them is evidence of *degrees* of taste, and, not forgetting that by education and important refinement the dictates of taste will be increased in power, in fine, that much talked of, but to me almost unintelligible phrase—"a standard of taste," will have a realization. Undoubtedly there exists a rule or standard in nature for trying individual *tastes* as there is for testing *morals*, and my comfort is, that after a time the search, however seemingly fruitless now, must be eventually successful.

Let me quote a page from Lord Kaimes' "Elements of Criticism":—"That there is no disputing about taste, seems to have grown into a proverb. One thing, however, is evident, that if the proverb hold true with respect to taste in matters of art, it must hold equally true with respect to other senses. If the pleasures to be derived from seeing works of art disdain a comparative trial and reject all criticism, then the pleasure to be derived from the sense of hearing must be equally privileged. At this rate, no one is within the reach of censure who shall prefer the beating of a kettle to the finest concert.

"And if thus all the pleasures of external sense be exempted from criticism, there would seem to be no reason why every one of our pleasures, from whatever source derived, should not be so; and that with respect to the perceptions of sense by which some objects appear agreeable and some disagreeable, there does not exist such a thing as a good or bad, a right or wrong—that every one's taste is to himself an ultimate standard, without appeal; and consequently, there can be no ground of censure against any one, if such there be, who prefers selfishness to benevolence, or wrong, for its own sake, to right.

"But to ascertain the rules of morality, we appeal not to the common-sense of savages, but to that of men in their more perfect state; and we make the same appeal in forming the rules that ought to govern the fine arts. In neither can we safely rely on a local or transitory taste, but on that which is the most general and the most lasting among polite nations. For, if we have recourse to general opinion and general practice, we are betrayed into endless perplexities. History shows that there is nothing more variable than taste in the fine arts."

The expression of common taste must be govered by common sense, and a work of art must be susceptible to rules of criticism. Nature has general laws, so has art—such, apart from their importance, are delightful from their simplicity, and by reason of the boundless applicability of their influence. Nature's laws we partly know; those of art unfortunately we have but framed into a skeleton code; but of rural architecture, the most binding art can teach, are reality, intention, and harmony. Reality, in the honest, simple use of materials and construction to effect the desired end; intention, in showing evident design and connection between the building and its planned purpose; and harmony with Nature's aspect and with the spirit of the place.

The influence that buildings so devised would have in educating public taste is incalculable. Scarcely a rural hamlet, where one house evincing some care in its design and treatment has been newly built, but its effect upon subsequent erections has been most marked. First one neighbor, then another, has discovered his own homestead requires refreshing; perhaps, merely to the extent of fresh painting, and a new roof; ideas for both of these are taken from the new model, and it may be somewhat ludicrously and inconsistently applied. Then another resident determines to rebuild, and his own experiences being enlarged, and a higher standard of taste erected for measuring his ideas of excellence, a very different structure is probably contemplated than he would ever have thought of at first. It is curious to see how any peculiarly marked features, or unusual details, are renewed in each fresh copy from the first new house that is built in a manner different from those usually seen in any small rural community. This remark equally will apply to the buildings of the middle ages, it generally being the fact that ecclesiastical architecture, when in its most glorious growth, developed itself alike all over a certain range, the mother church of the diocese almost universally serving as the type for the lesser buildings. Hence the gathered beauties of delicate spires in one county of England, and the quaint and battlemented towers of another; so, everywhere it seems, that the first presentation of any thing simply beautiful to the rural public, is instantly seized upon, and reconstructed in as varied ways as individual appreciation, circumstances, and means suggested. How careful then should those persons be who first attempt the introduction of an article of taste in a remote and simple district.

Apart from the increased beauty in the appearance of the country, there are other grounds for the advocacy of attention to its architecture. It is found that elevation in the social scale is commensurate with increased elevation in taste. Political economists have found in England, where the experiment has principally been tried, that the erection of commodious, and even elegant cottages for the country poor, has been followed by the most beneficial results. The laboring man that once found the ale-house the only comfortable roof under which he could rest his tired limbs after a hard day's work, driven from his own home by its squalor, its wretchedness, and miserable paucity of even the rudest necessaries of life—in his warm and convenient newly contrived cottage, finds a more airy and more cheerful room, and in the cleanly appearance of his wife and children, their happy labors and busy housewifery, a far pleasanter relaxation than the tap-room, reeking with the tobacco smoke of generation upon generation, could afford. He consequently spends his leisure hours at home, and naturally his thoughts dwell there with satisfaction during his labor-day; he contrives how this and that little improvement or additional comfort can be made; digs out his garden, and prides himself on its early promise of fruits and flowers. His children help him, and the man that in the rude hovel was assuredly striding his way to crime and misery, in the cheerful cottage is, step by step, mounting upwards in the scale of social worth. Thorough investigations by interested philanthropists have shown, in every instance where this has been tried, that the fruit has been one of promise; if so with the ignorant (comparatively), boorish day-laborers of agricultural England, how much greater will be the yield in the more intellectually fertile condition of the rural population here?

Common schools, improved means, a cheaper literature, unshackled freedom for acquirement of knowledge and advancement in position—all these are weighty advantages on the side of this people; and working on a better intelligence and appreciation, the benefit to be derived will be incalculably greater. Every heart is more or less alive to the impressions of beauty—when joined with utility it has an irresistible appeal, and it is not unfair to suppose that in the country, with Nature's simple or grand beauties scattered everywhere for contemplation, a more ready perception and appreciation may be counted upon than in cities. This may not everywhere be the case, but as a general rule it probably is; and at all events, in the country, there being less to distract, the quiet, unobtrusive lessons of constructive beauty cannot fail to work a quicker way.

But, not only cottages and cottagers are to be thus benefited; the country man-of-wealth, the professional man, the merchant, and the parson—all may be made wiser and better. "Sermons in stones," I have always read with its liberal meaning, and think an architect has a great and noble privilege in his power to preach by his works lessons of refinement, harmony, and beauty. The pertinacity with which every newly built house, if in any respect out of the common way, is discussed, the curiosity shown by the strollers around it during the progress of the works, and very speedily the avidity with which any scrap or morsel of peculiar detail is seized upon and copied, are proofs of the awakened interest it excites. When the finished whole stands fair and full before them, many a pilgrimage is made from some distant spot to contemplate its finish and proportions, and its beauties sink into no unfertile soil. And how with its occupants? The teaching influence soon shows its effects. The furniture, the internal plenishing and details take a tone from the dwelling. Articles in improved taste are demanded from the country store, or perhaps sent for from the distant city. There are some inquired for by others, and the building of one moderately good house (good in artistic sense) will often occasion the introduction of a thousand commodities of a better taste into a rural community. Perhaps the house has a quiet simplicity about it that shames the lovers of gaudy carpeting and showy upholstery into a better taste; perhaps its arrangement of rooms suggests an amended and more refined adjustment of domestic economy; a little plant cabinet has perhaps forced the love and attention necessary for the culture of a few flowers; a retired, quiet, little book-room, if merely, perhaps, from the pleasant view commanded by its windows, has tempted occupancy in an unbusy hour, and the mind, calm and unhindered by household cares, has found leisure to strengthen itself by inward contemplation or the study of books. Numberless are the methods by which this wholesome influence will work—lasting and limitless are its effects. The young girl that, finding no intrinsic pleasure at home, nor regarding it otherwise than as the sphere of her domestic duties, would seek away from its shelter, and with other companions, other than "those of the household," pleasures and excitements neither so wholesome nor refining as a fond parent could wish, would, in a rural home, find so much to attach her heart and give food to her mind, that the inducement to wander from it would have but little allurement. Young ladies, do not suppose that I insist you are naturally all gad-abouts—I only plead (and for this you should thank me) for making your homes pleasant and beautiful.

It has often seemed to me a matter of regret that country school-houses are not more generally made prettier objects. Rude, often incommodious, and generally situated in by no means a pleasant site, they have only their admirable intention to recommend them. With the number of books that have from time to time appeared on school architecture, one would have thought ere this that some more matured fruit would have been seen, but yet ever-present stands the bald, white, pedimented out-building, without porch, veranda, or inclosure of any kind; severe temples of learning to the little scholar, when they might be cheerful, smiling homes of the heart! But time, the great essential, is the only commodity wanted by the people of this country to do this and many good things; in the course of a few years the lessons they are teaching themselves will be fully learnt, and then the importance of rural architecture as an art, and its influence on mind and manners will be fully seen and acted on.

One remark of present and almost universal application I would wish to make, is on the too little care that is shown towards the preservation of forest trees. Many country places that now look flat, uninteresting, and bare, would, if Nature's leafy treasures had been preserved, have been beautiful and rich. Its groves, its hedges, and shaded lanes, constitute the rural charms of England; there the storm-worn memorials of the past are cultured, propped up, and cared for with as sedulous pains as the ruthless devastation with which the prodigal, strengthy giants of younger growth are here hewn away, and burned up, and rooted out. The inconsistency with which this is done is sometimes almost amusing, it being no uncommon thing to find some noble old elm cut low, and presently stuck out in front of the dwelling in formal soldier-like line, a row of saplings as stiff and shadeless as bean-poles. The "woodman, spare that tree" of the song-bard of America should be graven on every wall of a country house, or set up in public places where "he that runs may read."

The love of trees is a mark of a good and healthy taste; he who chooses his building plot by a preference for the trees that surround and adorn it, may very safely be trusted with the expression of his fancy in a house. The beauty of trees is in their simplicity, and this in a house is the chief and highest charm. Frequently a beautiful home may be formed by a building of most modest size and pretensions, economically, nay, even severely built, nothing more done than necessity absolutely requires, and that in the simplest way—if surrounded by trees; the grandeur and variety of the shade, the softened outlines of the building, and the partial concealment of its mass, with the ideas of retirement, protection, and endurance that they give, combine to throw a charm about the place, that denuded of trees, a costly building would fail to impart. Think then of this before destroying a tree, or neglecting to plant one.

---

The study of rural architecture is both pleasant and improving. As an art, it is susceptible of investigation through a wide range; painting, sculpture, ethnology, the history of taste—all these are kindred studies, and have more or less reference to the principles, practice, or history of architecture. Without pursuing the mechanical means of acquiring a practically useful knowledge, so far as to render education in an architect's office necessary, the drawing required for expression of the design is both easily learned and readily done. In my last chapter I directed the amateur in his first steps towards making a set of drawings, and can scarcely recommend him a pleasanter amusement for an hour of leisure, or a more profitable study for a long evening or wet morning, than endeavoring to elucidate with his pencil, scale, and compasses, the designs his architectural reading has enabled him to make. As a branch of education in public and private schools, as a mentally healthy and interesting pursuit at home, the science of architecture, theoretic and constructive, would prove very valuable; it has, in fact, been a matter of surprise to me that this, one of the most practical of the sciences, has not had its professors in the larger colleges, and its teachers in all schools of any merit. As a fascinating way of learning and practically applying the principles of geometry, as an incentive to improvement under the drawing-master, and as a pleasant exercise for the powers of calculation and ingenious contrivance, a more desirable study could not be found. The love of beauty, harmony, and proportion would thereby be fed, and the inborn taste fostered and refined, nor has it one objectionable element—as some have said of the studies of painting and music—that would tend to unhinge or sensualize the mind; the union of the practical with the imaginative, the sound judgment with the correct taste, preserve the balance, and the young mind whose perceptive and conceptive faculties were thus equally exercised, would acquire a strength and tone, leaving a character invaluable through life. Most of the great architects of whom history has left any records, have been men of exemplary lives, and nicely balanced, pure, and reflective minds; there is something in the study itself only appreciable to a simple and earnest heart; it is not sufficiently sensual for the voluptuary, nor chimerical for the speculative imaginist; enough there is of a practical business in its details to curb exuberant fancy, and enough for intellectual exercise and refreshment.

As a profession, that of the architect is a noble and useful one, and the day is not far distant when young men will commence its study, and diligently investigate the principles upon which its excellence depends. Heretofore, too generally, it has been taken up as a mere money-making pursuit, adapted to the lazy and the visionary, or still better to the broken-down carpenter, who, finding no credit to carry on his legitimate business, goes into the "drafting line" as he calls it, and in his own language becomes an "archy-tect." This latter class are greatly patronized by so called practical men; they think no architect can be trusted with their house who has not wielded the jack-plane, nor should they consistently read any author who does not set his own types. Architects undoubtedly should be practical men, that is, they should understand the whole theoretic practice of masonry, carpentry, and joinery, and be able to direct how work is to be done, and to appreciate it when done; farther than this is neither possible nor desirable. They should be familiar with the use and meaning of the technical terms of the different trades, so as to be easily understood by workmen, and they would find it to their advantage occasionally to suggest a different way of doing any particular work in which their experience and better theoretic knowledge enable them to point out improvement. This, with rapidity in making a clear, comprehensive working-drawing of any detail at large (if possible, before the eyes of the mechanic) will, with a presence of mind and coolness that are never at fault when any question or difficulty arises, inspire the workers with confidence, and greatly assist the designer in carrying out to the full, the spirit of his composition.

The rarest excellence of the artist mind, is when an architect can throw himself into the spirit of the builder, and see with his eyes, and reason with his reasonings; then, applying his own matured judgment and foreseeing experience to the design, he will be able to work out a composition appropriate and satisfactory; he should be able to identify his employer's interest with his own, to be tied by no undue pertinacity in favor of any peculiar designs, unless their adoption can be recommended by reasons so in accordance with common sense as to make it his duty, as much as may be, to insist upon them. Individuality is as much exemplified in a house as in personal character, and the architect's highest praise will be, that he has successfully *subli-mated* and embodied the peculiar views, habits of life, or circumstances of the owner. By so doing he will avoid mannerism, that curse of art, and show in his designs a power and curiously suggestive variety that will prevent them ever being common-place or tame. An architect of once considerable repute in England found it so entirely impossible to avoid the constant recurrence of a particular style in all his buildings, as to earn the *sobriquet* of "Ionic Inwood;" in fact, it *is* said, that in a Gothic church unfortunately entrusted to him, the *Ionic Volute* is very plainly perceptible in more than one of its details! Such mannerisms are common enough here; go where you will any where within fifty miles of New Haven, and you see houses, Gothic, Moorish(!), Italian, or Egyptian, with the same flat, thin roofs that look like box-lids shut down—so much so, as frequently to suggest to the observer a search for the hinges behind, whilst the fanciful garret windows in front not inaptly represent the key-hole. One of our best architects, and the one who, of all others, has had the largest and most liberal freedom for the expression of his designs, almost always makes his churches on one stereotyped plan, cruciform and with a broken-backed roof. A church in the form of a cross is beautiful in its symbolism and grand in its effect, if *vast;* but on a small scale, such a plan is unwarrantable, and if selected because of ancient *precedent*, is done so very ignorantly; only the abbey churches and ecclesiastical structures of the very largest class being thus arranged.

These are the mannerisms of individuals; the same charge

can be brought against a class. Every one must have observed how prone country people are to copy anything their neighbors have done, and in so marked an object as a new house, there is, of course, abundant opportunity for the exercise of this propensity. A short time ago it was universally the fashion to have columnar porches before hall doors—every one had them, and they seemed established as a fixed fact; then wide arches on consoles were resorted to, and almost equally in vogue; then again, every thing must be bracketted and richly carved, and frequently, in cities, as much was expended over the door-steps as would have sufficed to have built and almost furnished a decent house in the country. These fashions seem to have gone by, and others, like the changing forms and colors in a kaleidoscope, take their place. In country places the feeling is still more strong, and sometimes ludicrously evinced. Riding round the environs of Norwalk, Connecticut, I was amused with the frequent recurrence of a singularly formed attic window that looked exactly like the bows of a pair of spectacles, two oblong windows with their corners truncated being placed in couples side by side. I remember to have seen in London at the civic celebration of a royal visit to the powers that hold control in the city proper, a quaint and would-be-witty device these windows recalled. On one of the houses (an optician's) was a transparency, consisting of a gigantic pair of spectacles, and beneath, the words " a grand" in large letters, reading " a grand spectacle ; which pretty conceit the first builders of these houses must have read of or seen—though, whether the reading of the hieroglyphic thus transported here was meant to the house itself, or any peculiarity of its inmates within, I regret not to be able to solve.

Is it not a pity that drawing is not more strongly insisted on as an element of instruction in public and private schools? By it, the perceptive faculty would be strengthened, and whether as a means of pursuing an elegant accomplishment, or as an awakener of the powers of more accurately appreciating and comprehending the beautiful, would be an invaluable acquirement in after life. If not pursued beyond the limits of the class-room walls, still its refining influence would be carried into every after exercise of the mind, nor even would the merely business man, in the exercise it would have given to his young powers of calculation and arrangement, begrudge the time spent with the drawing-master. I know that at West Point it is considered, not only a most useful and advantageous pursuit, but admirable mental discipline, and the artist-mind, balanced by the sterner studies of mathematics, enlarged and made analytical by the acquirement of languages and the researches of history, produces a ripeness and refined elegance of scholarship which is as delightful as it is valuable. To go back to first principles, the more extended is the use of the drawing-master as a teacher of the young, the more rapid will be the advancement of a true taste, and consequently of a higher order of architecture.

Simplicity, as a source of architectural beauty, may thus be defined. Its dictionary meaning is the state of being unmixed, of not being complex, or of *consisting of a few parts*. This latter definition is the one usually applied to art, but it has not a sufficiently broad bearing, or else it would be the case that the smaller the number of parts, the greater the beauty. Thus a portico of six columns would be finer than one of eight, or a window with but two mouldings in its architrave more beautiful than one with six. Simplicity must regard not only the number of the parts, but their form and arrangement. Used in this sense, the word has a meaning synonymous with "breadth," as generally understood by painters or artistic critics. It is a general oneness of expression, in which, however multiplied the subordinate parts may necessarily have to be, the evident intention of one un-complex effect is plainly perceptible. Thus, in a plain, unbroken front of a country house, if the windows were small, many in number, and scattered over the *façade*, the breadth or simplicity of its effect would be spoilt; but change those for fewer in number and larger and wider in size, or group the smaller ones together into twos or threes, leaving broad, unbroken spaces between each cluster, and the breadth and simplicity are restored. In a more complex building, and one in which some peculiar and marked feature is attempted, the simplicity will be secured by such an arrangement of all smaller parts that may show evident subordination to the striking part that gives the character. Simplicity of effect is obtained by using one large mass and several smaller, so much smaller as never to distract the eye from the major body, as in a house with lower wings; or it is obtained by union of masses if two or more of similar size are used, as in an E-shaped building, in which the two similar ends are brought together into one whole by the central portion. The parts of each of these examples may be multiplied as much as needs be, but the effect being gathered by the general lines, and the minuter portions only serving as chasing, as it were, upon their surfaces, the impression of simplicity is secured. No matter how large or how ornate a building may be, the effect is produced by the outlines of the masses, seen from a proper point of sight; nothing can be more grandly, beautifully simple than the pointed cathedrals of

Gothic Europe, or the classic temples of Greece and Italy. St. Paul's, the metropolitan cathedral of England, is an instance in point, and though examined in detail, the wonderful fertility of invention and fanciful design of the exterior presents multitudinous forms of beauty. The general outline is so simply, intelligibly plain that its form, despite its myriad parts, can be sketched from memory by the merest school-boy who has seen it. Perhaps the shortest and truest paraphrase of architectural simplicity would be—freedom from confusion—and such is the definition I offer.

Reality, as an attribute of architectural beauty, I have before sufficiently explained. It consists in the legitimate use of materials and principles of construction to attain a required end. A building may appear beautiful in itself, its outlines may be harmonious, and effect simple, but if a material not suitable or method of construction not adapted has been employed, none but an undeveloped taste would sanction it. This is the reason that the wooden-classic, as a style, is doomed to an inevitable perishing before very long. The forms that carpentry copies are in themselves beautiful, and the study that they sometimes evince as spent upon their correct reproduction from the ancient model, commendable; but, inasmuch as the eye and sense know they are not of stone or marble, and that the fluted columns have been painfully cored, and glued up, and put together, and the carved capitals screwed on leaf by leaf about a clumsy timber block, the impression of sublimity is taken away, and one leading to ridicule probably substituted. So in the complicated Gothic contrivances sometimes seen, every one knows that the quaint and grotesque details have no meaning away from their own places, that the imitation "portcullis" (such has been seen and may be seen) never descends, nor do anything more warlike than nursery-maids and children with drums ever march across the "drawbridge." The "battlemented turrets" have no ordnance or bold archer behind, and the carved and crocketted chimney-shafts are only good, honest smoke-vents for a patent warming apparatus within. The funniest things are sometimes done by those who erect imitative Gothic buildings. A large and costly church recently erected in New York, shows upon its outside doors what apparently are very beautifully wrought-iron scroll-hinges, such as are frequently seen in old buildings, and worthy of reproduction now, but my appreciation of their excellence has lost its zest from the fact that, passing by the building ere completion, I found workmen carefully nailing on a wooden counterfeit cut out of stuff a quarter of an inch thick, and this, painted black and varnished, lies itself into an honest scroll-hinge, the real working fellow being craftily concealed in the door-frame, and getting no credit for the labor the showy humbug outside seems to perform. Once a week's labor would have been gladly bestowed on one such hinge if a means of adorning and enriching a beautiful doorway; now a pattern cut out of stiff paper, a few feet of thin board, a circular saw or a "jumping-johnny," with a little paint and varnish, will serve to turn-out a dozen in an hour—thanks to "progress"—not in *this* case, however, in "well-doing."

Meaning or expression of character in a building is a beauty not so easily obtained. Being, as it should be, an embodiment of the individuality of the owner, it can be subject to no rules other than those just explained. The house of the scholar, the man of leisure and refined taste, the follower of agricultural pursuits, or the sportsman, will have probably a character consistent with the peculiarities of each owner, and as marked as the residence of the showy *parvenu* who has brought his wealth from the city, and his taste from some not-so-easily-to-be-found place, to astonish the country folk. Whimsicality even in a building is not unpleasing if it has been obtained legitimately. A Chinese padoga roof has been seen to produce a very artistic effect, and used for evident purpose of shade; its shape, though fantastic and unusual, is not in itself unpleasing, nor could its use justly be reprehended if constructed of suitable and honestly used materials.

Frequently an architect may be called upon by his employer to advise and assist in embodying some principle of design not apparently entirely congruous with good taste: in such a case, not merely from motives of policy, but in order to secure that individuality a building should possess, he should not resolutely combat the owner's wishes, but sedulously seek to identify them with his own, and carry out the idea, transfusing at the same time therein so much of his own refined spirit as may assist in giving meaning to any whimsicality and simplicity of effect to the whole composition. Like a skilful performer in a duet upon the piano, who, in case his partner makes a mistake, does not steadily go on with his own part, leaving the other to catch him up and come in how he may, but by deviating somewhat in his own notes, covers up the blunder, and not only prevents its detection by the general company, but to the appreciation of the initiated produces a beauty by the dexterity and intelligence of the manœuvre;—so a competent architect over the suggestions of the owner will throw a masterly treatment, which will not only prevent inadvertent discord, but by the blending of the individual will, and the artist taste, will secure a beautiful and original effect.

At the risk of seeming repetition, I repeat the principles upon which architectural beauty in a rural home depends,—simplicity, reality and intention. Their importance cannot too strongly be insisted on, and so impressed therewith should builders be, that, in devising any plan, they should mentally train themselves to reply to a question that will soon be the query of the age—*is it honest?*

In a few years how beautiful may this country be made by its rural architecture! There are bye places, and nooks and lanes, fertile valleys and rich knolls, that only want the hand of taste and the clear eye to invest with the sentiment of beauty. No country in the world is so favored by nature, and by reason of the unfettered freedom for expression of individual taste, the lack of the restraint of precedent, and the presence of a common sense right-mindedness which teaches (or will teach) to judge of a thing only by its intrinsic merits, no land shows so open a plain for the advancement of art. Villages, now but assemblages of white boxes thrust as near as may be upon the street, may be made clustered homes of simplicity and beauty; the church, the culminating point and centre of rustic attraction, not a building with wooden quasi-classic portico and semi-exposed walls, but a modest and yet sublime structure, modest in its freedom from pretentious ornament, sublime in its simple dignity; the store no longer a red staring two or three storied barn, but a cool, cheerful, well-shaded erection with widely spread and sheltering roof, and interior light, roomy and airy; the school-house such as children would love to linger around, and in their very dreams to see enpictured as a place of beauty. The cottage, the parsonage, the farmer's homestead and the rich man's mansion each contributing, though each so differently, to the one effect of the whole; with noble old trees grouped here and there and avenuing the road, and around everything the air of thrift that it is pleasant to testify all American villages have; such will make lovely places of every hamlet. It is not possible that in erecting buildings so various as a country village is composed of, one general directing taste can be expected, beyond agreeing to retain the roads a certain width, appropriating a certain spot for a public square or common garden, and determining to spare all trees now standing, and, where fitting to plant new ones, an undivided action cannot be looked for.

But the general effect will be produced by the mass of individual effort; therefore, if each one fairly does his part, the result of the collected whole will show one harmonious design. The church-building committee having selected the spot for their structure, with reference not only to its convenience of access from all parts of the village, but to its effect in the landscape as seen grouped with the houses, determine to adopt a design and style of structure that shall harmonize. Probably standing on an eminence, but so placed that there shall be a background of trees or higher ground behind, with a bold sweep of sward in front, and roomy, rustic sheds for shelter of country wagons during service times, at the rear and sides, the building has a base upon the ground, and by these features has given to it a domesticity which is the very acmé of perfection in a country church. sympathizing as it does with our twofold nature, and drawing by ties of kindred with our human wants instead of standing apart in bare and cold separation, inspiring the spirit of awe rather than the feeling of love. It is perhaps a low wooden building, with high pitched roof, so made because strong, durable and simple, with its eaves projecting many feet at the side to screen from heat in summer, and give warmth in winter; on the front is a roomy porch of simplest construction, enclosed it may be at one end in winter and well warmed, so as to afford a comfortable resting room between services for those who have come from a distance. Somewhere from the building rises a tower for the bell, perhaps surmounted by a spire, no huge pile of box upon box and column upon column, but a simple square tower carried up from the ground and having evident support therefrom, (not striding the gable as so often seen,) and breaking with a few bold mouldings and perhaps a bracketted string course, into an octagonal spire, whose airy lightness gives finish to the tower and beauty to the whole structure.

Nestling amongst trees not far from the church should be seen the oft-alluded-to school-house, low, rustic and shaded. A distinct porch and yard for boys and girls, and above the roof a little bell cot. No columns, nor pediment, nor classic pretension; the village children make not the dead languages of Greece and Rome their study, why surround them with their architecture? Let me plead for a flower garden attached to the school-house—beautiful lessons of industry and love and reverence can be taught by flower culture—if those entrusted with the education of the young would but see this, and instead of tying them to droning lessons in the drowsy school-room, would cultivate their perceptive faculties and their inner sympathies with the beautiful, how much more eager to learn, and how much more benefited would the poor little school children be than they are now. Not far from this might be placed the parsonage—such an one as exhibited in this book;—unobtrusive, solid and simple, connected with the church by a something which distinguishes it from other dwellings, and yet possessing features in common with the people's homes. Then would come houses of differing size and character; the modest cottage of the working man with its gay little garden-plot and bright flower bed; the somewhat larger dwellings of the storekeeper, merchant and professional man; the great house of the village with its noble woods and lawns, and everything that can show appreciation of nature's beauties and sedulous cultivation thereof by art. The village inn, no flaunting, plate-glass bedizened temple of Bacchus, but a cheerful, spacious traveller's home. Wide should be its verandas, roomy its stable yard and offices, and if the travel of the place calls for a little external display, the good sense of the villagers must only allow it to be made in harmony with the spirit of the rest.

As yet there are very few examples of a satisfactory rural inn; this is singular when the partiality is considered that there is for an hotel life. Either such as we have are so extravagantly built and furnished as to cause a rate of charge far beyond what the general run of travellers ought to be able to afford to pay, or else are dingy and incommodious. Unfortunately an architect is rarely consulted in their construction; some speculating builder "runs up" for a certain sum a building to accommodate so many hundred persons, and provided the exterior be showy and as many floors as scaffolding can be made for are piled one above the other, and the whole is surmounted with a dome or an octagonal observatory and flag-pole, every one is satisfied. Showy carpeting, upholstery and furniture are looked for as matters of course, and compensate for unventilated and sometimes unlighted bed-rooms, —and "private apartments" at forty dollars per week. A country hotel should after all be merely a large, roomy house, with parlors, dining room, and spacious halls large enough for the *estimated number* of guests. Wide and airy verandas should be important features of the plan; they should be so arranged as to secure one large, retired shade-room for ladies, and the wider and larger they are, the better. The manners of the guests derive a coloring from the style of the house; in an over-fine, showy-parlored house, you will meet fair ladies with all their jewelry displayed at breakfast, and in ball costume at the one o'clock dinner, but in a house such as I would have it to be, I will venture to say those who have taste will, without fear of seeming to do differently from others, dress as they would at home, and those who have *not*, be shamed into simplicity by the homelike charm of the building, and the influence of its unaffected dignity. Such a house we will imagine in our model village.

On its outskirts are the usual appurtenances of a travelled road—the blacksmith shop, the town house, the toll house, and the covered bridge;—how pretty and yet how simple might they all be made! The bridge, I know, is a dangerous topic to touch upon—prejudice is decidedly in favor of making it a covered trough from bank to bank, and economy in preserving timber by its shelter is a powerful argument—in force till some kind engineer, inspired by a desire to improve and beautify, has shown how, at half the expenditure of material and money, a durable structure can be made, which, light and uncovered, shall not obstruct the view nor look unsightly in the landscape. One very great source of improvement in the appearance of the approach to a village, would be in a more careful attention to the fences and boundary walls that line the roads. Iron wire is now in course of introduction for this purpose; it is light, durable and inexpensive, and as a means of protecting from injury the hedges growing behind, can strongly be recommended. Wooden rails are too frail and too easily removed or broken, and walling is expensive and also takes up much room. Cast iron has a stiff and formal look, beside being liable to be easily broken by a blow or by a stone thrown by some mischievous urchin; but wrought iron wire, either simply run in a single strand through posts, or woven by machinery into some suitable pattern, is both beautiful and strong.

No country in the world possesses such facilities for the liberal and domestic use of water as this; the boast of the so much vaunted superior English cleanliness would receive a slight check if statistics were obtained to show the superior number of bathing arrangements in the private houses of New York compared with the private houses of London. Villages have frequently their own little aqueduct to supply their water-wants, and with the facility thus given for carrying the precious liquid over every house and adorning a few pretty places with sparkling fountains, there is an element of utility and beauty within the reach of Americans that is not attainable with the same readiness elsewhere. In no respect could the principle of association be so advantageously carried out as in supplying a community with water. The formation of an aqueduct (under ordinary facilities for water-supply) that would carry an abundant supply over every house, leaving still sufficient for ornamental purposes, would actually cost considerably less to the owner of each house than would the digging of an individual well and the provision of pumps or other water gear. The benefit to be derived by such a comfort is incalculable, and with a little taste and cheerful co-operation on the part of the residents, the public square, the school yard, and the church green, could each be adorned with some simple rustic fountain to give play to the sparkling and cooling waters. Near the school-house should be a covered bath of ample size supplied by the same aqueduct; this principally for the use of children, and supported by some small annual payment from all who participate in its benefits. No great expense would be needed for it; one properly made of brick or stone laid in hydraulic cement, with a deepening brick floor, and covered over at one end with a wooden erection containing dressing-rooms, of the dimensions of one hundred and twenty feet long by twenty-five feet wide, and six feet deep in the deepest part, would not exceed in cost two thousand three hundred dollars. It need not be entirely roofed over if placed in a sheltered spot where its waters could be concealed. A high fence surrounding it, and a building at either end for dressing-rooms would be sufficient, and the rest left open to the sky would be both better ventilated and more beneficial to the bathers. Were I writing on sanitary reform I would show the great advantages to be derived from the daily use of a large bath; or were I addressing parents I would comfort them by suggestions of the superior safety of such a bath to the open and treacherous river; but appealing as an architect, I can only show how easily such a luxury can be obtained, and the cost and means of securing it.

---

Such a village as the one I have sketched might be made of every rural hamlet throughout the land. Every class of builder, the cottager, the projector of the costliest mansion, has his part to do. Beautiful as are the reclaimed spots of this luxuriant country, they are tame in comparison to what a cared-for architecture may make them. Noble forests, rich expanses of undulating greensward and natural lawns, beautiful lakes and plentiful streams, are in boundless profusion; not a country town but has, within a five mile drive, some beauty so lovely as to make its neighborhood a precious place; not a single farm but has, somewhere on it, so glorious a prospect hill, so noble a wood, or so pretty a copse, as would render its possession a covetable object to every man of taste. Nowhere is there other than richest beauty. The sand plains of Maine are noble in their bold, unbroken extent, and in their sighing pines, and those places which at present man has not conquered, the swamp and lowland morass, only await skilful labor and untiring industry to yield the most grateful return. Mr. Ruskin says there is in nature no such thing as positive ugliness or deformity, only degrees of beauty; and where anything less lovely than another is permitted, it is only there to send a higher charm to the appreciation of the rest, "spots of blackness in creation to make its colors felt." Such being the case, what encouragement to the investigation of the principles of beauty in architectural form, and what incentive to their embodiment!

How beautiful is the description of Evangeline's Village, the "homes of the happy." "Still stands the forest primeval.—The murmuring pines and the hemlock" still whisper to us as they did of old; there is wanting only that tender love for nature; that sympathy with the simple and the beautiful, and, only differently employed than that of Mr. Longfellow's sweet heroine,—the "affection that hopes, and endures, and is patient," to make our gathered homes in the country more than a realization of the fondest "dream of Acadie."

---

Now must I draw my pleasant labors to a close, and bid my readers—farewell. In parting, I would again revert to the all-importance of embodying some fixed principle and meaning in each country dwelling. I would not go so far as to say that the individual character of its owner may be guessed by a glance at the building, but the general tone of mind certainly may. Reality—meaning—ornamental work serving a purpose, practical or poetic—suitability to material, situation and manner of living—these must be the beauties sought to be embodied in a rural home, and step by step, as such houses shall be built, will the high, broad base, for erecting a standard of true taste, be founded. It is a pleasant and a reasonable hope that the teaching of the public in constructive art will be commenced and steadily carried on by means of rural architecture. All know the influence of early home-teachings, youthful reminiscences and associations; if these were always of the simple, the beautiful and the reasonable in the home itself; if the very building never arose before the memory without confirming by its ever-speaking testimony the advantage of embodiment of these principles, and the harmony and loveliness of the result; how better armed to resist the temptations of a false and tricky taste, and to carry on the advocacy of the nobly true, the inventive mind of the artist and the appreciation of the amateur would be! Some old writer says, "the country is a perpetual sermon," so might be the dwellings it contains. Money is not needed as the only means to make them so; no, simple, almost homely treatment often secures the happiest result; their charm must rest in their appropriateness; their reality be secured by the stability and honest use of materials; so that the next generation shall say of them as was sung of the church-builders of old,

> "They dreampt not of a perishable home,
> Who thus could build!"

FINIS.

www.ingramcontent.com/pod-product-compliance
Lightning Source LLC
LaVergne TN
LVHW020229110826
845151LV00003B/873

* 9 7 8 1 4 2 5 5 3 1 7 4 4 *